What marks this book out as being a compelling
the overwhelming frankness and honesty on the p
of their lives is covered and it is a comprehensive look at life at an extraordinary time.
Yet nothing is sensationalised and nothing seems to have been held back. It is well
paced and structured with moments of real tension. It makes a fascinating, riveting
and also heart-breaking work.

Nicholas Purves, professional reader

What distinguishes this book from so many personal accounts of the Holocaust is that
it is the story of a whole family, not just one person – a family that lost 41 members!
The story is all the more powerful and moving because it reveals how these horrific
events impacted in different ways on a whole range of people.

Jeffrey Simmons, literary agent

This is packed with fascinating information and is obviously the result of a massive
research effort. The extent of Melanie's oral history work is impressive and the results
outstanding. She obviously won the full trust of the people she spoke with, and helped
them to recall episodes that must have been painful to live through, and tempting to
forget or suppress.

The pictures add a lot, particularly those of identity cards, letters of release from
army service and the photos of the people themselves at different stages in their lives. I
especially like the way in which the detail provides evidence of the gradual worsening
of ordinary Jews' situation in Holland. For the first year after the Nazi invasion it was
still possible for them to lead relatively normal lives, despite the gradual ratcheting
up of restrictions, and the sharp increase of persecution after the dockyard workers'
strike. Great details too, such as Tootje not realising that her mother was not Jewish
until they had been rounded up and sent for processing in Westerbork. The steady
accumulation of detail also creates the texture of everyday life effectively, and the
strange combination of planning and luck that led some people to disaster, others to
the resistance and survival.

Another wonderful aspect is that it explores the question of how the Nazis tried
to decide who should count as a Jew and who should not. They wanted the question
to be clear cut but often it was not, and this family is a perfect example of why it was
not. Some historians, albeit for very different reasons, have also tried to create a simple
Jew/Non-Jew dichotomy, which is dramatically satisfying, but misleading. The grey
area occupied by some of the Granaat family members might, in fact, be among the
most interesting aspects of the narrative for historians of the Holocaust.

Patrick Allitt, professor of history

WAR AND LOVE

A family's testament of anguish, endurance and devotion in occupied Amsterdam

Melanie Martin

With help from
Kitty Scheffer, Harry Granaat and Tootje Martin

Matador
9 Priory Business Park,
Wistow Road, Kibworth Beauchamp,
Leicestershire. LE8 0RX
Tel: 0116 279 2299
Email: books@troubador.co.uk
Web: www.troubador.co.uk/matador
Twitter: @matadorbooks

ISBN 978 1789016 307

British Library Cataloguing in Publication Data.
A catalogue record for this book is available from the British Library.

Printed and bound by CPI Group (UK) Ltd, Croydon, CR0 4YY
Typeset in 11pt Adobe Caslon Pro by Troubador Publishing Ltd, Leicester, UK

Matador is an imprint of Troubador Publishing Ltd

Dedicated to my beautiful aunt, Liesje

Acknowledgements

With special thanks to: Kitty Scheffer, Harry Granaat, Tootje Martin, Bob Martin, Fré Granaat, Erik Granaat, Marja Vuijsje, Yolande Schotel, Jeffrey Simmons and Jamie Wolfenden. Also Alice Wickham of New London Writers, without whose support and encouragement this book would not have been published.

Also thanks to: Bob Moore, Sebastian Van Lissum, Jane Stubbs, staff at NIOD Amsterdam, the Amsterdam Archives, Archivists at Westerbork, Joh Porck, Sue Elloy, Liz Thompson, Malcolm Allitt, Patrick Allitt. Finally, Rosie Lowe, Cameron Bonser and all the team at Matador.

Contents

Foreword and Guide to Family Members

During my teenage years I was fascinated by my parents' stories from the war. At university, part of my course led me to study the Arab-Israeli conflict and I became increasingly interested in what had happened to the Jews in the Second World War. In 1980 I wrote an essay, "Account for the strength of anti-Zionism in the contemporary Arab world", and began to realise the complexity of the region's history and the impact of the Holocaust. I read many books on the subject including, of course, *The Diary of Anne Frank*. Asking my mother more about what happened, I realised that my own family history from the war in Holland was just as interesting as anything that I had read. I decided to try to capture as much of it as I could. I bought a small tape recorder and asked my mother and her sister, Kitty, if they would tell me their stories. In April 1997 I began to record what they said and so the fascinating story began to unfold.

I understood from my mother that no other members of the family wanted to talk about what happened. But I persevered. I sent a copy of the story to my uncle Harry. At first he refused – he had not spoken about the war to anyone except the very few close friends who had shared the experience with him. Suddenly the following year he changed his mind and invited me and my mother to visit him and his wife, Fré (pronounced "fray"), in Baarn, Holland. So, in January 1998, we went with my recorder and listened to him for two days while he told his story.

For my aunt Liesje (pronounced "Leesha") the memories were too awful and she tried to shut that period away so that it would not ruin her life or affect her fun-loving and caring personality. She was sometimes called "stupid Lizzie", but I reasoned she must not have been stupid to have survived the war. Over the years I have pieced together her story, from the snippets that she and her siblings have told me about what happened and from the accounts of other survivors who shared similar experiences.

Through the story of one family, my book brings to life the impact of the German occupation to ordinary Dutch people who just happened to be Jewish.

The inputs from Kitty, Harry and my mother are taken, with minimum editing, directly from my conversations with them. These narratives have a different font to help distinguish them from the rest of the book. I hope readers will identify their different voices and recognise their individual style and personalities. The sections under the headings "Liesje" and "Willem" are written largely by me and in the third person (these have the same font as the introductory section, author's narrative and appendices).

The research I have undertaken included reading a number of respected history books, survivor testimonies and visits to the National Institute of War, Holocaust and Genocide Studies (NIOD) in Amsterdam and to Westerbork camp. This research has served to verify the accounts of my family and has provided interesting background about what was happening at the time. So as to not distract from the storytelling, the key historical events and factors which contributed to the plight of the Dutch Jews can be found in the Appendices and are indicated by endnote markers.

The number of Jews living in pre-war Netherlands was 140,000, comprising 118,000 Dutch Jews and 22,000 Germans and other nationalities. In 1941, the population of Amsterdam was 800,000, of whom 75,000 were Jews. From the Netherlands as a whole, just over 107,000 Jews were deported to concentration and extermination camps in the east and of these only 5,000 survived. Compared to its neighbours the mortality rate was disproportionately high.

"How such a disaster could have taken place in a country with such supposedly liberal values and one where people saw themselves as essentially resistant to the German occupation, continues to occupy historians, sociologists and political commentators." Bob Moore.

"While the general explanations for the high Jewish mortality in the Netherlands undoubtedly rest on a complex integration of factors, they tend to concentrate on the Jews as a homogenous mass. The danger is that in a quest for objectivity and answers, sight is lost of the tens of thousands of individual tragedies played out during the occupation as the Nazi's murderous policies were put into practice." Bob Moore.

"Those murdered on arrival are counted by the hundred thousand; those put to work by the ten thousand; those who returned by the hundred; and those who came

forward to tell their tale by the tens. It is on this scant evidence that historians have to base their work." Jacques Presser.

The narrative of these two respected historians and these passages in particular have been inspirational to me and have made me determined to see this project through to publication.

Family members

Willem Granaat
My grandfather, born in Amsterdam, 1892.

Lily (Lilian) Granaat-Hollingsworth
My grandmother, born in Hertfordshire, 1897.

Mary van Rood (pronounced Mar-ee)
My aunt; the oldest and illegitimate daughter of Lily. Born in London, 1914.

Kitty or Keetje Tertaas, later Scheffer (pronounced Keet-cha)
My aunt; daughter of Willem and Lily. Born in London, 1915.

Lizzie or Liesje Vuisje (pronounced Leesha)
My aunt; daughter of Willem and Lily. Born in Amsterdam, 1916.

Harry Granaat
My uncle; son of Willem and Lily. Born in Amsterdam, 1919.

Tootje Granaat, later Martin (pronounced "Toe-cha")
My mother, the youngest daughter of Willem and Lily. Born Amsterdam, 1926. Her real name is Cato, a name she never liked. It's shortened to Too (pronounced "toe") and affectionately known by her Dutch family as Tootje (means little toe!).

Maurice Tertaas
The first husband of Kitty.

Nico (Nathan) Vuisje
The husband of Liesje.

Kiki de Vries

Girlfriend of Harry Granaat and sister of Harry de Vries.

Harry de Vries

The first husband of Fré Pfister and brother of Kiki.

Fré Pfister (pronounced "Fray")

My aunt by marriage, firstly married to Harry de Fries and then to my uncle Harry.

Frans Scheffer

The second husband of Kitty.

Kari de Vries

Daughter of Fré and Harry de Vries.

Netty Vuisje

My cousin, daughter of Liesje and Nico.

Wim Vuisje

My cousin, son of Liesje and Nico.

Erik Granaat

My cousin, the son of Harry and Fré.

Robert (Bob) Martin

My father.

INTRODUCTION

Before the war in Holland

"I can remember sitting on my mother's lap and being cuddled as a small child. She used to wear a grey overall. It was a slightly shiny material – probably dirty and shiny from handling the metal and other items in the shop. It's a happy memory. I also remember her coming in from the hairdresser. I told her that her hair looked like an Easter egg. It was very flat with fine grooves in wavy lines – the fashion of the time I suppose. Another time I said rather unkindly that the large pores on her face looked like the skin of an orange."

Tootje (my mother).

My grandfather, Willem, was named after the King of the Netherlands (the father of Queen Wilhelmina). He went travelling as a young man, firstly to Germany and then to England. He could speak English fluently and German very well. He met Lily when he was about 22 and they fell in love. She was attractive and pretty with a bright personality. She liked to party.

Lily had worked "below stairs" as a maid for a wealthy family in London. At the age of 16 she was taken advantage of by either the man of the house or his son and became pregnant. She had a daughter, Marriette Emma (Mary), in May 1914. It was said that Mary's father had been killed early in the First World War.

Lily and Willem in 1915

When Lily fell pregnant again, Willem proposed and they got married at Lambeth registry office in July 1915. Their marriage certificate stated Willem's occupation as an Electrical Engineers Fitter. Their respective fathers were Hijman Granaat ("Ironmongery Stores Proprietor") and Oliver Hollingsworth ("Motor Engineer").

Kitty (my aunt) was born in October 1915. At first Willem and Lily intended to stay in London, but with the advent of war, even though Holland remained neutral, my grandfather was required to return to do national service in the Dutch army. He had been working in a factory in England, but this had been bombed and all the foreign workers were sacked in case they were spies, so many returned home at that point. But, rather than return to Amsterdam, Willem sailed to South Africa to spend a few months more as a merchant seaman, working as a cook. This enabled him to get enough money together to relocate the family to Holland.

So, with Kitty as a small baby, they went to live in Amsterdam. Willem's family was quite well off and owned several shops. However, being Orthodox Jews, him marrying

Lily, who was not Jewish, was a terrible thing for him to have done, according to his family. Also, because there was another child, Mary, who was not my grandfather's child, they disowned Willem from then on.

In the early years of my grandparents' marriage the family moved house several times. Willem took advantage of subsidies available for families to help with the first six months of rent in a property. The records show they moved 12 times between 1916 and 1938, eventually settling in the Oudeschans (pronounced "owderskanse"), in the beautiful old part of Amsterdam.

Kitty described Willem as a pacifist with communist principles. The army paid very little. With a wife and children to support he faced an ethical and practical dilemma. So he feigned illness in order to get a discharge from national service. The army officials visited him at home to check if he was ill. He was in bed at the time and quickly took off his glasses and pushed them with the newspaper he had been reading down the side of the bed. They took him outside to get a good look at him and the cold air made his eyes water. This together with his quickened heartbeat (due to the feeling of panic when they had turned up) led them to believe he was very ill. He was taken to hospital, where prayers were said in case he was dying. That was how he got out of joining the army.

Willem then started his own shop from next to nothing in premises belonging to the family. My great-grandfather (Hijman Levie) allowed them to live at 15 Oudeschans, but did not provide any other form of support. By that time my grandmother, Lily, was pregnant again with my aunt Liesje (Lizzie) and they went on to have two more children, Harry in March 1919 and Tootje in November 1926.

My aunt Mary had remained in England and was brought up in Ware in Hertfordshire by her grandparents until she was ten years old. Lily would sometimes visit her and money was sent from Holland to help with her upkeep. When they brought her over to Holland my grandfather adopted her. The other children liked it when she came to live with them because they had a new older sister and she spoke perfect English. But, to help her learn Dutch, Willem would not allow any English to be spoken at home. There was no English spoken at school either so of course she learnt to speak Dutch fluently in quite a short time. Although more than a year older, Mary was put in the same class as Kitty. There she would sometimes sing songs in English, which the other children thought was great. As well as learning a new language, Mary also had to adopt the Jewish faith. At her first Christmas she bought some pretty glass baubles for Christmas decorations. This made Willem angry and he threw them down and broke them all. Poor Mary, it must have been very tough for her and as soon as she was old enough she left home and went to live in The Hague.

At first my grandparents struggled and business was not good, but Willem was hardworking, strong willed and very determined to manage somehow. He would buy bent nails and straighten them. When the war was over in 1918, things got better and he did very well. He had a shop, and then another shop and he had three shops at one time. He had a special nose for business, especially buying – for getting a very good price. But he was not so good at selling. They called the shop in the Oudeschans "The Iron Man". But the people he got in to manage the other shops swindled him and he nearly went bankrupt. By the time my mother was born in November 1926 it was hardship all the way round, and by then they only had the small shop in the cellar at number 15. There was just no money coming in. Willem spent many hours in the shop, keeping it open until 8pm, hoping for customers. At that time it was often difficult for people to pay and too often he gave credit. He was not tough enough, only a hardnosed businessman when it came to buying. My mother could remember the accounts book from the shop detailing sales and money owed. When all the people on one page had paid he would put a big line through it, but most pages had lots of names of people who had not paid. The Depression in the Netherlands was as harsh as anywhere else in the Western world following the Wall Street Crash in 1929, so this was a time of hardship for many people.

My great-grandparents had nine children in all. Their names were: Carolina, Marcus, Louis, Simon, Jacob, Samuel, Cato, Willem (my grandfather) and Elias. A family tree is provided in the Appendices.[2]

The rest of Willem's family were better-off and they all had shops, given to them by their parents. One brother had a babywear shop; another a grocer's, and another an ironmonger's shop in a different part of Amsterdam. Two brothers ran the famous ironmonger's shop on the Oudeschans, at number 11 (FA HL Granaat on the shop sign was their father, Hijman Levie).

Erik, with some other members of the Granaat family, attended the 125-year anniversary of the shop in November 2005. The shop was dated from November 1880, 12 years before Willem was born. At the ceremony, the Mayor of Amsterdam awarded it the status of "purveyor to the Royal Household", on behalf of Her Majesty the Queen. Unfortunately, instead of being restored to its former glory, the building was demolished.

For a few years Willem and Lily were allowed to live at number 15 Oudeschans, but when my great-grandfather died in July 1935 the older brothers inherited number 15 (with the small shop in the cellar). They came in while the family were out and emptied all their belongings. As they were coming home they could see from the other side of the canal all their furniture and clothes on the street. Lily fainted.

The shop sign for 15 Oudeschans (before demolition). The top of the Montelbaans tower is reflected in the windows

Fortunately they were able to move across the canal to number 20 Oudeschans. This was a stroke of luck as the owner allowed them to take the shop on the ground floor rent free and charged a low rent for the second floor. This was because the whole building was under threat of demolition as it was leaning forwards. It suited her to have tenants and so they were able to come back to this better shop and the Iron Man returned. Though now there was stiff competition from across the canal.

The apartment they lived in was quite small for a family of their size. Willem and Lily slept in a small bedroom at the back. The three older sisters shared a bed and Tootje slept in the same room in a cot until she was six years old – at which point Mary left home. Harry slept on the sofa in the living room and there was a tiny kitchen. There was no bathroom or hot water. They had a small oval tin bath, which they used once a week. My grandparents had a much larger one, which took a lot of filling with hot water boiled on the stove. Later they all went to a bath house towards the Waterlooplein and had a weekly shower.

Willem had very strict principles – he would never borrow money and would never buy anything on credit. So they didn't have much and hardly any clothes. Recalling this, my mother found it almost unbelievable how we can live now so well and how they lived then, so poor.

When my great-grandfather died, Willem followed the Jewish custom of showing respect in a bereavement by sitting on the floor for one week, not shaving for six weeks and tearing his clothes a little bit – just a small piece of the lapel. But his nasty brother, Louis, at number 11 would stop people before they came into the Iron Man and say to them "can't you see he is a thug?" In those days men would never have stubble on their face.

Willem was very innovative. He rigged up a communication tube between the apartment on the second floor outside and then down to the shop on the ground floor, which they could whistle down and later talk through. He had got this idea from working in the merchant navy. My mother recalls a funny incident when Lily, who was upstairs, talked through the tube to a customer, but he thought she was on the telephone. Even after he had hung up the phone she called down the tube, "Oh by the way, Mr Davidje," and he picked up the phone and continued talking!

Pre-war Oudeschans. Number 20 is second from left.
Below is number 20 today

My mother, Tootje, remembers her father making some scales from two frying pans! She was so bored looking after the shop one evening that she put their tabby cat on the scales and wrote down his weight in an exercise book. There was a display in the window of clay mice that my grandfather had made to advertise his range of mousetraps – he took some of my mother's hair to make its whiskers.

Another memory from before the war was when Willem and Lily were on a trip to England and Kitty was left in charge. She was quite strict and wouldn't let Tootje stay up late to listen to her favourite radio programme, *Snip and Snap*, on Tuesdays at 8pm. So Tootje prepared a document and persuaded her father to sign it, giving her permission to stay up later that evening. The next time they were away she prepared a similar letter and used tracing paper to copy his signature. But he found out and gave her a long lecture explaining about fraud!

There was a Zionist movement in Holland that started before the war. There was a little tin collecting for them in the shop, but they were looked upon as a bit cranky and left-wing – like "ban the bomb" or Greenpeace nowadays. They wanted to go to Israel. That's why they raised money – so that they could start up a farm. But the family thought "Jews don't do farming – they strive to be doctors and lawyers: they don't go and be farmers". That was a common opinion towards Zionists before the war.

There was another tin to collect money for the Jewish Hospital (Joodse Invalide). This was a very popular cause founded in 1911 to provide shelter for frail and elderly Jews. At that time there was no such thing as government-funded care for the elderly. Many years were spent collecting the necessary funds and radio appeals asking for donations. By 1938, there was enough to pay for the hospital's relocation to Weesperplein. My great-grandfather played a key role in raising money for the sick Jewish people and later for the establishment of the Jewish Hospital for which he was officially recognised.

The Granaat children all thought their mother was Jewish and that is how they were brought up. My grandparents took Harry as a baby to England to be circumcised because you couldn't become Jewish, not in Holland, not in those days. It was not like the Catholic faith, where they try to convert everyone to become Catholic. As my mother put it: "The Jewish faith doesn't want anybody to join. They just want to stay with their own faith and their own religion and nobody else."

During my mother's childhood she suffered from ill health and often missed school for weeks at a time. She had mumps and then diphtheria. Once she was sent to a Jewish children's convalescence home in Hilversum. During the day she had to stay in bed. At one point she was so skinny they thought she was dangerously ill and the next thing she knew, she was put in an ambulance and taken to the hospital in Amsterdam.

At the age of 10, Tootje was at a school that, because it was on the edge of the Jewish Quarter, was closed on Saturday mornings. To make up for this they had to stay half an hour later, to 4.30pm, during the week. The Jewish Sabbath is observed from Friday sunset to Saturday sunset. In winter, when it gets dark by late afternoon, they would go home early on a Friday because of the Sabbath starting. Some of the children would leave but not all, because most were not Jewish. Some of the children would say, "Not you, you're not Jewish." Tootje used to wonder, "What are they talking about?" She couldn't understand why they said that – perhaps they could see that Lily didn't look Jewish.

Willem did his utmost to make Lily appear Jewish and she in turn, being devoted to him, did everything she could to support him. She never mentioned her Christian background and adopted all the rituals and customs of a good Jewish wife. But the wider family still did not accept Lily as Jewish, so Willem and Lily returned to London to settle the whole thing in, they hoped, in a more proper way. In November 1937 they had a Jewish marriage ceremony ("Choppe"), which it was not possible to do in Holland. I have the original certificate from this marriage from the East London Synagogue. It reads in Hebrew on one side and English on the other:

"On the third day of the week, the 26th day of the month of Yislev in the year of 5698am, corresponding to 30th November 1937 the holy covenant of marriage was entered into, in London between the Bridegroom, Willem Granaat and his Bride, Lilian May Hollingsworth.

The said Bridegroom made the following declaration to his Bride: "Be thou my wife according to the Law of Moses and of Israel. I faithfully promise that I will be true husband unto thee. I will honour and cherish thee; I will protect and support thee, and will provide all that is necessary for thy due sustenance, even as it beseemeth a Jewish husband to do. I also take upon myself all such further obligations for thy maintenance, during thy lifetime, as are prescribed by our religious statute."

And the said Bride has plighted her troth unto him, with affection and with sincerity, and has thus taken upon herself the fulfilment of all the duties incumbent upon a Jewish wife.

This covenant of marriage was duly executed and witnessed this day according to the usage in Israel."

There is proof that Lily was a member of the English Church when she came to Holland. There is the excerpt from the Council Registers, which shows an amendment in the column "Religion": what was there originally, "EK", Engelse Kerk (Church of England), has been changed to "NI", Nederlands Israelitisch (Jewish). While we are not very familiar with Jewish laws, we know that you can't be considered Jewish by just having a Choppe with a Jew. However, the effect of the Choppe was that Lily promised to fulfil all the duties of a Jewish wife, that she would follow the Jewish rules in the housekeeping, upbringing of the children and so on. In this way, Willem could demonstrate that, although he had a non-Jewish wife, his household was Jewish.

As a consequence, Lily and Willem's children were always expected to marry Jews, even Mary. Kitty's boyfriend, Maurice, was out of work when he wanted to go out with Kitty. Willem said that was no good because he was unemployed. But Maurice was determined; he had a lovely Norton motorbike, or another famous make. He sold that and started a shop that sold bicycles and did bike repairs; it was also a place where people could keep their bikes overnight. It became quite a good business.

Harry's childhood memories were happily recalled. His school results were good and at the age of 16 he spent four years at a technical college to train as a mechanical engineer; later on he did a correspondence course in hydraulic engineering. Harry's girlfriend, Kiki, was also Jewish. They had been together from their early teens.

Liesje was more rebellious. If she came home late Willem would slap her across her face. He would be furious if she went out with a non-Jewish boy. Rather hypocritical, given his own behaviour and the fact that he had got Lily pregnant.

Source: Jewish Monument

Before the war and before she met Nico, Lizzie went out with a boy called Max (Salomon Meijer) Kannewasser. He was very keen on Lizzie but was a very low-wage worker, packing bags in the Bijenkorf department store. Perhaps it came from Willem or from Lizzie herself, but she said he wasn't good enough. We think Lizzie thought he was too short and not very good looking. She certainly didn't look up to him in the same way she did with Nico, so she said to him, "You don't earn enough." That spurred him on and he started off with his second cousin, Nol, to become the comic duo Johnny and Jones. They sang funny songs and became very famous – like a top-ten artist would be now. They made records and were in shows.

Liesje was described by my father, Bob, as being very beautiful with thick dark blond hair. She was kind-hearted, generous and sympathetic, but also gullible and thus possibly easy prey to men. She could have had any man she wanted, but the man she fell in love with was Nico. She didn't see him as a nervous self-opinionated little baker, which is how he has been described. He wasn't little in stature and she loved his sense of humour and generosity and the way he showed his affection. He worshipped the ground she walked on. Nico could sing and play the trombone. Part of Liesje's appeal to Nico was her view that Jewish rituals such as blessing the candles, the bread and the wine, were nonsense.

Nico playing the trombone
Source: Marja Vuijsje

Nathan is a Jewish name, and is what he preferred to use after the war, rather than Nico, which is short for Nicolas, a Christian name. Nico worked in his family's successful bakery business making bread and lovely Dutch cakes. Liesje worked in the shop as an assistant and that is where she first met him. Nico had several brothers and his parents had the main shop, in Weesperstraat in the mainly Jewish area, where the bread was also baked. Coincidently, now there is a monument to those who helped the hidden Jews in the exact spot where the baker's shop once stood.

Liesje and Nico got married on 2nd August 1939, just a month before the declaration of war, she was 22 and Nico 29. Because the business was doing well, Willem was able to afford a traditional Jewish wedding.

Their Choppe was in the Grote [Large] Synagogue on the Jonas Daniël Meijerplein. This now forms part of the Jewish Historical Museum. Afterwards, there was a reception with a lavish kosher dinner in the Hotel Hiegentlicht (Nieuwe Hoogstraat 9).

So the Granaat family's way of life in the couple of years before the war was good; they were no longer struggling financially and they were able to eat well. They observed the religious customs and on the Jewish holidays the shop was shut. Every Friday night was like a party. Lily would cook a chicken or piece of beef. There would be soup and then a separate course of peas, runner beans or carrots cooked in sweetened water. She would serve sautéed potatoes with the meat. For dessert they had "tutti frutti", dried fruit such as plums and pears mixed together or a tin of pineapple. Lily didn't make custard, as Jews were not allowed to have milk and meat in the same meal. There had to be a half-hour gap between any meat and milk products.

After dinner they would clear the table and sit back. They would eat oranges, bananas or other fruit, and then chocolates. Every Friday night was a really happy time, with all the family together, including Kiki, Maurice and Nico. There would be discussion about politics and other topics.

At Easter the festival was two nights. They would go through the whole story of why the Jewish people were taken and why they were freed, Exodus and all that. Tootje and Kitty have good memories of that. At the end of the evening they would say "Next year in Jerusalem". In those days no one had any intention of actually going there; it was just part of the ceremony.

Although he did not have much schooling, Willem knew about lots of things. He was clever. My mother remembers sitting on his knee on a Friday night and him explaining about Einstein and splitting the atom. On Saturdays there would be outings. They would go to the Rijksmuseum to see the "Nightwatch" and the other paintings. He taught Tootje how to play chess and play cards. They would play a game like bridge, called whist. If there were an odd number of grown-ups, my mother would be partnered with somebody.

For Liesje's wedding, beautiful dresses were made for all the sisters and Tootje was bridesmaid. When she tried on the bridesmaid's dress in the bridal shop on the Kalverstraat, she was so enchanted by the whole experience that she suddenly wanted to become a dress designer, even though she was excellent at maths and not at all good at drawing. This was a decision my grandfather went along with, partly because Kitty, who had gone to the grammar school, was struggling to find enough

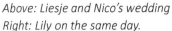
Above: Liesje and Nico's wedding
Right: Lily on the same day.

time to do her homework. Later my mother came to bitterly regret not going to the grammar school.

So, after leaving primary school at the age of 12, instead of being sent to the school where Kitty and Harry had gone, Willem decided that a more practical education would be better for Tootje. He secured her a place at a school specialising in designing clothes and dressmaking. Prior to that she had a year at another school, called Prinsen, starting at the beginning of September 1939, this was known as the 6R class. The Prinsen School was where children were made ready to take their high school scholarship. Whereas at Montelbaans junior school there had been 40 children in her class, at the new school there were only 20, and of these, just five girls. Tootje did very well at that school and excelled in her favourite subject, maths.

It was here that my mother first met Willy (full name: Wilhelmina van Wolferen, born 13/8/26). Willy sat next to Tootje and they became best friends. She was really talented; she could play the piano, skate and ride a bike. All the things my mother couldn't do! And she was a real tomboy. She was pretty and could be described as a typical well-built Dutch girl. She later married and had two children. My mother unfortunately lost touch with her and would love to know what happened to her in later life.

When my mother saw a TV programme in the 1990s with Vanessa Feltz, about Jewish people and what the Passover meant to them, she was really upset. Although she had seen many programmes about the Holocaust, she had remained dry-eyed. But this programme made her realise what she had lost. The evening when you eat the matzos and hear the whole story about the Jews leaving Egypt. Everything is done in the same order and the youngest asks the four questions, "Why is this different from all other nights?" It was a wonderful family get-together and gave a feeling of great warmth and belonging, such a nice thing to have.

"And then these Germans came and destroyed it, destroyed the family, destroyed everything. Remember when you were children and how you loved Christmas? Christmas after Christmas. Then no family any more, no nothing any more. I sobbed and sobbed – privately because I didn't want to upset Bob. It was the only time I really cried about the whole thing. It made me realise how much it all meant to me and how deep the impact of it was."

Tootje.

CHAPTER 1

The Beginning of the War in Europe

Tootje

The war in Britain started on Sunday 3rd September 1939. Germany had already annexed parts of Europe and there seemed to be no stopping them. Then they wanted Poland. The British said, "No – you must not do this." They took an ultimatum to the Germans: if you invade Poland, we will be at war. It was thought by Prime Minister Chamberlain that this would be enough, but on Friday September 1st Germany did invade Poland. A final ultimatum was sent that, if you have not retreated by 11 o'clock Sunday morning, Britain would declare war. I think there was a time difference so in Holland it must have been quarter past midday when my father and mother went upstairs to listen to the BBC and the declaration of war was made. I looked after the shop, which was open on a Sunday – because being Jewish we were closed on a Saturday. So I was left on my own and stood in the doorway. It was lovely weather and I held my kitten in my arms. A little later on they told me the news from London that the war had started. My mother was crying because she was worried about her family in England.

Kitty (talking in 1997)

In 1939, Hitler was invading different countries. Before Hitler there was a treaty – no army etc. The "Polish corridor", which had been part of Germany – he wanted back. It was his answer to high unemployment. On 3rd September war was declared but to begin with life carried on as normal because Holland was neutral.

Harry was called up for the army on 6th May 1940. This was normal conscription, not because of the war. It was a bit of a lottery whether you went in or not.

Our oldest sister Mary's husband was Isaak van Rood, Ies for short [pronounced "ees"]. He had been unemployed – but had joined the merchant navy on 6th May and sailed to Canada. Because of that he survived the war. When Holland was invaded Mary was 26. They lived in The Hague and had a son, almost three years old, called Aby (pronounced a-b).

Suddenly on 10th May there was a lot of noise in the middle of the night. There were planes flying over – we knew they were German – and the Nazis had invaded Holland. We heard them but didn't see them. No warning was given in any of the countries. They didn't declare war, just went in.

We had thought we would be safe because Holland hadn't been invaded in the First War. But the British ambassador had phoned Father and Mother, because Lily was English, and advised them to get away. Because the Embassy knew what had happened to the Jews in Germany, he had warned them a few times.

Father also knew very well what was happening because of the work he had been doing to help the Jews coming out of Germany. This was not resistance because before the war it didn't need to be "underground". From 1933 it had started, but we felt it was "far from our beds".

We were not allowed to listen to German radio or buy anything made in Germany. Father wouldn't have it. He helped many people and had therefore heard a lot of stories from German Jewish refugees. Not about the real concentration camps, which came later. They killed people, though it was on a smaller scale, but still nasty enough. There were already concentration camps, but not with the gas chambers. Our parents hadn't left Holland because of the family – Harry in the army, Liesje married with her husband, Nico, also in the army. He'd been in a year by then and they were expecting their first child any day. And it was also difficult to leave the business – the successful ironmonger's shop.

Tootje

After the war started in Europe, nothing much happened in Holland for some time. Harry was studying, so to begin with his national service was deferred. But he did have to go into the army on 6th May 1940 and he was sent to Rotterdam. On 10th May, without any warning, the Germans invaded Holland and Belgium. For most people it was such a surprise: being neutral in the First World War, we thought we would stay neutral in this war too.

There had been many German Jewish refugees. My father spent a lot of time collecting money and looking after them. My mother was not very happy about it because she had to look after the shop while he "swanned off" and did all this refugee work. Anyway, he heard what was happening in Germany with the Jews from the stories they told. Especially after Kristallnacht (night of broken glass) in 1938 when they smashed all the Jewish shop windows and burnt synagogues. So he must have known.

Harry (my uncle, talking with Fré, Tootje and me in January 1998)

My aim in this is to tell you about what happened to our family. So, with this in mind, I will just try, as a member of that family, to remember what happened. After a gap of 50 years or more I am not sure if it is all in the right sequence, but it is all true.

Talking about the war after so long, things can get mixed up in your mind. Certain facts might not be in the right order and often Fré and I have discussed points, saying "Why did we do it that way? What was the reason to do it?" Sometimes we remember the facts but not the reasons why.

Some events have completely gone from my mind – mostly the worst ones and these are forgotten. You still remember the facts but the details have been pushed down in your mind or erased.

So I will tell you what I remember and I am sure some things will come back to the surface. Some already have over the last few days and from reading the stories you have written down from Kitty and Tootje.

I was very grateful to my parents because they gave me the opportunity not only to be educated, but also to develop independence. Some of the key points my dad forever underlined were:

16

"Don't believe what is written, have your own opinion about it. Question things and make up your own mind."

"Make sure you are not following people just because it is the easier option"; and

"Of all the things you do, the only one who is responsible is you. You can't say I have to do this or that someone made you do it. You decide to do it yourself and sometimes that leads to conflict, of course."

One of the other things he often told us children was about our roots in the east of Europe and what was going on there. He always told us to get the most education we could.

"What you have in your head can never be lost. If you are a good craftsman, they can cut off your hand and then it is impossible to do those things again. But the things in your mind they can never take away. Only by chopping off your head! You know why there were so many Jewish violinists and not so many piano players? For the reason if you have to go away from where you are living you can't take the piano but you can always take your violin."

Later on, we came to realise how true those kind of words were.

In Holland there was no anti-Semitism evident. Of course it was there, as it is now and it was in Britain too. But, in principle, in Holland, you could get any sort of job, go to any firm. There were some employers who didn't want Jews, but in general you could reach the highest ranks. Ministers of State were Jewish and the highest man in the courts was Jewish. So there were possibilities enough. Therefore, the stories Father told us at that time seemed to be hypothetical. Again, it is only afterwards you realise how true they were.

Nowadays, if there is something on the television about the war, I always switch it off. We don't want to be reminded of those kinds of things. And what they show you are always the worst things that happened. Generally speaking the five years of war for Fré and me were not the worst five years of our lives. For we were young and being in the "resistance" meant you are active.

One of our golden rules was to have nothing to do with the Germans. What they want us to do we don't do if we don't like it. Of course, some things we had to do.

We had a circle of people in the same organisation and of the same ideology. This had started before the war. Fré was in the union of youngsters –

there were several groups which were all linked together. She was very socialist and became a member of the OSP [Independent Socialist Party], a left-wing group of mostly young and rather revolutionary people. During the war some members like Fré also joined the Group Gerretsen (see Chapter 17). Among them, Miep who was her close friend for 77 years, from the age of 16 until Fré's death in 2009.

All our friends and especially the friends of Fré were of the same mentality and had strong ethics about what do to: what is right and what is wrong behaviour. They became close to each other and because they were doing some illegal activities together they developed a very strong bond of friendship. So we had a lot of fun during the war which did compensate for the bad things that happened. It was dangerous but our aim was not to "survive"; our aim was to "live" and do what our conscience told us to do was right. Of course, the consciences of young people are not hampered by experience.

I just had finished my studies in 1939. So, for the last year before the war in Holland I was already working – I had to do a year's practice and then I got my certificate. I had left home on 9th January 1939 and lived in Vlissingen. I was 20.

When the war started in Europe, I had a feeling of relief because the Germans had been doing such nasty things to the Jews in Germany – we thought, "Now at last there will be an end to it. It will be resisted." My father was not earning much money because he was so involved in collecting money for the refugees from Germany. This was more or less the beginning of his early resistance work and he told us a little about what was happening there. So at the moment of the official beginning of the war in Holland we had the feeling that now something would be done about it.

Everyone knew there would be a war; there was not suddenly war. We could feel that it was coming. So my dad said, "Can I give you some advice? Ask for a deferment of your national service."

I asked, "What reason can I give?"

He replied, "Say you are the breadwinner, because the businesses are going very badly, and you are living with us. You earn a certain amount of money and we need that money." It was not completely true, but they accepted it and I got a deferment.

War came for the Dutch on 10th May 1940. Before then the Germans had invaded Denmark and, a month later, Norway, just a month before starting on

Holland. Both times I was told that I had to go in the army. Again I asked for a deferment because I was the breadwinner. At first I got it but the last time, when they had invaded Norway, they refused and I had to join up; I had no choice. So I joined the army just four days before our war started. I had to go to Rotterdam.

Tootje

Our neighbours at 20 Oudeschans were the De Hond family, on the first floor. They moved out early on in the war and the Boekelman family moved in. We tended to keep ourselves to ourselves, but were quite friendly with them. We didn't think the Boekelmans were NSB [National Socialist Movement] but later their daughter went out with German soldiers, so we were very careful. One of the daughters, Kitty, came to my wedding in Newbury in 1948. In the flat above ours lived an artist and his family.

Next door on the corner was a tobacconist shop See the photo of me holding a dog in about 1936 – this was their dog. On the other side, close

by, was a narrow lane leading to the playground at the back of the houses. On the corner of the lane was a paint shop. We were friendly with them too.

Further up this lane was a blacksmith we were also friends with. He used to joke with my father: "If a spark goes in my shoe I can quickly slip it off". My father would respond, in his laced-up boots, "Well a spark can't get into my shoe!"

After the war started we had a big shock as all these friendly neighbours turned out in their black NSB uniforms. They knew we were Jewish because we closed the shop on Saturdays.

CHAPTER 2

The Netherlands Invaded

Harry

In the centre of Rotterdam there was a school which was empty and this became our barracks. This is where I was when the war started. One of the main objectives for the Germans was to take Rotterdam so there were a lot of parachutes coming down near the bridges and Dutch soldiers were posted at the bridges to try to protect them. There were four bridges of great strategic importance. The people of the regiment I was with, the Engineers, were sent to repair damage to the bridges. People who had already been in the army for three months or more had to go to the bridges to fight. So I was very lucky that I had nothing to do with it.

On 10th May I woke at four in the morning to the sound of planes flying over. They bombed the bridges and so we knew the war had started. This was not a shock to me. In the first place, they had published too often in the paper, "Don't worry". Even the night before they had said that nothing would happen. But we knew they were concentrating their forces on the borders so it was not really a surprise.

I was not afraid. I was 21 and liked to be active and when you are young you like a touch of adventure! So we were in the school, which was our barracks. We listened to the radio and had nothing much to do. We had some training and did some exercises in the playground. For uniforms we had only blue working clothes. They gave us a very long, old-fashioned rifle with a bayonet (probably from the First World War), but I was never taught how to handle it. The only thing I learnt was how to put on the bayonet and take it off, how to take out the moving parts, clean them and put them in again. Because I was on a training course for a higher level of rank in the army, most of the instructors were already fighting with their guns and what was left was second-class – probably in terms of the guns and the instructors! We got our food, of course, talked together, played cards and chess. The war was going on outside.

Then a German ultimatum was made to the Dutch government that the Luftwaffe would bomb Rotterdam if the Dutch did not surrender. In the meantime, our queen had gone to England.

How they knew what to do I don't know but the officers at the school I was in went to Rotterdam to collect all the iron from the shops. Pickaxes and shovels. So there was a big heap of that stuff collected in the playground.

Holland started to negotiate their surrender but at lunchtime on 14th May the planes (50 Heinkles) still came and bombed the port and the centre of Rotterdam. From the roof of the school the officers were following events and at one point the bombs were falling just three or four hundred metres from the school. They said we had to go out and take a shovel or a pick. To ensure that I did not have to do the heaviest job, I chose a shovel because using a pick is very heavy work and the shovel was also lighter to carry. I don't remember what the picks and shovels were for.

We also took with us our rifles with bayonets – no ammunition. In fact, it was a dangerous thing what they did. They sent us men out of Rotterdam. We were military people and the Germans could have killed us, but fortunately we didn't see any. No one knew what to do – not the military leaders or even politicians and certainly not our sergeants. They were only aware that the Germans were coming. You can make contingency programmes and plans in advance but in this case they would never work out. Nobody was expecting the invasion to happen so quickly. They thought the enemy would be fighting from the borders, bit by bit. They didn't know they would target Rotterdam or issue the ultimatum. They were surprised by the drop of all those parachutes. In just a few days we were completely overrun and it was completely unexpected.

When a country has not had any war for 150 years, they have no experience at all. We were just playing at being military people. We still had one brigade of soldiers on bicycles! We believed that the two big rivers would save us – they had always been our defence in the past and had never been crossed. They remained uncrossed – the Germans knew this so they just bombed Rotterdam and parachuted over the top. Yet, in 1944 the Allies couldn't get across…

There is a famous piece from one of the history books. It tells of a telegram sent from an officer, who said, "We are in retreat."

They sent us out of the school and we had to go to a certain place and there waiting for us to collect was a military overcoat and a helmet. It was about 2.30 in the afternoon. Then came my first big shock. It was May and wonderful weather but the whole area was full of smoke and little pieces of burnt paper. A little later I realised it was ash. We hadn't known about the extent of the bombing because we'd been inside the school. There were thousands of people leaving Rotterdam and we came in among them. We were walking and walking. At one point the planes came over. I think we were in a park and we had to take cover. I remember that I held my hands over the end of the shovel. The shovel was grey but the end was very shiny. I was afraid they would see it and recognise us as a military group and shoot at us.

We walked for hours and came to some small villages. The citizens we had met thought we had come back from fighting in Rotterdam so they gave us cigarettes and food, which we accepted – they thought we were heroes. At dusk we came to a barracks. This was nothing to do with the military; it was a factory which made wooden shelves. There we heard that Holland had surrendered, but we didn't believe it so the officers went by car to The Hague to be sure about it – because we couldn't trust the radio. We were worried that it was in the hands of what we called the fifth column. That means there were a lot of people in Holland that were *with* the Germans and were supporting their cause. There were a lot of German people in Holland before the war started. They were picked up and usually deported, but you can't pick them all up. Especially the ones who were spying – they went to great efforts not to get caught. These were the "fifth column", or Henneicke column, who passed information to the Germans. How much of this is true is not sure. It happened but the scale was unknown. But at the time we thought anybody could be a spy – so you could not trust what you heard. So they went off by car to The Hague and there they heard it was true: Holland had surrendered. It was the Henneicke column who later specialised in ferreting out Jews who had gone into hiding.

We could see that Rotterdam was burning – we were about 15 kilometres away. From that distance we could only see flames. Not individual flames, just one big fire. Then the trolleys and tools were confiscated and we went back to

Rotterdam. We got back to the school and we could see that it had been visited before by some people. We did not know who. This was 11pm – the same day, 14th May.

So we were in the school. Nobody knew what to do next so we just went to bed, exhausted. At 4am it was already daylight. We got up and came down to see what was going on. There was only one of the lowest-ranking officers left, just one sergeant, and there were 40 or 50 of us boys. We asked him what had happened. He said, "I don't know, all the officers have gone, the cowards."

So I asked, "What should I do?" and he said, "If I were you? I would desert. Get out of here and find your way home."

I had been in plain clothes when I had arrived, but I couldn't find them anymore. The reason for this was because the soldiers at the school who had been fighting in Rotterdam had come back to the school to exchange their uniforms for plain clothes and disappear. My raincoat had been left behind in another room. Somebody had taken it but maybe the quality was not good enough so he had got a better one!

So in my blue working military wear we went into the centre of Rotterdam. I was pleased that sleeping next to me in the school had been a man also from Amsterdam. His family were funeral directors and they had a branch in Rotterdam. He said to me, "Perhaps they can lend us a car to go to Amsterdam, and anyway I want to find out what's happened to them". So we decided to go there.

It was terrible to walk through the city. Everything was destroyed and it was still burning. In one square mile all the beautiful old houses had been burnt and 1,000 people killed. We found neighbours of his family who had not been bombed out. They told us that part of his family had gone to a part of Rotterdam called "the Golden Mile", the area where richer people lived. They told him, "You can't have our car because, of course, we will need it". So we wondered how to get there. There was a shelter with lots of bikes nearby, from military people. So we said to each other, "Let's take a bike!" I remember I had always wanted a bike with hand brakes so I took one that had them. Before we set off I lowered the saddle down. He looked at me and said, "You have some experience in picking bikes!" When I was back in Amsterdam I found an address label on the bike so after two weeks I sent it back to its Rotterdam home.

Then we tried to find his family and amazingly we did. They had broken into a house because the people there, also relations of the man, had gone to the South of Holland. I remember the food left there was only preserves such

23

as bottled peaches and all kinds of fruit. But we were really hungry so that was our breakfast.

Then we set off by bike to Amsterdam and, as simple as that, we succeeded. We didn't follow the main roads so that we could keep out of the way of the Germans. Once we spotted a military group. They were shaving, in a camp by the outskirts of Amsterdam. We told them we were going to Amsterdam. They didn't realise we were military.

At one point we had to cross the Rhine in a small rowing boat. The ferryman asked, "Where have you come from?" We told him and he asked how terrible it was there, and did we know if this street – such and such a street was destroyed? He knew a bit about Rotterdam so we could tell him how it was. On the other side he gave us some food, so we were "reinforced" to go further.

We arrived in Amsterdam at about 2pm. It had taken four or five hours. We had set off just after 4am from the school and found the people (his family) at about seven in the morning. So we got to Amsterdam, via Amstelveen. From there we could see the fire brigades from Amsterdam were on their way to Rotterdam. From all the big cities of Holland the fire brigades went there to help.

Tootje

Harry was near Rotterdam, but had only just gone into the army. You could write them a letter every day, whatever you wanted, and you didn't have to use a stamp. I wrote a letter to Harry saying, "I'm going to write every day because it doesn't cost anything." I posted it but it was the only letter I sent because on the Friday morning our war started.

Kitty

Harry's army career was very short. He hadn't even been taught how to hold a rifle properly and had not yet been fully kitted out in army uniform. He was in the soldiers' school, close to Rotterdam. When the war started we heard that Rotterdam was being bombed and we were worried about Harry because we didn't know exactly where he was. The Germans threatened to bomb Rotterdam unless the Dutch capitulated. The Dutch did capitulate five days after the invasion but the Germans bombed it anyway. When the Germans invaded they (Harry's lot) fled – moved further south. But the war was over quickly so he just came home, probably the next day.

CHAPTER 3

Trying to Escape
"A Day in the life of Ordinary People"

Tootje

It was Monday, 13th May 1940, in Amsterdam. I was 13 and I was frightened. Without any warning last Friday we were invaded by the Germans and we were at war. A war was something you learnt about at school in history lessons. Also parents would talk about the 1914–1918 war. It was something vague and terrible and I did not like it happening to us now.

Harry, my brother, had just a few days ago been called up for his national service in the army. He was in Rotterdam. On our radio we kept hearing that lots of German planes were heading that way, a fact that we kept trying to hide from our English mother. Her Dutch geography was not so good. I remember often she was quietly crying as she was worried about her son and what would happen to her people in England. Although she'd had several warnings from the British consul to get back to England, it was easier said than done: we had a shop full of stock, a house full of possessions, lots of family and friends.

Looking back, one would say of course we should have gone, but at the time we hoped things would turn out okay. We didn't know our war would last only four days and that Holland would be occupied for five years. We didn't know that in those years the Germans would slaughter nearly all the Jews. We had led ordinary, secure Jewish lives. At the time it seemed inconceivable that any harm could come our way. Also, leaving the country would mean breaking up the home and we were a close-knit, loving family.

There was Mary, 26, whose (Jewish) husband a few days before had joined the merchant navy and was now on his way to North America. Next was Kitty, engaged to Maurice (Mozes Tertaas), also Jewish of course.

He was a good-looking, kind-hearted man with a great sense of humour. Maurice had a bike shop at the other side of the IJ [the water between Amsterdam Centre and Amsterdam North, pronounced "eye"]. The shop was called Bakfiets. Bakfiets are types of trolley used to transport goods from shops or to come round selling vegetables or flowers. They are still used today. The shop did repairs and also included the renting of cycle racks – safe storage for the many people who lived in flats. As they were not yet married, Kitty was still living with us in the Oudeschans.

Maurice

Then there was Lizzie, whose husband was also called up in the army: we were not sure where he was. Lizzie was expecting her first baby, which was due on 12th May.

Finally, there was my brother, Harry, who was in the army in Rotterdam. He was 21.

I don't know what we did for a couple of days after the invasion. I was only a child so wasn't consulted on anything. Then, on 13th May, Father decided we had to go the next day, after four days of the war. This was after another phone call from the consul. Dad found out that all was going wrong with the war in Holland and we were finished. So Mum and Dad decided to leave Holland and go to England after all.

The plan was that we would go to the town of Ware in Hertfordshire, where my mother's parents and brothers lived. I had never met them but Kitty had. The family used to go to England on holiday before times were bad. We didn't know what else was planned.

First we made a trip into the city to buy suitcases. We also needed a large bag for all the paraphernalia for a confinement and the needs of a new-born baby. We could not take too much as we had no car and everything had to be carried.

We had to make our way somehow to the coast. The 14th May was a beautiful day; the sun was shining, the trees were lovely and the birds were singing. How they could sing! They didn't they know we were sad and frightened and our world was in turmoil. So off we went, Mum, Dad, Kitty, Maurice, Lizzie and me. Normally a day at the seaside was a rare and exciting event. But that day I was full of apprehension.

At first we went to Zandvoort on the special seaside "blue tram". There were no boats to be seen. So we made our way to IJmuiden, a busy port with its own fishing fleet, where we joined thousands of Jews who sought to escape Holland by sea. As we walked through IJmuiden we saw and smelled the smoke of the burning oil of the refineries that were being destroyed by the Dutch so the Germans could not use them.

The sirens were going several times heralding air raid warnings. Dutch soldiers in the streets with pistols in their hands is another one of my memories of that time. With every air raid warning we had to find shelter where we could. Once we dived into a grocer's shop. I remember looking at the sweets and chocolates on display. Did we eat that day? Another time we dived into a doorway, and some kind people took us inside. They said if things go wrong and we could not get away we should go back to their house.

At last we got to the harbour, where one fishing boat was tied up. Many hundreds of people stood on the quay, hoping to get away the same as we were. A man with a megaphone was shouting that they were short of a crew member for the boat. If enough money and jewellery was collected they could get a captain. Presumably they got what they wanted because after a while the man was shouting again that now they found they were short of a first mate. So it went on. A lot of people who stood there with us were German refugees who had come to Holland to escape the persecution and concentration camps. They had thought they were safe at last because Holland was neutral and they would be left in peace. A lot of these refugees were well-to-do people and presumably provided a lot of the money and jewellery that the man with the megaphone asked for. It was, of course, terrible for them, finding themselves at the edge of Europe on the North Sea coast and with a mounting sense of despair.

As the boat did not seem to let us on, some people must have thought all was lost. So several cars, with whole families in them, just accelerated and drove straight into the harbour, accompanied by the screams of the people who witnessed this terrible event. They screamed because they nearly got run over and they screamed when they saw the water close over the tops of the cars. Some people held hands and just jumped into the sea. This was both Dutch and German Jews. It was very eerie and something I will never forget.

After a long time we were allowed to go aboard the boat. I remember sitting on the metal deck and feeling the rivets through my dress. I had very mixed feelings. I had never been away from Holland and I had never been on a sea voyage. Would I be seasick? What about all those mines floating in the sea? Would German planes shoot at us? What would it be like to live in England? Mum used to buy the English newspaper *News of the World*. As a little girl I would point at the photographs and ask her why these people had their picture taken. Knowing now what sort of newspaper it was these people were probably in sex scandals! Mum would say "she was murdered", "he was drunk" or "they were murderers". So it was not surprising I was slightly worried by the prospect of living in a land populated by drunks and murderers.

After we sat there for a while, Dad and Maurice made a tour of the boat. The crew was fast asleep, perhaps drunk. They must have already made several trips that day and on the days preceding. They were exhausted and refused to sail. Perhaps the captain was afraid to venture out in case he was shot at or hit a mine. Dad and Maurice found lots of guns and rifles. By that time the mood of the people had become frantic and volatile, bordering on mass hysteria. So they thought it best to throw the weapons overboard, which they did.

Another long time passed. It seemed we were not going anywhere. I don't know who made the decision to get off the boat – I can't remember – but we found ourselves back with the kind people who we met earlier. We were told Holland had capitulated. The people were the Porck family and they had made beds for us on the floor. My father cried. I did not know that men could cry. I remember very well that he said through his tears, "It won't be so bad when the Germans arrive here, it's when they stay it will be terrible, a catastrophe!"

After our rest we returned to Amsterdam the following day. That return journey is a complete blank in my memory.

Of all the happenings of that day, what I remember most of all and made the biggest impression was the acceleration of the cars, the screaming of the onlookers and the splashing of the water and what that meant. It stays with me forever. We were never ordinary people again.

It is only in the last few years that that I have identified our situation with the scenes on television of refugees, walking with just a few belongings, and I thought "that was us".

Kitty

I had been working for the British Tobacco Company, which had all English managers. My own manager had a number of warnings to leave, which eventually he did, with his family. He had asked me, "Aren't you going?" But this was difficult for us – to leave the business and the family. Mary had a little boy, Aby. With her husband in the merchant navy, she was on her own and did not want to come with us on our attempt to escape. Liesje's husband was in the army, and Harry too. It was hard to take the step to leave all our family, our friends and our country to become refugees.

Dad had heard that the Queen had gone to England on 13 May and I think that is what finally helped him make the decision to go. Liesje was due to have her baby so we took sheets and nappies in case anything happened. We took the "blue tram" via Haarlem to Zandvoort. Dad thought we could get a fisherman to take us to the other side. Perhaps the fisherman had already made some trips or was afraid to venture too far or be shot at. But there was only one boat and the fisherman said, "Oh, no, I'm not going across the sea." A man, something like an ambassador or consul, very rich, from Germany was trying to do the same thing with his family. He had a lovely big car. So Dad said to him perhaps we can do this together to persuade this fisherman. But although this man had much more money to offer, the fisherman wouldn't do it.

So Dad thought we'd try IJmuiden, which had a large fishing fleet, and we managed to get a lift part of the way there. On the walk into the town – still carrying our large bags – the air raid siren went. We had to find shelter, but of course we didn't know of any shelter. We passed a church and a man came out, who was the church warden, and said, "Come on in here, come on in here! You can have shelter here." So we went to his house. Alongside, there was a meeting room belonging to the church and he said we should go in there. He and his wife made us tea, took care of Liesje for us and made us comfortable. They felt so sorry for us as we had to flee from our country. That we were at the end so to speak. This was the first time we met the Porck family.

Mr Porck got us a bakfiets trolley (fixed to a cycle) which Liesje could sit in with her heavy bag. We went to the harbour. You couldn't believe it: there was only one ship. We stood a long time on the quay with a whole lot of people – many hundreds in number, mostly families, but we didn't speak much to each other. Everyone was too upset – leaving their country and their home.

A man was shouting through a megaphone "You are welcome to come aboard, but I can't let you on because we haven't got a first mate or a motor driver. But if we can raise enough money the man will do it. There is someone available but he wants paying." So we all gave money or jewellery. Then after a while we thought, "Why don't they let us on?" Then he'd say, "We haven't got an engineer or a captain." This happened two or three times and each time people gave more money. Someone would say, "I know one who lives in the town – he's bound to do it, if I only get 200 guilders." So people gave him the money but he walked away and never came back. So they conned us. The people who lived near the harbour were even charging us ten guilders for a glass of water!

This just showed us how unbelievably awful people could be, exploiting the most terrible situation. Dutch people often say, "Ahh, we were good during the war," but sometimes I tell them off and say, "You should have seen the people in IJmuiden and how they treated us when we were trying to flee from the Germans." So in that 24-hour period we had witnessed two opposites of human nature – the extreme kindness of the Porcks on one hand and such nastiness on the other. There we really learnt what people were made of.

At one point Maurice covered my eyes to try to protect me from what was happening around us. While our family stood on the quayside, cars were being driven into the water as some people had no hope left at all. Whole families going off the quay to their death. Some of these were likely to be German

Jewish refugees who had already fled years before from Germany. In Holland they had believed that they were safe. But, that day, they had been trying to flee again but failed. They were more aware what would be in store in a Nazi-occupied Holland.

A lot of people killed themselves in those first few days, over 300 we learnt later from watching World at War. In Amsterdam some jumped from the third floor or gassed themselves. The news had come through at that time that Holland had surrendered. In all the years nothing much was said about these events. Nothing written about it either – but Tootje and I clearly remember it.

At some stage we were let on the ship. It was a fishing boat, a trawler, confiscated by the Dutch Navy. So on board were sailors, but they were all asleep on the floor. They must have so busy, at war, for five days and nights. Or maybe they had been busy ferrying people to England? Anyway, they were just lying there in deep sleep next to their guns. All the people now seemed to be in the boat. It was very crowded and well down in the water. We were on the boat four or five hours.

Maurice and Father had gone for a walk around the boat. Past all the soldiers or sailors asleep, who were armed. They threw the guns overboard. It was a dangerous situation and they were concerned that in the atmosphere someone might do something crazy and start shooting.

After a few hours we got off the boat again. It was now late in the night and dark. Mr Porck came to fetch us back again with the trolley when he realised the boat was not going. So we returned with him to the church. They had said, "If anything goes wrong and you cannot get away come back here." Father cried. He felt despair; he had let everybody down. He and Mum had been warned to leave, they could have fled, but he had left it too late.

The next morning Maurice and I left the others with the Porcks. It was later we found out that they had 12 children! We hadn't seen any of them. We arrived in Amsterdam and took a look round to see how things were. There was nothing unusual at all. Everything was as we had left it at home. It was all quite surreal, so Father said the whole family should go home later the same day.

I was aware that the Dutch queen was broadcasting from England. I didn't hear it myself because we no longer had the radio but friends told me all about it. The Queen stayed somewhere near Newbury and Queen Mary used to visit her.

CHAPTER 4

Harry's Army Discharge

Harry

Then a new phase of my history started because I came to our home in the Oudeschans and nobody was in. A neighbour saw me and told me the news. She said, "All your family have gone to England. Here are the keys from your father for the house and shop." It was always a very big bunch of keys. Inside on the kitchen table was a note which said "We are fleeing to England. Join us if you can."

I thought about what to do. I went out again because I was excited – very keyed up about the situation I was now in and wondering what to do about the empty house. So I went to the house of my girlfriend, Kiki de Vries, and stayed there. In the meantime I was wondering about the future – no job, no family. I believed they had really gone to England. We didn't think in terms of were they "safe" or not. At that time we didn't know. But I fully agreed with their decision to try and go.

I think it was the 15th May when my parents and the family came back from IJmuiden. I remember that my dad was very down about what would happen next. The family of my girlfriend were also Jewish. Dad came in and Kiki's parents asked, "Why are you making so much fuss? Just stay because nothing will happen."

My father started to cry. He said to them, "We are all ruined." He said we would not be having a happy time under Nazi rule, but they didn't believe it, so we went home.

As was said, life goes on, or starts again.

The next thing I remember was that there was an order given that all the military people had to report to a certain place [probably the Oranje-Nassau barracks in Sarphatistsraat] in the centre of Amsterdam.

My father urged me not to go because he was afraid we would all be captured. But I went there, still in my plain clothes.

There were lots of people from all over Holland who had fought there. I remember that I took with me a man from Limburg because he didn't know where to go and had no place to stay, so I said he could stay with us.

In the mornings we had to report to the kazerne and in the evenings we could go home again. Until a certain time, when we were told we had to stay there. There were no beds so we had to sleep on the ground, which was not good.

That first evening we had a concert. The school where we were staying was surrounded by very big houses. They knew that we are all military people. How it began I don't know, but certain people started singing the famous songs from operas. Some people out of the group were good singers. So there was a very nice one-hour concert.

I was still in plain clothes. Every day trucks came and put things on the playground of the school. Uniforms, socks, shoes, all that kind of stuff. A lot of people took those things but I didn't want to have them because I didn't want to show I was a military man. They went out with two or three pairs of shoes. Afterwards I realised that it was the military staff who put the stuff there, to get rid of their stocks before the Germans took them. In fact, I should have taken some shoes – they would have been really handy later on.

Everything turned out all right. I was there for four or five days and then it was declared in the newspapers, which were already controlled by the Germans, that military people who had a job could go home and back to work. But first we had to return to the place where we had been at the end of the war. So I had to go back again to Rotterdam. There were special trains and a special station at Rotterdam because the main station had been destroyed. We arrived and went back to the school which had been our original barracks. I think it was a Saturday, I don't remember exactly. That evening we went out to see Rotterdam again. Now there was no smoke anymore and we couldn't find our way anymore. There were streets but they we unrecognisable. There were no landmarks. So it was terrible and the smell was terrible. It had been hot weather and I think there were still bodies lying underneath the rubble.

We returned to the school. I said I had a job and they said on Sunday you can go home within a day or so, but only if you have a uniform, i.e. as a real military man. So, with another sergeant who had no uniform, we went to several other barracks to try to get some uniforms but they had all been taken away. But I just had to get home. I went to the cellars where the stores were located: there I found some trousers, which were much too wide, and a military coat, which was also very big with long sleeves. And a cap which was twice the size of my head. So I filled it up with newspapers and put in on – but when I turned my head it twisted round. I had to put a wad of more newspaper up my arms. It was very comical.

One by one we had to go to the office and I remember when I came in, apart from the officer in charge, all the others at the table saw the hat and started laughing. The officer said, "But you can't go like this!"

I said, "I must have military uniform, and I have, so you have to let me go. But I can assure you that I won't go far in these clothes – as soon as I am out of here I'm changing back into my plain clothes!"

So they said okay; all was nice and neat and they gave me papers for my release and a free ticket for the train. I then changed back into my plain clothes – but I had to take the other stuff with me of course. There was a cushion. I opened it and took out all the straw stuffing and put the uniform in.

Often I am joking – and still do – that I had a wonderful military career. I had my first military exercise – for four days. Then I went to war and I was christened by war. Next I deserted and then I became a prisoner of war and finally I was sent for release. A whole military career in four weeks!

Later on they tried to make soldiers prisoners of war, but I had my papers and I was okay because I was working for Werkspoor, which was part of the German war industry, so I was free from this.

DEPARTEMENT)
 VAN) AFWIKKELINGSBUREAU .
DEFENSIE)

VIIe Afd.Nr.316 V.   's-GRAVENHAGE, 5 Maart 1941 .

O N D E R W E R P:
Vrijstelling van den
dienst,licht.

    Hierbij verleen ik U als dienstplichtige der lichting
1939 uit de gemeente AMSTERDAM
met ingang van 10 Maart 1941
voorgoed vrijstelling van den dienstplicht wegens
k o s t w i n n e r s c h a p .
    Voor den duur van deze vrijstelling is U buitengewoon
dienstplichtige.

    Tegen deze beslissing kan elk der in genoemde gemeente
voor dezelfde lichting ingeschreven personen of hun wettelij-
ke vertegenwoordiger uiterlijk den tienden dag na den dag,
waarop de beslissing door den burgemeester ter algemeene
kennis zal worden gebracht,in beroep komen.
    Het verzoekschrift,dat met redenen omkleed moet zijn,
moet worden ingediend bij den burgemeester,die dan voor de
doorzending zorgt.

       HET HOOFD VAN HET AFWIKKELINGSBUREAU,

A A N.

 den Heer

Eijman GRANAAT,
Oude Schans 20, II,
AMSTERDAM(C).

 1510

The document issued by the Ministry of Defence, dated 5th March 1941 declaring
Harry's deferment from national service for ever, because of "breadwinnership".

CHAPTER 5

Restrictions

Tootje

On our way home from IJmuiden in Paleisstraat, close to the Dam Square in the centre of Amsterdam, I remember very clearly seeing for the first time a whole troop of German soldiers marching in their uniforms. Of course, it became very commonplace to see them so I soon got used to it.

I remember lying in bed hearing large groups of German soldiers marching and singing. The "Horst Wessel" song (the Nazi anthem) or "Wir Fahren Gegen Engeland" ("We Go Against England") seemed to be the favourites. They sang very well. Just after the war I would lie in the same bed and hear the Canadians singing "Oh You Beautiful Doll". I liked that much better!

On returning home we found our gramophone was gone. Our neighbours, who had a key to our house, had come in and taken it, thinking that we would not be back. But when they heard us arriving they quickly brought it back, so that was all right.

In September 1940 I started at the school for tailoring and dress design in Weteringschans. I was still keen on the idea of designing clothes and the more technical side of dressmaking, but I was very disappointed that there was only one hour a week on design and half an hour drawing, which was what I enjoyed the most. We did some maths but it was so simple for me. The rest of the time was spent on sewing, which I wasn't so good at. There was a very sensible schoolmaster who advised us how to find a safe place in our houses in case a bomb fell. So I took this advice and chose a passageway, a small area with a door which had reinforced glass in it. This was in the middle of our house and seemed a perfectly safe place to be. The rest of the family were always hanging out of the windows looking, trying to see the planes.

One night (30th September 1940) a stick of four bombs fell. One fell in front on the canal where the boats were moored. The coal merchant lived there on his boat. He was getting out of bed and putting on his trousers to go out and see what was happening and a piece of shrapnel hit him in the thigh and it killed him. One fell in a corner by the canal – a woman from the baker's shop on the corner was hit and killed. Another fell in a playing field (this is now the playground round the back). The last one fell round the corner from us in Recht Boomssloot and a little girl and her father were killed.

Report of the bombing Recht Boomssloot 99

08.00 Report detective Jansen states that it appears that a bomb has hit the highway at the Recht Boomssloot near Oudeschans bridge. Also in the plot Oude Waal 31 and in the playground located behind the houses of Oude Waal and Oudeschans. All other plots received damage as a result of the windows blowing out. So far, three deaths have been transferred to Binnen Gasthuis. The barge resident lying in front of plot Oudeschans 12, who was in bed, got a thigh wound by broken glass. He was transported to the hospital.

The debris from that house all fell on to our house. We had a four-storey house, but the back was only two storeys and the wreckage fell on the part where our bedrooms

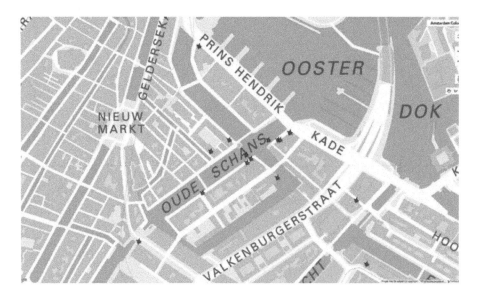

Positon of the bombing
Source maps.amsterdam.nl/woii

were. I was okay but the others! Kitty remembers it: hanging out of the window with her mum and dad, watching the planes and the searchlights. There was shooting and all of a sudden the whole house was in turmoil. They were lying on the floor, thrown by the force of the blast and there was glass everywhere.

I was pleased with myself for being the clever one to have worked out the safe place to be, but they could have been killed. After that our father replaced the big glass window in the shop with a window with six small panes of glass instead, in case the same thing happened again.

Next door some Nazis lived and there were more nearby (they lived on nearly every corner). On 10th May, after the invasion, they had all turned out in their black uniforms – it was a real shock to us and of course they knew we were Jewish because we closed our shop every Saturday. These were Dutch people that the family had known for a long time. They were Nazis all the time but we didn't know. One particular family of neighbours had a tobacconist's shop. After the bombs fell we had a tarpaulin put up outside our large broken front window. The tobacconist wrote on this in white chalk: "This we have to thank our English Allies for". It was true: it was a British bomb. They would have been targeting something else – the nearby docks or oil refineries in North Amsterdam. Or they could have been hit and had to get rid of their bombs. It was just one of those things you lived with – we didn't blame the British.

Liesje's relationship with Nico was sometimes stormy and I know there were arguments, but I can never remember Liesje being in a temper. Nico had been called up and went into the army. He was stationed at a camp in the middle of Holland, near Apeldoorn. Sometimes he came home on leave. By then I was at the sewing school, but most weekends I stayed with Liesje because she hated to be alone. I think she was a good housewife; her house was always tidy, but perhaps that was for visitors. She had her alarm clock set for 3am as it was an early start in the bakery business and she worked long hours in the shop.

Somewhere around this time I saw a dogfight between a German and English plane. This was on a visit to Liesje's house. I remember the very large green square with houses on one side, which was close to the bakery shop.

By then Harry had come out of the army and was working in an engineering firm. He was in the resistance. But not Father, at that point.

In October 1940 university lecturers, musicians, artists etc., and also some lawyers and judges, had to sign a paper to swear allegiance to the occupiers. Most signed and regretted it later. Many refused and could not work anymore. I don't know if they were punished or not. In fact, all civil servants and teachers had to fill in the so-called Aryan Attestation. The Dutch government-in-exile recommended civil servants stay in post as long as they felt they were serving the best interests of the people. This put them in a difficult position.

Liesje

Initially, Nico was in the army defending the Gelderse Valley. He served a total of eight months until, like Harry, he was discharged. On 24th May 1940 Liesje had her baby. She was called Jeanette (Netty), the same name as Nico's niece, the three-year-old daughter of Nico's sister, Alida, and her husband Gerrit Agsteribbe. Jeanette is a modern version of Nico's mother's name, Schoontje.

Despite the invasion, the bakery in the Weesperstraat was doing well. A total of 14 people were employed by then and bread deliveries were made to more than 1,000 customers. The bakery was especially popular

Source: Amsterdam City Archives

with the many German Jews who had settled in the area and would buy the specialty sourdough bread, plain or with aniseed.

Nico's parents opened a new branch of the bakery, in September 1940, and gave them this shop to manage. This was at Scheldestraat 139, a nice part of Amsterdam, where the richer people lived. Liesje served in the shop, Nico ran the bakery.

This was known as the river area because streets were named after rivers, not because it was near the river. After the war, streets nearby were renamed "Churchilllaan" and "Rooseveltlaan". Not far from this area there is also a small street called Granaatstraat! That is in the so-called diamond area, which is close to the diamond factory of Asscher, the man who became later the president of the Jewish Council. There are also a Saffierstraat and Smaragdstraat, all based on the names of precious stones like Granaat [= Garnet].

*Advertisement for the bakery from the Jewish Weekly, 18 December 1942
(joodsmonument.nl/isaac-vuijsje)*

Kitty

Maurice's mother [Sophia Velleman] had died in May 1924 when he was a child and his father had married again in March 1930, to a Christian woman [Louise Eichbergen] from Osterfeld in Germany, so Maurice was not so worried. Most Jews had not even thought of leaving.

After we got back from trying to escape from Holland life carried on much the same as normal. People went back to work. The shop reopened and Tootje went back to school on 1st September. Early on there were not many visible signs of the occupation. Sometimes you would see Germans walking about. But the Germans gradually introduced decrees to limit our freedoms one by one.

Jewish shops were only allowed to open between 3pm and 5pm. With each change we thought, "If this is all, we can bear it." Our nature was to try to make the best of it, but by 1942 there were restrictions on just about everything we did.

Tootje

Kitty and Maurice got married in January 1941 at the same venue as Nico and Liesje, the Grote Synagogue, and afterwards had their reception at the Pension Hiegentlicht. It was a quiet, typically Jewish wedding. Kitty borrowed Liesje's wedding dress and I wore the same bridesmaid's dress.

Kitty remembers going up the stairs of the synagogue and catching the seam of her wedding dress in her heel. This is bad luck in Holland. There was no honeymoon, but Dutch people didn't in those days. They were happy. When people got married in those days the woman gave up work – so Kitty left her job at the factory, and they worked together in the bicycle shop. This was at number 19 Wingerdweg, a street which runs alongside the Florapark. Their house was on the corner of Ribbesstraat and there was a school opposite.

Things were not so bad then and it didn't occur to us that marrying Maurice put Kitty more at risk. My mother had become Jewish so at that point my father would not have considered her to be anything but Jewish.

It was quite soon after this that I remember walking home from school with Willy and there would be notices put up in certain places with all the new regulations – e.g. all the Dutch people had to hand in their radios, Jews were not allowed into parks and then they introduced a curfew.

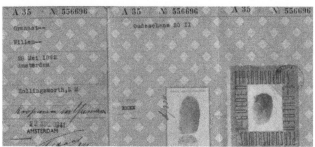

We all got identity cards, which we had to carry everywhere, with our photograph and fingerprints on. Everybody got them and they were the same except the Jews also had a big "J" on theirs.

After a while they brought in another rule that we had to wear a star. These came in a row on long rectangular pieces of yellow material with a black Star of David printed on them. When they came, you had to cut the stars out. They had J.O.O.D. printed on each. We had three or four of them and I cut them around using my sewing knowledge. I lined them by putting other material on and sewed all round, turning them inside out to make nice neat stars. I did this for all the family. For the backing I used some yellow and white checked material – this was left over from some frills I made to hang below some shelves in Kitty's house. Also there were safety pins so you could wear them on a coat or a dress and that's what we did. Stars had to be worn at least chest height on the left side of outer clothing in such a way to make it difficult to conceal them, although we all did try to conceal them by putting our hand on our handbag strap. Then Jews were not allowed to go in cinemas or on the tram; there were lots of different things that we couldn't do.

We didn't realise this was part of Hitler's master plan, his "ultimate aim" being to destroy the Jewish race.[3]

Harry

When I got back from leaving the army, life was going on in an almost normal way. There were various measures introduced but the biggest measures the Nazis introduced were not intended to shock. They tried to get at all the important people from the socialist and communist parties. But the really important ones were not there anymore. They were already in hiding. A lot of people had killed themselves – some very important ones, and some not important – they did not want to live in that situation. It's all in the history books.

I started to work. My job was to make technical drawings – a special kind of drawing to design tools for manufacturing. For example, I designed precision tools to make holes in machinery. I was designing these tools. We made the drawings and someone else wrote the work description of how to do the job. But there was no work for the first two months so they brought down our wages and gave us free time. Then the firm had to do work for the Germans. The drawings came in and we were always the first ones to take action in order for the tools to be made, otherwise the others couldn't work. So we had to work overtime, which was nice. We were offered a meal from the company as recompense. But we refused it because we wanted to be paid for the extra hours. The reason we gave was that they had cut our pay when work was short. So, as we were all youngsters, we came in and ate our own food and then started to play chess or cards, but didn't make the drawings. It was the first kind of resistance or protest and, indeed, from that time overtime was paid. Before the war, overtime was never paid to engineers. Also, before the war there were no checks made when you were ill. You just said you were ill and it was a matter of trust. The first controls only came after half a year, which we didn't mind too much. But when they cut our wages enough was enough!

And so it went on for a while. Then all kinds of restrictions were introduced by the Germans – and more and more measures came to the Jewish. Then, in early February 1941, it really started. The Dutch people who were pro-Germany were called the NSB (National Socialists); they had uniforms and went into the Jewish quarters. This was the area of Amsterdam where the largest part of the Jewish population, mainly the poor and unemployed, lived. Overall, approximately 40% were communists and 40% were socialists and there were a number of smaller parties. I don't know how many people were fascists. In certain quarters it was high but at that time most of the general population didn't accept that people were provoking the Jews. The NSB were hoping the people would respond to their provocation so they could take reprisals.

There was already a communist underground (resistance) organisation, which was very well organised. They were prepared in advance. From several parts of Amsterdam people came to end the provocation. They started fighting each other, just with their hands as they did not have guns. As a result of this fight, one of the NSB men was badly wounded. And as a consequence there were reprisals. It happened on a Saturday afternoon in the middle of the Jewish centre, where all the synagogues were and where children were playing. They shut all the bridges and they picked up all the people. They asked them "Are you Jewish?" Or else it was clear from their faces. They were honest people so they said "yes". Those who were not Jewish they let go. That afternoon it was a terrible situation – they took them out and did very nasty things: so different from just the previous day.

My father was also there, but at that point they were looking for young men and he was too old. I was at the house of my girlfriend and my father phoned a colleague of his in the same street, to warn me not to come home. So I stayed there, out of the way. In the evening we saw all the trucks going to Schoorl. On Sunday I wanted to go home so I went home and it happened again. They came out once more, because they said they did not have enough: their aim was 425 men and they only had 360. So they made a second run. They did it at the Sunday Jewish street market: Waterloopleinmarkt.

So they did it again and all the people were sent to Germany. So far as I know, only one or two came through. At Schoorl, the place where they went, a selection was made. People who were ill or disabled went home (the first time). All the others were sent away – at the time nobody knew where they were sent. Now I know they were sent to Mauthausen. But this is only from what I have read; it is not from my own memory.

At the Sunday market a lot of non-Jewish people used to come every week. It was very popular with all kinds of stalls. A lot of the stallholders were like comedians. They were selling their products but gathered an audience because it was very entertaining. One of the best – there were two who were very good – sold razor blades. One of his "talks" went like this: "You buy this also in the Kalverstraat, but if you go there, there is very nice shop – this already costs you 25c. Then there is nice carpet – another 25c. Then a nice lady with a lot of powder on her face. This is at least 50c. So you have a price of five guilders. But I am here – a poor man; you are standing on the street and if it rains you get wet. So my price is not five guilders, not four" and so on.

This gives you an idea of what that market was like and its atmosphere. It was quickly resented by the Germans.

Another one was also with razor blades; he bent them to demonstrate how flexible they were. Sometimes the blade would break accidentally and he would say, "So you can see how it looks like inside." He would mostly have an audience of 50 or 60. If he saw someone with the mark NSB among them, he would say, "Ladies and gentlemen we stop the performance as there is one rotten apple in the audience." So it stopped until the NSB person left. No one from the NSB liked this so they took revenge on him.

This is just to show you that, even before all the measures were brought in, there were Jewish people who had the guts to stand up and defend themselves, who had the character not to be intimidated, although they knew what the Germans and NSB were capable of.

It is significant that they made the second raid on a Sunday afternoon, at the market which was not just Jewish stallholders, although the majority were. But many of the visitors and customers were not Jewish. There were thousands of people there every Sunday and now they had seen the round-up of innocent Jews. They were upset and so after two days, initiated by the illegal Dutch Communist Party, who as I said were very well organised, there came to be a strike, a general strike in Amsterdam. No trams were running. Everything stopped including all the factories. People walked out. I remember one of the big bosses said to us, "Don't do that, it's dangerous. Please stay at work." But we went out on strike too. And that was the famous February strike. It was the first time that such a big group were saying "NO"… and the Germans didn't know what to do. There were proclamations, of course, and, as always, a small group of people who did not strike. So a few trams came through. But these were stopped and all the people taken out and the whole tram was tipped over. I don't know what the impact was of that strike, but afterwards there was an alteration in the attitude of the Germans. They didn't believe they could win the people over, or lots of people, with their theories alone so after that the measures grew sharper, but were less overt to the non-Jews.

At least three of the organisers from the strike were captured and they were killed later on. Up to then no one had been killed by the Germans, but after those terrible events it became an operation. They realised they would have to remove the Jews "under cover" if they were to succeed in their policy to win the Dutch population over and to become part of Germany.

It's not true to say this was the first strike because there were two proper strikes before – both won by the strikers. One by a shipbuilding company in Hamburg which did not have enough people to do the work, so they wanted labourers from the Dutch shipyards to go to Hamburg. The Dutch shipbuilders went on strike and the Germans said forget about it. The other one I can't remember – something to do with working in the woods – but it had the same result.

Liesje

When anti-Jewish measures were implemented in 1941 the Vuysje bakeries were obliged to close on Sundays. This went against normal Jewish practices because Sunday was not a holy day and bakeries were normally open – in fact, Sunday was one of the busiest days of the week because it followed the normal closure on the Sabbath, when all Jewish shops were closed.

Along with many other businesses in Amsterdam, the bakery participated in the 25th February strike and closed both shops that day. But notwithstanding the huge support from many sections of Amsterdam society for this event the February strike turned out to be the first and last big protest by the city's population – both Jewish and non-Jewish – against anti-Semitism. The occupiers realised that they needed to be more circumspect and started to operate more covertly against the city's Jewish population. Early solidarity for the Jews seemed to melt away.

Kitty

In February 1941 the Germans suddenly went with lorries into the Jewish Quarter. On a Sunday morning there was a Jewish market, a sort of flea market on the Waterlooplein. This was close to our house and the school [see map[4]]. The lorries came and German soldiers picked up a lot of Jewish boys – 20 and 21 years of age – I suppose they could see who was Jewish. They picked them up and took them away. That was how the first trouble started. They went to Mauthausen.[5]

It was first time Tootje and I heard the term and name of the camp. Some postcards came back – Maurice's two brothers went and sent a letter back.

Maurice's brothers were good-looking young men. They survived partly because they worked close to the kitchens and managed to get some extra food. One was called Harry (Hartog). He was younger than Maurice and went to Poland. He had a wife and child, who unfortunately didn't make it. The other brother was called Levie (dob 12/10/14). The records show that he died in Tenerife on 17th April 1983. He was married to Sophia van West, who died in Amersfoort in 1985. There was a further brother, David, who died as a baby. Dad [Willem] was also caught in this raid, but because he was elderly (not yet 50, but looked older), they let him go.

Although Kitty asserts that this was true, she remembers Maurice's brothers sent a letter or postcard back from Mauthausen and survived because they were selected to work in the kitchens. However, from my visit to NIOD in April 2015 I found handwritten accounts made by both brothers after the war. Levie Tertaas wrote on 5th July 1945 that he went from Westerbork in April 1942 and then spent two and a half years in Auschwitz. On 22nd January 1945 he went to Buchenwald and was liberated by the Russians on 8th May. Harry Tertaas's account, written on 19th September 1947, is very detailed and describes nine different camps where he was held between 23rd October 1942 and his liberation in May 1945, also from Buchenwald. So neither of the brothers went to Mauthausen but both were very fortunate to have survived so long in the camps.

Hartog (Harry) Tertaas #30244
Son of Joseph Tertaas (13/7/1890–22/11/1964) and Sophia Velleman (19/2/1890–15/5/1924). Following Sophia's death, Joseph remarried 26/3/1930 to Louise Eichbergen.

Married to: Reine Franschman #30243
Born 2/12/1922, Amsterdam (source: Gezinskaart Amsterdam; Overlijdensverklaring WO II Amsterdam), died 26/10/1942, Auschwitz, 19 years. Occupation: seamstress (source: Gezinskaart Amsterdam).

Child: Sophia Louise Tertaas #30245
Born 1/04/1940, Amsterdam, died 26/10/1942 Auschwitz, 2 years.

Source: In Memoriam

After that, everyone had registration forms to fill in – eventually this would lead to identity cards. The Dutch had not had ID cards before then. There were all sorts of questions: "Where do you live? What is your job?" About your grandparents – "How many are Jewish?" Everyone filled them in, although afterwards people said we (and all the people) should never have done it. Or we should have left a lot of blanks.

So all this was done rather obediently by the Jews, because not enlisting meant Mauthausen. In any case, Dutch people were law-abiding and if you get a form from the authorities, especially the Germans, you fill it in. Also, most Jews were aware of the fact that their neighbours knew that they were Jewish, so denying it was very risky and probably pointless.

Father put that we all had four Jewish grandparents. Even Mary, who was not even Father's child, she married a Jew. It was unheard-of not to. Liesje sometimes went out with non-Jews and got into a lot of trouble with her father, who had been known to try and beat this behaviour out of her.

After the forms were filled in, Jews were required to wear a star. ID cards, which had a photograph on them, also had a big "J" on them for those with three or four Jewish grandparents. That's when the restrictions started. We couldn't go in the park, the cinema, sit on a street bench. We were restricted in all public places and, later on, we saw them put up the big yellow boards "Jewish Quarter". It was mostly but not all Jewish people living there. The non-Jews stayed there, although later Jewish people were required to move. Liesje had to move to a Jewish Quarter. So she and Nico moved to Scheldestraat from the Plein. Later they had to give up the shop and move again – closer to the Plantage area. It became a ghetto with barbed wire round – people could go in and out as they pleased but the Germans could shut everyone in very easily when they wanted to, using the barbed wire and raising the bridges. Fortunately, the Oudeschans was close to the Jewish Quarter, though not in it.

All radios had to be handed in, firstly those belonging to Jews in April 1941 and, much later, everyone. Newspapers were censored. People could have cable radio, which was subscribed to, for so much per week; this was also censored. So it was all German music with a couple of Dutch stations.[6]

Tootje

There was a market – like the famous Petticoat Lane market in London, on a Sunday morning near where I lived. One Sunday the Germans came along and picked up all the young men who looked Jewish – this was before we had ID cards. The two brothers of Maurice Tertaas were picked up and taken away. They were forced to work in salt mines – they were the first people who went off. We didn't know where to, but I think they survived. We heard the name "Mauthausen". That's the first concentration camp name I ever heard of.

And that was of course terrible but nothing happened again for a while and after the strike the Germans didn't do any more picking up of Jews from the streets. The Germans may have thought that the Dutch would like the Jews being picked up, but then they saw that they didn't like it. Then there was an order that some Jewish people had to go and pack their belongings to be sent to work in the east and they had to come to some point or other, probably at Central Station. And that was that for a little while with a certain number of people having to go every week.

Meanwhile my father knew what was happening and sent me to IJmuiden, where I lived for about six months with the Porck family, who we had met when trying to escape. He went to The Hague and started his resistance work.

Although Amsterdam was the centre of the resistance, especially when it came to helping Jews, we think my father did his resistance work in The Hague because it became too dangerous in Amsterdam. He could easily be recognised by neighbours. Also, with less "resistance" activity in The Hague, he would more easily get away with his procurement of ID cards, and with Mary there it meant he had a base there too.

Harry and Fré started to use the opening bars from Ode to Joy (Beethoven's 9th symphony) as their "call sign" when visiting. Willem would whistle "Keep the Home Fires Burning" for his. Harry went to live in a bedsit somewhere, and so my mother was left alone in the house. Lizzie, Kitty and Mary were all married.

Because I wasn't in Amsterdam, I didn't know exactly how it all went, but I think the next thing was that Jewish people were buying rucksacks. There was good trade in rucksacks then! They had to pack and be ready to be collected from their homes. There was a curfew. From June 1942 all the Jews had to be indoors at eight o'clock. For the non-Jews it was 10 o'clock at night, until six in the morning. They made a division so that after 10pm, when everybody was inside, they could go round in their large lorries to collect up the Jews. There was a whole lot of Jews so it took a long time – months and months. Every night some more went. For those living in the Jewish Quarter it must have been terrifying. They'd take them to an old theatre, where they had to stay for a couple of days and then they were put on a train to the transit camps. I don't ever remember going to the Schouwburg theatre before the war, but I often went to the cinema, called "Tip Top" theatre.

CHAPTER 6

Early Resistance

Harry

In April 1941 they decided that every Dutch person should carry personal identification papers – before that we had never had them.[7]

They wanted it so you could show who you are and those held by Jews had to be stamped with a "J". And those stupid Dutchmen in the government offices cooperated. As a result Holland lost the highest percentage of its Jewish population. This was in contrast to Denmark, where nobody cooperated – led by their king, who stayed in Copenhagen throughout the war.

One Dutchman (Jacob Lentz) was in charge of designing the new identity card and he put all his effort to make a card which was impossible to forge. It was so perfect that even the Germans were surprised how good it was. It took a long time for the resistance to be able to print them themselves – the first success was not until 1944. It was only then possible because they had stolen the paper, they had the ink and a lot of the glue, using people on the inside who were willing to help, who worked in the factories.

That doesn't mean that we didn't have false ID cards before 1944, but they were not very good – if you looked at one, it seemed all right, but if you used a magnifying glass you could see it was wrong. But it was good enough to pass normal controls just on the street. If you were arrested and went to the police station or somewhere like that, they wouldn't accept it. They also had a copy of your papers. You had to give your photo and your fingerprint – you had to do it three times and the photo was in colour. Plus they had all your personal details and dates. They held all the copies in a central archive. So it was very easy: if they stopped you and they saw it was not the right person they can check your fingerprints or just ask for a copy of your card.

So that man who made the identity cards harmed a lot of people without realising it. He was not NSB – he was just so proud of his profession. You could say he was just doing his job. If there had happened to be another, less skilful man then it might have been easier to make false papers.

This map shows the concentration of Jews in Amsterdam in May 1941.
Each little black dot represents ten Jews (source: Verzetsmuseum, Amsterdam)

As an example of something that happened to me, later on in 1944 I was in charge of the department in the company I worked for, who were doing work for the Germans. They wanted to have certain important items for the war effort. They said they must be ready by a particular date so they asked me to make a plan to see if it was possible. I did my job and found a solution after just a week of trying. We had to start manufacturing straight away so I gave it to my chief, who said, "Very good, but isn't there a possibility that we do it another way from how you suggest?" And I understood that this would cause a delay, i.e. to deliberately take longer. That's what I mean by doing a job. I mention this to make it clear that by doing his job well one man can harm so many.

In 1941 the aim was for the total population of Holland to have an ID card and it took half a year before everyone had one. First we had to fill in a form. We had to put down all kinds of things, perhaps the same for Jews as everyone else. One of the questions required us to state the number of Jewish grandparents we had. There was the law from Nuremberg, where it was stated that you are only Aryan if you have four Aryan grandparents. It was the same for Jewish: if you had four you were Jewish; if you had three, you were also Jewish; if you had two you were half Jewish and if you had one you were nothing.

We all thought, not knowing anything to the contrary, that in our case it was four Jewish grandparents. We filled in our own forms – though perhaps it was done by the man of the house (e.g. Maurice for Kitty, Nico for Liesje, and Willem for Lily and Tootje). Only Mary, who knew better – as far as I know she only put two. Tootje later added that she recalls Mary did wear a star and she thinks she put down four Jewish grandparents. This is likely because Mary had married a Jew. As mentioned before, everyone thought, "Well, if this is all we have to do we must do it. We'll get through."

It was from then on very easy to catch Jewish people. They could just ask for the ID papers. There were always Germans at railway stations looking at people's papers – and other places like that. Normally they were looking for young people to send to Germany. I think the ID cards were completed in February 1942 and by then they had excellent lists of all the Jewish people: where they were living, what they were doing. They started to say, "This area is forbidden to Jewish people. This shop, this café is not allowed for Jewish people." And now with the ID cards they had the means to control it. Of course if you did not have a Jewish look about you, you could mostly go through without being stopped.

Then in early May 1942 they said that all the Jewish people had to wear a star – a yellow star with "Jood". They shaped the J, O and D to look a bit like Hebrew letters.

From now on if you are walking in the street they could recognise that you are Jewish. If you don't have it on your clothes and they check, if you have a "J" on your paper, then you would be arrested. Stars even had to be worn when standing at an open window.

I never wore the star on my clothes because, after that February, I had more or less already left home. I was coming home to visit but slept at other houses. I had said to my boss and to the personnel department, sorry I have to leave the firm: I want to go in hiding. And they were so kind they gave me a year's salary to live on. Ha!

After a few weeks, I asked a good friend and colleague of mine to help – it was someone I could trust. I said, "You know I have a "J" on my ID card, can I have yours so you can help me make it through this?" He agreed and gave me his card, reported that it was stolen and got another one.

I then made my own false card in a very simple way. I stuck my photo over the other one but without sanding it down first. Just put it over the top and with a pencil made the stamp circle mark. I didn't do anything about the fingerprint. It was false and if you put it up to the light you could see two photos. And it was thick in the place of the photo. I took the name of the man – Filip Voortman – and I memorised his date of birth, the name of his father and those kinds of things.

Harry

You have to understand that this was only the beginning of the resistance – the hiding in order to try to survive. Always at the beginning these things were very primitive. Until they – the enemy – found out how it worked when they looked at the false papers. So then we had to make them better, to try to keep one step ahead. For the resistance, they used the same method as I did, though more professionally, with sandpaper. Later they even had the possibility to steal blank papers so they could make really perfect ID cards and even when they checked they couldn't see that they were false. Only there were no records – they did not match up with any of the lists at the station. To get round this problem we had to break into the town halls – this was part of the resistance, to break in and steal the blank paper (blankos). But you have to understand there were 80,000–100,000 Jewish people and if they break in they might get only 50. They couldn't break into the Amsterdam office, because of high security. So it was only a few. All the other ones were made as I already described.

Kitty

Rationing of food had started from the beginning of the war. Placards were put up with notices of what was happening, but the German influence and its visibility was very gradual. There was clandestine radio – after a while Father didn't want the cable radio anymore because it was censored. Our big radio was given to Willy's parents at the beginning of the war, and they had it taped underneath their dining table. The resistance workers had a copier and published pamphlets, which gave us news. And of course there was the German news! Heavily censored. There was also Pathé News at the cinema (also censored). Plenty of news about the German victories at that point in the war so not much need for propaganda. Tootje remembers watching the news when the Germans arrived in Paris, which was 14th June 1940.

Life went on pretty much as normal, especially for the non-Jewish population. Sometimes German soldiers were seen walking around. There was a 10pm curfew – until six in the morning. It was later (11pm) for the Goyim. In June 1942 it became 8pm for Jews and in the last part of the war during the hunger winter it was 8pm for everyone. People were not too frightened in those days, although occasionally there were bombs dropped by the English.

Harry

It was soon after the restrictions were starting to have an impact, in early 1942, that a terrible event happened. The Nazis came in the night to the home of my girlfriend, Kiki. She was living with her parents in Amsterdam (Haarlemmerdijk 65). Her father had a shop in household goods. They came in quickly and they asked me who I was. I showed them my Filip Voortman papers, which looked okay, and at that time I wasn't wearing a star on my clothes. But then they turned on Kiki and demanded to see her papers. My heart sank to the floor and I asked myself then, and so many times afterwards, why I had not arranged a false ID for her. Regret and dismay remained with me ever since, for if I had given her false papers perhaps she would still be alive. Or if she had managed to escape out the back. But she had no chance and they took her away.

I remember that the next morning, from six o'clock, I was hanging out the window, looking for her. I was there for ages with her mother hoping in vain that she would come back. These are the thoughts that you want to go away. You just don't want them.

Harry was too emotional to continue at this point.

During the war the illegal press was also in Amsterdam (*Het Parool*), and later on I found out it was made by Jacques Presser. A similar situation happened to Mr Presser, a prominent member of the resistance. Although Presser was in hiding for the duration of the war, writing, reading and studying, his wife, Deborah Appel, was caught in a regular control. She was carrying a false ID and Presser blamed himself for this because he should have known better. She had very bad papers and he should have warned her not to travel with those.

Kiki (Rika de Vries) had lived with her parents and at that time her father, who had a useless hand, was 60. Every day he had to go to help run the shop. In the evening he would come home and the next morning he had to go there again. I am certain he thought that Kiki would come back. Of the people I was close to, she was the first one to go. I found out much later (after the war) that she was gassed in Auschwitz on 5th November 1942. She was just 22 years old.

There was still her mother and her aunt, her mother's sister. The husband and wife looked after the shop and her aunt did the cooking – she was a very good cook. We can still remember the dishes of different food. Kiki was not a close friend of Fré, but of course she knew her very well because at that time Fré was married to Kiki's older brother, Harry de Vries. They married just before the war, in 1940. Kiki was at the Jewish high school.

Erik has a picture of the Joodse HBS, school year 1937/1938. My father kept it all his life. Probably because Kiki is on that picture, but we don't know which girl is Kiki.

Salomon de Vries (head of family)
Leeuwarden, 20 July 1882
Auschwitz, 28 September 1942

Dora de Vries-de Groot (wife)
Leeuwarden, 16 November 1888
Sobibor, 23 April 1943

Rika de Vries (Kiki) (daughter)
Amsterdam, 29 October 1920
Auschwitz, 5 November 1942

Sara de Groot (relative)
Leeuwarden, 23 October 1882
Sobibor, 23 April 1943

Kiki had another sister, who was very nice looking, I think she was called May, who had a husband and a little child. They were living in the south of Holland. They were also at a certain moment deported and did not come back. At that time, the old lady, Kiki's mother, said in her heart she still believed Kiki was still alive. Fré and I both went to her house of the sister to clear it out – to see if we could find the stamps and distribution cards. We took some things with us, and took a horse and carriage. We asked the neighbours what had happened.

Harry de Vries was the brother of Kiki and first husband of Fré. He was one of the few people in Holland who had a passport. Otherwise you couldn't leave the country. Before the war, unless you went abroad for a holiday you didn't need a passport. So he had a passport and in it his name was Devries, which is a normal Dutch name. And on the passport they ask what job you have. He didn't want to say he was a pharmacist, so he said he was a carpenter. Fré: "But he had two left hands!" Harry: "Three left hands!" He went to help build the fortification walls in France. But his colleagues there were real carpenters and builders and found out quickly that he was not. Luckily he had other skills and one of them was very useful. He was very musical and could play the accordion. So they liked him and were happy to cover for him. After three months he came on leave to Holland – again with the false papers, so he had to hide them again, in case he was picked up.

One evening on his way home he was stopped by the Germans – but he was very good at languages and spoke excellent German. So he said, "I am from the secret police," and walked through. They accepted it because of his good pronunciation. He had "Gotspe" as we say in Dutch (a Yiddish word now in general use in the Dutch language: it means something like "lots of front", but with a certain extra meaning, namely that your action is completely illogical and therefore completely unexpected.)

There were some Jewish people who said the best hiding place is in the nest of the wolf. I know a couple of our age, who with false papers went to work in Germany. It was not expected.

After that Harry de Vries went back to France, but that was also dangerous so he wanted to get away from the occupied area. His behaviour was like a French man and his face was dark. He went to Vichy France and there he joined the Maquis, who were active in many forms of sabotage. His pistol is still upstairs. I've made it so that it can't work. It's for Kari. He was the only one from Kiki's immediate family to survive the war.

Harry de Vries was a chemist and a pharmacist and he was very clever. He was active in the resistance, using his chemistry skills for "burning" up. He destroyed the papers belonging to the resistance. It turned out that all the records of the Dutch serving in the war were destroyed, but the book doesn't say how. The implication is that it was the resistance who took steps to destroy the papers (perhaps it was Harry de Vries!) so the Germans couldn't trace or persecute anyone who had been in the Dutch forces. That's why the Germans at a certain point wanted all the Dutch soldiers who had fought them to turn themselves in to be prisoners of war or go to the labour camps. But at the same time all the offices holding the papers were destroyed. So it was total confusion and they couldn't tell who was in the army and who wasn't. This was a type of resistance for the soldiers of Holland. There were such good records kept by the Dutch. They could only rely on people's honesty and it is a natural instinct to comply and complete the forms. For generations in Holland we had been law-abiding and well organised. We had not been at war for so long.

So I think now I have to tell you more about my relationship to the family. At the point when I came back from Rotterdam (the second time) I learnt that Kitty and Maurice wanted to be hidden and they couldn't get an address. This had been completely unknown to me, because if they had contacted me about it, perhaps I could have helped them and taken them somewhere. But I didn't know that they had false papers, they didn't tell me – why they did not, I don't know. They didn't advertise what they wanted to do and I was never advertising what I was doing. It has nothing to do with the relationship. I told nobody apart from the group where I was working, what we were doing.

As I mentioned earlier, because I was employed by Werkspoor, a firm that was working for the German military industry, I was able to get a "Bescheidigung", a certificate, declaring that I was working for the German war effort. Because of that I was a so-called "Rüstungsjude", that is, a Jew who is to be spared. Erik still has the Bescheidigung. This was different to the red exemption stamps on the ID cards, but like them would also eventually be worthless.

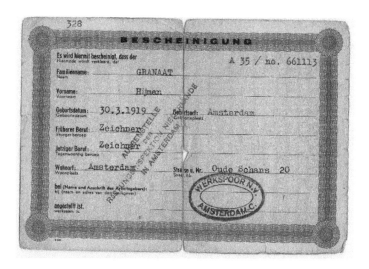

Tootje

In the same year that Kiki was taken, Fré's husband, Harry de Vries, left for France and Fré discovered she was pregnant. My brother Harry was there for her, first as a friend. They fell in love – I think he had always found her attractive. By the time Kari was born on 16th March 1943 they were very serious about each other and already living together. They both took care of Kari. Harry de Vries divorced Fré in May 1943 to make her safe from deportation. Fré married Harry in November 1946. They were very happy together until Harry's death in 1999.

There was a receiver for the piped radio in the flat below us. Our neighbour piped it up to our flat because we didn't subscribe to it. It's not often talked about that during the war no music by Jewish composers was ever played. So for five years we never heard any Mahler, Mendelssohn, Bruch, Schuman, Offenbach etc. But music was still a very important part of our lives. I remember there was always a series of concerts during the winter at the Concertgebouw. There was an abonnement (which means a subscription where you pay for a whole series of concerts). As students we could choose four concerts at a much-reduced price. Willy and I would look at the programme and choose the ones we both liked. I remember an incident when I had handed this to one of my teachers who said, "What does your brother say about you going to concerts?" I was dumbfounded and just pretended to ignore what she said. The thing was that my father was very principled and would not have gone to concerts or German films. But Harry and Fré used to go to films and concerts. I remember queuing some mornings for cinema tickets for them. Cinema tickets were available early on, before the restrictions started. So how did she know Harry and how did she know he was my brother? She must have been in the resistance too. I don't know why but I never mentioned it to Harry, until a couple of years before he died. I suppose I had forgotten about it and Harry did not like talking about the war until the start of this book project. Harry asked what her name was but I could not remember, though I did recall she was in her 40s and had very thin hair.

At least once a week, usually on a Saturday night, my parents, Harry and I went over on the ferry across the IJ to Kitty's house to play cards. Sometimes Maurice and Kitty hired a film projector and showed little films. Occasionally Lizzie and Nico were there too as Maurice and Nico got on well together and sometimes the two couples would go out as a foursome. Or Maurice organised other entertainments. For example, one time he got a glass blower to visit who showed us how to make little glass animals. Maurice was so nice; he was the real organiser. His birthday was the same day as Bob's, 2nd February. And he had a similar temperament – always helping people. Nico's birthday was on 1st Feb. We had lovely evenings together. The card game was whist, similar to bridge, and we gambled with cents. We had lots of laughs and drank tea or coffee. We rarely had alcohol in those days, just wine on religious or special occasions, or an advocaat on New Year's Eve. The wine was Spanish. When the war started you couldn't really buy it anymore. But our lifestyle was still good. We had pretty much what we wanted and we were not too affected by the rationing. Business was quite good too – following the recession it had picked up before the war started.

In the ironmonger's shop the Germans often came in – always in twos – and would ask: have you got so and so? Father would always say, "No, sorry." Or the German would say, I'll take that, but Father would say it was already sold to someone else. Once he did sell something and found out afterwards that it was for the Germans. He gave every penny away – I don't know how much – but he went with my mother and gave it to anyone who was busking in the street (playing the violin) until all the money was gone. He had very high and strict principles. Although my father was a disciplinarian, he was also a very loving man and was very fair. It was a happy, contented family home.

We used to buy the *Jewish Weekly* quite often, though not every week. We rarely went to the synagogue.

Kitty

The next thing was the Germans had letters sent to Jewish people – telling them they had to be ready. Young people aged 16–17 had to prepare and go with some clothes, in a rucksack, to assemble at a meeting point. They were to be sent to work for the Fatherland. That's how it started, with the youngsters being "resettled". It was awful. That's when, and why, Dad took Tootje to IJmuiden in about May 1942. She stayed with the same family that had helped us before, for about six months. We had kept in touch with them in between – had become friends and maybe went to visit them once or twice.

One thing I will never forget. To mend punctures in tyres you have to use a special resin-based glue, which was no longer available when the war started. So we couldn't mend tyres without this rubber solution, though we knew how to make it using pieces of rubber and petrol. Across from our house there was a large Roman Catholic church and school. The Germans had taken this over for their soldiers to live in. One evening a young German came over to the shop with his motorbike. He was 18 years old and the son of a farmer from the mountain area of southern Germany. He had never been away from home before. He asked my husband, "Can you repair my bike?"

My husband said, "Oh yes, I can do that but it will cost x amount, but you could give me some petrol instead of money, and then I can make some glue to repair tyres."

So he agreed to give my husband some petrol. The conversation went on and at one point Maurice told the German that he was Jewish. The boy said "No, that's impossible, you are not a Jew."

My husband said, "Of course I am". He had dark hair etc.

The boy continued, "But that's impossible, Jewish people don't work." It turned out that he had been brainwashed. He had seen propaganda films where the Jewish people had rat faces. They didn't work except as bankers, making money from lending to others etc. He couldn't understand that this friendly, helpful person could be Jewish. The boy was nice about it, though, and gave us a lot of petrol.

The Germans had taken away our ironmonger's shop early in 1942, at the same time they were confiscating many Jewish businesses. Sometimes they put a manager in. Others they just emptied. For our shop, they turned up and out we had to go. Tootje remembers that all her school books and exercise books were left behind. So we lost everything, including any personal possessions that might be in the shop. All the stock went to an ironmonger's shop at number 15 across the canal, which until recently was still there. This had also been confiscated and was being run by Dutch Nazis. This had been anticipated by the family and the most valuable goods, such as copper plate, was hidden in the canal. Later, they were able to reuse this copper for the restoration of the shop.

Liesje

Life was increasingly difficult for the Jews, but it was still nothing compared to what was to come. In September 1941 signs started to go up "Für Juden verboten" (Prohibited for Jews) at all non-Jewish cinemas, theatres, libraries, shops and museums. Liesje, optimistic by nature, would have thought, like many others, that if nothing worse happens they could live with this. Other than some already deported, Jews were still in their own homes and there was hope that Germany would eventually lose the war.

At the beginning of May 1942, all Jews over six years old had to wear the star. It had to be clearly visible even if they were standing on a balcony or in a door opening. Public transport, parks and zoos were forbidden to people with three or more Jewish grandparents. Cinema owners were forced to show German propaganda films such as *The Eternal Jew*, where Jews filmed in Poland were compared with disease-spreading rats.

This was depressing for Liesje, who was a naturally outgoing person. She would have been relieved that Netty – only two years old – didn't have to wear the star and she wasn't deterred from her wish to have a second baby.

CHAPTER 7

Willem's Resistance Work

Harry

Our dad, Willem's role in the resistance was to obtain, by various means, good identity cards from non-Jews. [An identity card without the "J" was eventually worth between 300 and 500 guilders, worth about £100–£150. But, at that stage of the war and with Willem's ability to negotiate good prices, he was able to acquire them more cheaply.]

When he was in hiding with his own false papers he would drink with them or talk to them and if he thought it was someone he could trust he said, "Could you help me?" He bought them in bars, up to ten or 15 different bars. He then brought them to Amsterdam and I took them from him. I gave them to the resistance groups who started to falsify them and if I needed one I only had to ask. And they gave me the money that my dad was paying.

You may be thinking, where did the money come from? In fact, it was coming from the big banks that had connections with the free Dutch. The Dutch government in England also gave money. It was called the NSF, the Nationaal Steunfonds, which translates to "National Support Fund".[8] Of course, this was also illegal but it was much easier at that higher level. Few people knew where the money came from and we never had to explain what we needed the money for because we were trusted. So I took the money to pass to my father. As far as I remember, I gave 25 guilders for each one.

So, for the people giving their cards, the amount of money would have been quite attractive and an incentive. They could get 100 guilders for four cards and at that time 100 guilders was a lot of money. So they liked us to do it and we got off to a good start.

When I took them from my father I hid them in my socks. Then I passed them on to certain people in our circle of friends, but they didn't know who it was that had given them to me. This was the Group Gerretsen.

Afterwards, we found out that they were going to a central group. Not only did they make the identification passes, but they also made other false papers, German papers for the German Jews who needed to show they belonged to the SS or the Gestapo, if they were checked. They were not so difficult to falsify – because they were not designed by the Dutch!

So, they had all kinds of stamps and became a very important group. They would make false SS papers, for example, so they could go in German uniforms and infiltrate the prisons and take out the prisoners they wanted to liberate. So there was a group who specialised in forging at a very high level.

Sadly, the best man who made them – it was one man – couldn't stop what he was doing after the war. He was so crazy [Harry pointed at the side of his head] inside he didn't accept that it was wrong. So he started to get involved with the Algerians when they were fighting against the French. He made false money for them and for that he got imprisoned. This shows you that it was sometimes difficult after the war to get back to normal.

[Erik: Harry was talking about Sal Santen, a famous revolutionary in the Netherlands. He was a Trotskyite and involved in the Algerian conflict. He made counterfeit French money, trying to disrupt the economy. He got caught and was handed over to the Dutch authorities. Because of his great bravery during the occupation his punishment was mild and after 15 months he was a free man, still very respected by the people and society in general. He was a close friend of Miep, one of Fré's very old friends, who spoke at her funeral. Sal Santen was also the son-in-law of Henk Sneevliet, an internationally renowned revolutionary and one of the founders of the Chinese Communist Party. Still a hero in China.

"From my experience, I knew that such a scrap of paper could mean life or death."
Sal Santen.

CHAPTER 8

Tootje in Hiding

Tootje

From early May 1942 I was in IJmuiden. And that's how it was. The Porcks, who had shown us such kindness when we had attempted to escape two years earlier, now risked their lives sheltering me. My identity card had a "J" on it and I should have worn the star, which of course I didn't. They had 12 children between one and 20 years old and a foster child, plus an old grandfather living with them. Even so, they gave me a little room of my own. I didn't have to be "hidden" as they let everyone think I was another foster child. Looking back, this was another great example of my father's ingenuity. He'd kept in touch with Mr Porck and remembered the offer of help. This meant I didn't have to live in a cramped space like Anne Frank and I could go outdoors every day. I became very fond of the whole family and especially friendly with their daughter, Klasien, who was the same age as me – 15 years old. She was in a wheelchair from having polio as a child and often had to stay in bed. I remember once we walked all the way to Santpoort to visit a friend or distant relative of Mrs Porck, taking it in turns to push the wheelchair. And then all the way back again. It was a long way. Although I had a good life there I was homesick for Amsterdam and missed my best friend, Willy.

Tootje (right) with the family in IJmuiden

Mrs Porck was a very good cook. I used to help peel the potatoes, which was a lot of potatoes for 17 people! She had bad varicose veins which were very itchy. It was better for other people to scratch them for her so as to do it gently. This gave her some relief and sometimes I did this for her. Mr Porck was the verger at the church and deeply religious. The family always said the Lord's Prayer at mealtimes. But he also had a sense of humour. If there was a funeral he would walk alongside the cortege and as it passed by their house he would surreptitiously give a thumbs-up sign because he knew we would be looking out of the window. All the while he would be looking very serious – he was very good at that. Despite everything he was optimistic and often said good will prevail over evil. The last time I saw him, after the war, he took me to one side and told me that I had lots of goodness in me – he was very complimentary.

Bob remembers visiting IJmuiden and meeting the family after the war and Mrs Porck serving little glasses filled with berry fruits. Delicious!

I stayed in touch with Klasien after the war. Her legs improved and for a while she worked as a receptionist in a nursing home. In 1988 I went to her funeral with Kitty and Frans. Since then I have been exchanging letters with her brother, Joh. We remembered each other very fondly. Joh continued to live close to IJmuiden, until he passed away on 25th December 2015.

Up until this point my father still managed to keep his business going, though without the shop, but at least he did some work. His resistance work

The Porck family: From left to right (starting back row) Jan, Greeth, Frans, Rie, Joh (Johan Hendrick), Henk (father), Betsy, Gerrit, Henk, Francina (mother), Gonkel, Klasien, Theo, Diny

consisted of going to a café in the evening and saying to some poor-looking people, "If you lose your identity card I'll give you some money. And you can go to the police and say, 'Oh dear, I've lost my identity card,' and they will give you another one". He took the cards and, like Harry, hid them in his socks because railway stations were dangerous places and he wasn't wearing a star. He used to travel from The Hague where he was doing this work. He would regularly make a detour on his way to Amsterdam, via IJmuiden to visit me, and would show me the ID cards in his socks. I suppose he must have paid some money for my upkeep, but I don't know about that. And then he went on to Amsterdam and handed the ID cards over to Harry and Fré. They had the cards altered with another photo stuck on there to help Jews to go in hiding. Later on, a while after that, they managed to print their own identity cards, but not in the beginning. I think Kitty

Tootje and Joh reunited in October 2014

and Maurice had ID cards without the "J", but I don't know why the whole family didn't have these false cards.

Kitty

Anyway, so things were hotting up and Tootje had gone to live in IJmuiden. It was the first time she had been away from home.

It wasn't long after that Father stayed away from home too and went to live in The Hague. It was Father's birthday on 28th May 1942. Liesje and I had decided to buy a present together for his birthday; he was going to be 50. I came over the water on my bicycle to my mother's house. Liesje had not arrived yet but there were two men (Dutch Nazi SS) in long leather coats. They were looking behind the pictures and in all the cupboards, and the sideboard. I don't know what they were looking for, but someone must have said he was a communist. Mum took me to one side and whispered, "They are waiting for your father, they want your father." He had probably already started doing resistance work and someone must have given him away. The Germans didn't usually *search* – they just came and took you away.

My mother took me into the other room and told me where Father was. He had gone to a farmer, Mr Bugining. He was a customer for whom he made some special ironwork (metal clamps that fitted over the noses of young calves to stop them drinking milk, though they could still eat other food). He had gone to deliver these on his bike. I thought to myself, "well, when he comes home he must come over the bridge; I'll go and stand near the bridge so I can warn him." In the meantime, Liesje also arrived. The men asked, "Where is your father," but Liesje said, "I don't know" – because she didn't. Liesje and I said we had to leave to do some shopping and they let us leave. I said to Liesje, "We must stay by the bridge." There was a Jewish butcher just there – in case we missed him, we went in and I said "My father will be coming over the bridge, but there are people waiting for him. So if you see him, please warn him not to come home."

Liesje and I kept on standing there, but in the end Mum came and said the men had gone. She said, "They couldn't wait any longer, but as soon as he comes home he must go to the SS bureau." We knew if he went in there that he would never come out again. So us sisters went home to our husbands and when he eventually came home he left again very quickly and after that he never came to the Oudeschans again. He went to The Hague and began doing his resistance work full-time. From then on he would just come for short visits after seeing Tootje in IJmuiden; usually they would meet at Fré's house. Apart from that, our mother and Father rarely saw each other again until in the camp. So the whole family was split apart. Harry may have been in hiding also – he was even more at risk as a young man.

Harry had a couple of friends who helped with the false ID cards – one was a photographer. He would make a photo and another who would make a new stamp, matching it in to the original one, so you couldn't see the difference. This was the beginning of it all. Later they began to print their own ID cards from scratch. Sometimes they stole them and once they raided some offices and stole a few hundred of them to give to Jews who needed them.

My mother used to be cross before the war because Willem was always helping others (German Jewish refugees), not the family. We were poor and she thought he should spend more time on the business. Perhaps he thought other people had to have them as they were at greater risk. Maurice and I tried to find somewhere else to stay, where we were not known. It sounds an easy thing to do, but we couldn't. I can remember going out, with the star on my coat. I would put my handbag on my shoulder, holding it in such a way to hide the star.

Liesje

In the summer of 1942, not long after Liesje found out she was expecting her second child, the systematic deportation of Amsterdam Jews started. The Jewish Council[9] sent out warrants in alphabetical order. These stated that those named had to make their way to Westerbork for "possible participation in the work expansion in Germany under police supervision for a medical examination and personal investigation". The luggage allowed was limited and a list was provided: two blankets, one set of bed linen, nourishment for three days, toiletries, a plate, cutlery and a mug. The *Jewish Weekly* published the following: "All Jews who do not comply with the call for work expansion in Germany will be taken prisoner and taken to Mauthausen concentration camp."

It is hard to believe that the Jewish Council believed those being deported would really be working in Germany. How could anyone explain why the very young, the very old and the infirm were included? Members of the Jewish Council were given exemptions because they were deemed to be already doing labour service. Some Council members rejected the idea that leading Jews should be reprieved. Those justifying the Jewish Council's role believed that:

1. *By continuing this work they might be able to delay implementation.*
2. *Obtaining exemption for leading Jews would mean the retention of a strong core on which to rebuild Jewish society.*
3. *Winding up the Jewish Council would play into the hands of the rougher elements and give the Germans a pretext to intensify measures.*

Nico's sister Alida and her husband, Gerrit Agsteribbe, were among the first to be called up for labour service. They decided to comply, taking their children, Marcus, nearly ten years old, and Jeanette, age four. Belongings which they could not take with them were divided among their cousins. Netty was given her namesake's ring. Once they had gone they were never seen or heard of again. Their Jewish Monument records are as follows:

Gerrit Agsteribbe (Head of family)
Amsterdam, 13 April 1908
Auschwitz, 30 September 1942

Alida Agsteribbe-Vuijsje (wife)
Amsterdam, 28 September 1908
Auschwitz, 29 July 1942

Marcus Agsteribbe (son)
Amsterdam, 26 August 1932
Auschwitz, 29 July 1942

Jeannette Agsteribbe (daughter)
Amsterdam, 12 November 1937
Auschwitz, 29 July 1942

Radio Orange broadcast from the BBC on 29th July: "Just how does it help the German war effort to herd thousands of defenceless Jewish Poles and do away with them in gas chambers? How does it help the effort when thousands of Jewish Dutchmen are dragged out of their country?"

The numbers reporting for deportation decreased as Jews became suspicious owing to the lack of letters from Germany. Among his family, Nico was the most suspicious about the Germans' real intentions and began to fear the worst when the Germans evacuated firstly the Jewish Hospital, and then the mental hospital at Apeldoorn. This is covered in more detail in Chapter 12.

Tootje

After I had been six months in hiding with the Porck family in IJmuiden they had to move house. The Germans wanted to make fortifications along the seafront (part of Hitler's Atlantic Wall). When they moved, perhaps because Father kept coming to visit, they thought it was getting too dangerous having me there. So I couldn't stay with them any longer and I went back to Amsterdam. It was early November 1942. I was only home a few weeks.

CHAPTER 9

The Arrests

Kitty

On 2nd December 1942 Maurice and I were taken away by the Germans. It was late in the evening. A lot of people had a key to our shop because they used to bring their bicycles in and out of storage, so we didn't have to keep opening it. They were all people around us that we knew and trusted. There was one friend, a man Maurice had known since his youth, Herman, who was often going out to visit a farmer who would sell him apples, which were already becoming scarce. He would often return late with his bike. We were still up and we heard knocking on the door of the shop and we thought it was this friend with the apples.

We opened the door and were shocked to see a couple of German soldiers standing there, with guns. They spoke to us loudly, in German. We had a dog called Rooky, who started barking, and I started screaming. One said, "Take the dog away or we'll shoot him." So I quickly took his lead and went outside to take him to our neighbour upstairs. This gave me time to tell the neighbour what had happened. We had two doors at the corner of the house. The Germans came in one door, but there was another. I rang the bell and said, "The Germans are here, they've come to fetch us!" I had already packed a special suitcase with clothes and some other things, in case this happened. Because we had two entrances, we thought we would have a chance to run away. But, at that moment, because we never thought it would be Germans – we thought it was a friend, we just opened the door. I told the woman, "Please will you tell my mother that I have been taken away with my husband by the Germans?" I told her the address and gave her the suitcase, and the dog. So she went the next morning to my mother, which was very nice of her.

We were supposed to have a rucksack to take with us, which most people did, but I don't think we had one. I can remember they had fetched all the Jewish people to the same part of town. We were all in rows, walking along Prins Hendrikkade, where the spire is over the bridge which is so near to my house, where my mother lived. I was screaming and shouting and crying, "Oh, Mummy's tower," referring to the famous landmark. We were very frightened. We were taken to this place, to the Schouwburg theatre, where all the Jews were kept together. We slept there overnight in the auditorium – with many others.

My mother-in-law, Louise (Maurice's stepmother), who was a German Christian, sent me a letter, smuggled in by the Jewish assistants. In it she told us that Mum and Tootje had also been arrested and were also going on the train to the camp, so I knew they were coming.

Tootje

I had been home from IJmuiden about four weeks when Kitty was arrested with her husband, Maurice. Mum and I were woken up by a ring on the doorbell early that morning by one of Kitty's neighbours, who said they'd been taken away. It was fairly early as Mum and I were still in bed. Well, my mother went into hysterics, as she used to do. Kitty was her favourite, always had been and always would be. I had a bit of a job to quieten her down. But, when she seemed a bit better later that morning, I went to try and find Harry to ask him what we should do now that Kitty had been arrested.

But I couldn't find Harry. I went to the address where he was in hiding, but he wasn't there. So I went to where Kiki's parents lived but he wasn't there either. I didn't know where else to look. So I thought I'd better go home and see what Mum was up to – because of her hysterics – and to look after her. At that point I still didn't know about her not being Jewish.

Unbeknown to me, Mother had already been trying to establish officially that she wasn't Jewish. She'd been going to the headquarters of the German Gestapo, in the Euterpestraat, which was the main building of the Dutch/German security forces. She told them she was not Jewish and she could prove it with papers from England, but they had to go through the Swiss Red Cross and do all sorts of things to check if it was true and it took a long time, so nothing was happening about that. But she had been visiting the Gestapo headquarters several times.

Looking back, it seems that my mother was attempting to declare herself not Jewish without telling her husband or her children. We know she did not tell me or Kitty and probably not Harry either. If Harry had known about it he would have followed up this line of enquiry first. We don't know if she told Willem or whether he had encouraged her or even suggested it. We know that Willem was very astute and was aware more than most of the threat the family was under. But, overall, I think my mother acted on her own initiative. With him gone to The Hague she had to start looking after herself and perhaps she had begun to feel "abandoned" by him and her loyalty to him eroded.

When I got back, my mother was all right, so she said, "Let's go to the Euterpestraat". She was going to tell them that she was not Jewish and that Kitty was born in England. But she did not tell me this until later. I didn't know what she was going to say to try to get Kitty released. I suppose I thought she was just going to say she was English. In fact, she was even going to say that Kitty was not her husband's child so she was not Jewish at all and they should let her go. So off we went.

Indeed, there was a declaration signed by the Mayor of Amsterdam, dated 11th December 1942, stating that Lily belonged to the Anglican Church. This was probably delivered to 20 Oudeschans just ten days or so after our arrest. But we didn't know about this.

Kitty

Mum had already been to the German authorities and said, "My husband wanted me to be a Jew, but I am not a Jew. He forced me to say that I am Jewish, but I am a Christian woman and I am not Jewish." They believed her and gave her a special stamp and with that stamp you were not sent to the camp.[10]

So she asked the man, "Can I also go without a star?"

One said "Yes" but the other said "I don't think so."

Tootje

So that day (Thursday 3rd Dec 1942), the day we tried to get Kitty out, Mother decided we would both go out without stars on our coats. We went to the Euterpestraat, about a 50-minute walk.

While my mother went in into an office, I stood outside in the corridor to wait for her. As I looked along the corridor I recognised one of our neighbours from the Koningstraat nearby (now the restaurant Van Beeren, a favourite place to eat in Amsterdam). It was Mr Koeman – he was our milkman, who was a very nice man, or so I thought! He had a lovely wife and his mother, who had died before the war, I had liked very much. The son had taken over the shop by then. Father and I used to shop there always; we went every day for milk or for cheese because we had no fridge. It was raw milk, which had to be boiled before use.

Our house was in a very small area, just about five or six houses, but it turned out there were at least four Nazi families there. I think it must have been a terrible place after all. I used to love Holland but those memories, especially the thought that Mr Koeman probably got the reward for dobbing us in, have made me go off it more and more.

Anyway, our milkman turned out to be a Nazi too and he was there in his black uniform and happened to see me. He said something to someone. I think he told the people that I wasn't wearing a star and that I was Jewish. The next thing I knew they started pushing me about, punched me (though not hard) and threw me into the room with my mother. And that was that. They arrested us both because we were not wearing a star. They said we were going to be sent to Westerbork. We were put into a gym – the building had been a school originally. During the day, more people came in dribs and drabs.

It wasn't a place where you were kept overnight, but they collected Jews there during the day. There were soldiers with big dogs and guns.

Kitty and Maurice were in the theatre (Hollandse Schouwburg), which was in the Jewish Quarter, and the people who were collected every night were held there. They were held there for, say, two or three days as there was a transport twice a week to Westerbork. From the place we went to, as it happens, there was a transport on the same day. So we didn't have to stay overnight.

Late that night – it must have been about midnight – we all had to go with German soldiers with guns and dogs. I can also remember going along the tramlines, over the same bridge as Kitty to the railway station. It was cold and pitch dark everywhere because of the blackout. There was nobody on the streets because of the curfew. We were put into darkened trams (the "dark tram"), all locked up and we went along to the Central Station. I went over the bridge, so close to where we lived, and saw my tower, the Montelbaanstoren, and wondered if I would ever see it again.

Although I can't say that I was particularly worried. I was sort of pragmatic and just waited to see what would happen. This is typical of me – always worrying about the small things that might go wrong and never do, rather than the big events.

Anyway, we got to the station and were loaded onto the trains. They were those old-fashioned trains which had little compartments with a door each side and you couldn't walk from one compartment to another. There were about eight or ten people in each compartment and we sat there in the dark all the way to Westerbork. It was a long, long journey, all the way round Utrecht and Apeldoorn, which took at least six hours. We arrived at Westerbork in the early morning, when it was just about getting light. Kitty and Maurice knew we were on the same train as us but until we got there we didn't know. They found us and we were reunited.

CHAPTER 10

Arrival at Westerbork

Tootje

When we arrived at Westerbork we had to give up our money, our ration cards and our house keys. We had to strip and were then searched and after that we were checked to see if we had any lice on our heads. At another office we went to we were lucky as there was a distant relative working in the office. His name was Jacob (Jaap) Granaat. This was Tante (Aunt) Mietje's son, who was also in the camp. Mietje was the widow of Isaac Granaat, who died in 1917. Isaac was the son of Simon Granaat, the older brother of my grandfather [Hijman Levie – refer to second family tree showing Simon Granaat and his family].

Jacob said, "You shouldn't be here. I'll see that you are kept here and not sent on to Poland." This was the first inkling I had that my mother was not Jewish.

Some people who came there had a special stamp in their identity card; if they were doing work for the Germans or, like us, said they were foreign nationals or any other reason, they would stay there at Westerbork until their case was sorted out. Eventually they would either be sent on to Poland or go back to Holland – to Amsterdam or wherever they came from. Of course, most of them were sent on. If you were ill they kept you at Westerbork until you were healthy again. I knew a boy with only one leg; he was about ten years old. His artificial leg was being repaired in Amsterdam and when we went home I was given a letter by his parents to send to the person at the clinic who was doing the repair, not to send the leg back, because as long as he did not have the artificial leg he could stay at Westerbork until he got it. I suppose in the end he went anyway.

But, crucially, Jacob Granaat helped us to get this special stamp on our ID cards. Unfortunately, he had no way of saving himself, his mother or his wife, Aleida.

Mietje Granaat-van Kreveld
Eemsstraat 8 II, Amsterdam
Hoorn, 31 October 1874
Sobibor, 9 July 1943

Jacob Granaat (Head of family)
Amsterdam, 14 December 1909
Auschwitz, 10 September 1943
Address: Niersstraat 1 III, Amsterdam
Occupation: Representative

Aleida Granaat-Groen (wife)
Amsterdam, 3 November 1907
Auschwitz, 10 September 1943

In addition, a Jokos* file (#30016) on this family reveals that a claim was lodged for compensation for valuables surrendered to the Lippmann-Rosenthal looting bank. More information can be found in *"Counting My Steps"* by Jakov Lind and Therese Cornips (Amsterdam 1970).[11]

* The Jokos foundation was a partnership arrangement between various Jewish organisations. The files are stored at the Amsterdam Municipal Archives.

We stayed on and for the first two or three days we were there I slept with my mother in one very narrow top bunk. They were bunks three high and of course she kept worrying that I would fall out. Every time I fell asleep she would shake me awake again! Then it was sorted out a bit and we could all have a bunk each. That would have been after the first "transport" to Auschwitz the following Tuesday. I stayed in the top bunk. The bunks were all three high and there were two side by side with another bunk on the end, so there were nine people sort of in a little group.

Photo from trip to Westerbork Musuem April 2015

I think there were about 200 or 250 women in our part of the barrack and the same amount of men on the other side of the barrack. It was one long barrack. We had no belongings with us, but we were given some clothes and some other items which had belonged to women who had already been sent on to Auschwitz.[12]

Kitty

Shortly after we arrived, Mum said, "Stay with me, I'm going to the office." She had said to someone I have a claim that I am not Jewish. In the office there you had to queue up and when it was your turn you could tell your story. She started telling them, "Kitty is not the child of my husband," that I was from another man who was not Jewish and that she was a Christian woman. The man she told this to was Hijman Bromet, the son of Simon Bromet and Carolina Granaat (Willem's eldest sister). He was the sales manager of the Bijenkorf in The Hague. He lived in Wassenaar, very close to The Hague. We think he had already been told of our arrival by our distant cousin, Jacob, who had seen us when we arrived. Hijman listened to it all and knew there was some truth in the story. Because he was our cousin, he would have heard about my father being the "black sheep" of the family for marrying the English woman now standing in front of him. The secretary next to him had to type it all out. Then we got the stamp on our papers and as long as this was looked after we were free from the transport (to the concentration camp). Sort of temporary papers. It was very fortunate for us that Hijman, because of his standing in the community, was able to get a position of authority in the camp. For now the four of us were safe (including Maurice, as it was claimed he was married to a non-Jew). Maurice went along with all this, of course. Father agreed to it as well by then. He went with Harry to a lawyer to swear an affidavit that it was true. It had to go through Switzerland – and then letters to England to verify it all – and that all took a long time.

Later on we found out (I think Harry told me) that the solicitor acting on our behalf thought it was a such a weak case that he kept putting the papers to do with our claim underneath – to the bottom of the pile of all the other cases. Every time it came to the top he said, "Let's put it underneath again," and he ordered his staff to do this. But it took such a long time that everyone was getting worried. Harry went to see him again and he told Harry that all the time he had been using these delaying tactics. Harry said, "You'd better not do this anymore because she's in the camp and it's too risky." The solicitor was worried he'd lose the case and thought that, so long as the case was under investigation, they were safe from being sent on. He thought this was the right thing to do but in fact it was very dangerous for them, because you never knew with the Germans. There was a lot of people who paid perhaps 30,000 guilders to get on a certain list not to be sent away, but all of sudden maybe after three months they were gone (and therefore dead).

For example, there was a factory where they made army clothes. The Jews who worked there thought they were quite safe as they had the special stamp. A relation of Maurice worked there [this was likely to be his sister-in-law, Reine Franschman, who was a seamstress]. All of a sudden, one Friday afternoon they closed the factory and brought all the people to Westerbork. They had no spare clothes and no belongings with them. Many people were trying to get these stamps but in the end, in the Germans' eyes, ultimately everyone was going to go so there would be no more Jews. But in the meantime they wanted and needed Jews to help get the other Jews away.[13]

The whole camp was run by Jews. Our cousin, Hijman, was one of the Jewish Commandants in the camp (there was an overall German Commandant and a number of Jewish Commandants) but he did nothing more to help us. In the end he died too.

Portrait of Simon and his wife, Caroline Bromet-Granaat, taken in
Studio William, Damstraat 34 Amsterdam (circa 1896)
(source: Collection Jewish Historical Museum)

Carolina Bromet-Granaat (Willem's sister)
Amsterdam, 22 September 1876
Theresienstadt, 24 September 1944

Husband (Simon Bromet) survived the war
One child (Cornelia) survived the war
Address: Harstenhoekweg 39, Scheveningen

Son: Hijman Bromet and his family
Address: Jonkerlaan 43, Wassenaar, The Hague

Hijman Bromet (Head of family)
Amsterdam, 25 June 1904
Extern kommando Grünberg, 31 December 1944

Alice Bromet-Flesseman (spouse)
Rotterdam, 10 December 1905
Auschwitz, 8 October 1944

Yvonne Carla Bromet (daughter)
Den Haag, 25 November 1932
Auschwitz, 8 October 1944

Madeleine Alice Bromet (daughter)
Den Haag, 2 December 1934
Auschwitz, 8 October 1944

Philip Emanuel Bromet (son)
Wassenaar, 12 June 1942
Auschwitz, 8 October 1944

People have asked me, "How did you feel when your mother said you were not Jewish?" It was such strange times that we did not really care. It didn't make much impression on me. Because of everything else that was happening to us, it was not so shocking. I did wonder how could she ever make up such a

*Cornelia Bromet and Jacob Polak on their wedding day, 29th July 1942, in The Hague.
Cornelia is sitting beside her parents, Caroline Bromet-Granaat and Simon Bromet,
Jacob beside his parents, Rebecca Polak-Hacker and Joel Polak
(source: Collection Jewish Historical Museum)*

story! I knew it was all made up, but because I was born in England I suppose it was plausible.

I know I was conceived before they were married but both Mary and I believed that I was his real daughter. But we didn't discuss it at all at the time. It was typed out and we got the stamp and then we didn't talk about it anymore. We thought Mary was our real sister too. In those days things like that were not talked about. We took it at face value and didn't ask questions.

CHAPTER 11

Tootje at Westerbork

Tootje

A couple of days after we had arrived at Westerbork we would witness the first "transport". We were fast asleep and the door was thrown open at two o'clock in the morning. A German soldier came in with the Jewish barrack leader. I soon found out this was the German Commandant of the camp, Gemmeker. They shouted the names of the people who had to get ready to go on transport to Poland. So a whole family – Jonathan Meyer, Marie Meyer, Jacob Meyer and we would hear the names of a whole family, sometimes with four or five children. Of course everyone was worried in case they were going to be on the list. So the first night everybody was crying and screaming and then when it was over we would give each other a hug and go back to sleep. At about six o'clock in the morning you would see the people whose names had been called walking past the little window. We would watch them go, all bedraggled and bent over, carrying their belongings. They went to the trains and, as you have seen on television, they were cattle wagons and goods trains, not ordinary passenger trains. The railway track passed right through the middle of the camp, so when the train was there it dominated life at the camp – physically and mentally. It was such a grim symbol of being deported east. There was a weekly transport every Tuesday, with about 70 people with their rucksacks crowded into each wagon, with just two buckets in the middle; one with water and one for the human waste. It was really awful. It took hours to load everybody onto the trains and then three days for the journey to Poland. In all, about 1,000 people went on every transport. Afterwards, I realised that the filling of the trains was the main objective of the camp and the machinery of it all ran like clockwork. It was more important than getting supplies to the forces at the front.

We couldn't go near the trains when they were being loaded. We were kept locked in the barracks. But on a Monday when it arrived empty I could go right up to it and touch it. I did this one time.

Westerbork – Auschwitz train sign
Source: campwesterbork.nl

Later, the people in Westerbork knew of Auschwitz and heard from the resistance, who had heard on the BBC that it was an extermination camp, but when I was there we didn't know where the train was going or what would happen to the people on it.[14]

"Millions of Jews were being murdered and the civilized world heard about it and either disbelieved it or stood aghast. Possibly the Allies could have done little about it, but they failed to do even little. Every initiative founded in ocean of political, economic and military excuses." Presser.

I think there might have been two transports like that after we arrived and then somebody got scarlet fever and we were not allowed out of our barracks for three weeks. We were quarantined, so we would not spread the disease. In that time we got to know everybody really well, as you can imagine. After the three weeks was over we were pleased to be able to go out for a walk in the fresh air. We saw the chap, who we slightly knew, who had had scarlet fever. I believe he died afterwards from the disease. But anyway somebody else got it on that same day and there were megaphones everywhere announcing that we had to go back inside for another three weeks! As I said, we knew everybody inside out and after the six weeks of course most were sent off to Poland. We were very upset when they were sent on the next transport.[15]

There was a woman who looked very posh. During the two lots of quarantine she would sit up in bed, in the bottom bunk, during the day. She had a large fur coat, all silver fox, which she had draped over her. She would sit there filing her nails. Her little girl, about three or four years old, was beautiful like a little film star, with lovely curly hair. Everybody loved her and I was her special friend. She would run around making friends with everyone. One day they found she had nits in her hair and it all got shaved off. They were both sent on.

Another friend in Westerbork was in the next bunk to me, Hannah Frankel [or Frankle] and we became good friends during the quarantine because for six weeks we were cooped up together. We always talked in the evenings. She didn't come back. Her father was very upright and nice.

I remember a dear school friend called Esther. She didn't come back either.

Meanwhile, it was cold and freezing weather. It was horrible. There was just cold water to wash in and very occasionally, if you asked for it, you could get a little coupon so you could have a hot shower but you had to be very quick – in a few minutes the water would stop. They would shout out a warning in German after three minutes that there was "zwei minuten" left. Usually Mum and I would go in together. But it was nice to do that occasionally. By then Lizzie and Harry sent clothes and other things from Amsterdam for us, and some food parcels.

You were allowed to send a postcard with five words to say, for example, "thanks for the parcel". So I got the idea to thank them for something that we wanted. Once I said, "Thanks for the pancakes." They understood, so sent us pancakes. In addition, we were allowed one letter per month. I wrote how much we enjoyed the pancakes and I continued to sniff the empty paper. That made Lizzie cry, she told me later.

The food at Westerbork was reasonable and similar to what we used to have at home, for example stamppot, a typical Dutch dish of mashed potato with carrots and gravy poured over.

I did not work much. My mother and I peeled potatoes sometimes in the kitchen. Often I was not very well. I used to be ill quite a lot when I was young – high temperatures and sore throats – and frequently missed school, usually for about two days at a time. Anyway, in Westerbork I had very low temperatures and the doctor would come round and say I must stay in bed. Early in the morning the nurse would come round and say (indignantly), "I don't know why you have to stay in bed with a low temperature." So I would get up, but then the doctor would come back at about ten and say, "Oh, no, you've got to stay in bed." So that went on for a while – perhaps he was trying to save me. All the doctors and nurses at Westerbork were Jewish.

One day I had to go to the hospital in Groningen, which is a town in the north of Holland. There's a big hospital there, a university hospital, and I had to go there to be looked at by a specialist. This was quite an event, to get out of the camp. We were taken in a big lorry which had a tarpaulin all over it and was open ended. There were Germans at each end of the lorry with guns and some other people who had to go to Groningen too for one reason or another. It was quite a long drive. I thought it was so strange; we could just look outside and when we got to Groningen I could see people going around on their business, on bicycles, walking, shopping etc. There were gleaming shop windows and I realised that the world was still going on normally outside. People were buying things and there was food on display. I remember seeing sausages hanging up. I had forgotten that life was still going on. Nothing much was done in the hospital – dental or throat, I can't remember. Afterwards I think the specialist must have sent a report back.

Another thing that happened was to do with a mental institute in a town called Apeldoorn. You know we used to say a joke, "Oh, yeah, you should be in Apeldoorn", if someone was a bit silly. Anyway, some people were in a worse condition than others, as happens in mental institutes, but they all seemed to be left alone by the Germans. Nothing was happening to them. So some Dutch Jews thought, "Ooh, I'll go there, like an in-patient and I might be safe then because nothing is happening to them." It was a beautiful place with lovely gardens and until January 1943 the Germans left it alone. Well, one day Maurice and some other strong young men in Westerbork had to go and be ready early in the morning, to go to Apeldoorn. The entire hospital of 869 psychiatric patients was emptied out, plus 50 nurses (20 had volunteered to go and a further 30 were forced to). Maurice had to help get the people out of the institution and onto the trains. He saw the German police ransack the building and beating many of the patients, who were completely defenceless. They were loaded into trucks and then put on the train and were transported straight to Auschwitz. They didn't even go to Westerbork. So all the people, whether they were mentally ill or not, adults and children, were sent like that, all mixed together and straight to their death. Maurice was very upset when he came back to Westerbork, having had to do this and seen such brutality first-hand. Following this he transferred to the section of the camp which looked after the kitchens. He worked as a server delivering food to the barracks in little trolleys.

My period in Westerbork was only a fairly short time – 4½ months in all – but it seems such a very important part of my life. I don't know why – I've had a whole lot of life at 74 years (92 at date of publication), but that little bit is so important, I often think about it and can remember lots of details. We were there during the winter and, round about March 1943, Mother and I were able to spend more time outdoors and I remember the sun shining and standing against one of the barracks and feeling the lovely warm sunshine on me. That was good. But I also remember the squelch of mud when it was wet – there was a great deal of mud.

There was one toilet in the corner of the washroom, no partition or door. This was for use at night and during the six weeks' quarantine. There was one long sink with six cold water taps. That washroom was used by all 250 women.

Source: campwesterbork.nl

Outside were latrines with partitions between the eight seats. So when you entered you saw the women sitting but when you were sat down you couldn't see each other. In Amsterdam just before the war an Italian-style ice cream parlour opened with about eight different flavours. Quite a novelty. The tubs were set in a long counter with eight holes. The shop was called "Gamba". There was one set of latrines at Westerbork which had no partitions – these were nicknamed Gamba! So we could still laugh and joke. There was plenty of Jewish humour. This ice cream parlour "Gamba" was there until late 1990s.

Westerbork was run by German refugees who were Jews. Because it had been built for refugees before the war, there were nice little houses just for them. Afterwards they built the great big barracks for the whole lot of Jews – the Dutch ones.

There was a little camp hospital that was run by the Jews and the barrack leader was a Jew. Of course, there were German soldiers and the hierarchy was there – the Germans and high-up Dutch Nazis. There was barbed wire and watchtowers like you see on television with a soldier at the top with a gun. And soldiers with dogs patrolled around the perimeter of the camp. There were Dutch Nazis who were high up in there, in their offices. They seemed to run the place as well.

There used to be a boy, a teenage boy with a bicycle, like a courier and he would come to the barrack to bring us messages that we had to go and see them in their office. German Jews were investigating the claim that my mother and Kitty were not Jewish and that I was half Jewish. We would go there and they would ask us one or two questions about our case and then we would go back to the barracks again. And perhaps a week later another message would come by courier and we would go again. It took ages before it was all sorted out and the story could be verified.

Kitty's husband, Maurice, worked in the kitchen. He was a very nice man, full of fun and jokes and good-looking too. They were very much in love. Kitty also worked.

My mother and I occasionally went for little walks during the daytime and in the early evening – I think the curfew at Westerbork was eight or nine o'clock – I would go around and have a little walk on my own and see what was happening in the other barracks. There were tables in between all the bunks. Like I said, nine people in the three bunks stuck together and then a table and then another nine and then another table. Sometimes it would be somebody's birthday and there would be a white sheet used as a tablecloth on one of the tables. Dutch people enjoy their birthdays very much and even in Westerbork they would celebrate them in their own way as best they could. Also there might be a cabaret in one of the barracks and I would stand outside and watch through the window. Sometimes there would be famous people there who were singing songs or had a violin they brought with them or do a bit of opera or operetta. Some of the songs – when I hear them occasionally, I still remember: "The Merry Widow" and that sort of thing.

One song was called "My Yiddish Mamma". Before the war it was quite a popular song – like it would have been in the top ten nowadays. Some of the words in there are "We kneel to you" and that sort of thing – all about kneeling – and when the song was finished, the Master of Ceremony said, "Well in the song we talk about kneeling but we never kneel!. We don't kneel in our religion and we never kneel for anybody and we will never kneel for anybody!" And we were all cheering and feeling so uplifted – you know, when I come to think about it, most of the people who were cheering and feeling something like patriotism, they all went to their death anyway, but of course they didn't know that – we didn't know what was happening in Poland. We thought everybody had to work – of course, there were babies and old people who clearly would not be able to work. What about them? We didn't want to know what was happening after they left. We just didn't think any further.

Anyway, there must have been quite a few Zionists in our barrack because one morning, at six o'clock, among all the people who were going to the train on transport, there was this group of Zionists and they marched. They didn't walk all bent and bedraggled – they marched with their head held high and they sang the Jewish National Anthem, which is about hope. It is called the Hatikvah. Whenever I hear this song now, it brings tears to my eyes – you know, the memory of it. I want this and the hymn Jerusalem to be played at my funeral!

Another vivid memory I have is of two nuns in their black, long, flowing habits walking about in Westerbork with the yellow star on their chests. These were genuine nuns who had converted to Catholicism before the war, but they were of Jewish origin of course. I expect they went the same way as most other people there.

My cousin, Hijman Bromet, was one of the top people in Westerbork. He had been one of the directors of the Bijenkorf in The Hague and was probably one of the last to be deported. He did not come back. His parents, Uncle Simon and Tante Lientje (Caroline), lived in one of the nice little houses in Westerbork. We used to visit them sometimes, two or three times in all. Eventually they were sent to Theresienstadt, a better concentration camp. At nearly the end of the war they were going to be exchanged for German prisoners and so get to Switzerland. But Lientje died in Theresienstadt in September 1944. Uncle Simon came back to Holland and lived in The Hague. Bob has met him, and remembers him being very well dressed and elegant. So, apart from Uncle Simon, most of the family were killed. Simon lost his wife and his two sons (Hijman and Joseph), together with their wives and all his grandchildren (ten of his family in all) were killed.

CHAPTER 12

Willem's Arrest and Escape

Harry

The war moved on and we now understood about Mum: that she was not Jewish but was in Westerbork with two of my sisters and my brother-in-law. So I tried to find a way to get them out. I didn't know about the declaration signed by the Mayor which would have proved that she was not Jewish. It was far too risky for me to be seen in the Oudeschans. I knew too many people, and after my mother's arrest I couldn't trust any of the neighbours not to inform on me.

Then my father was arrested. As I have already told, he had been buying the identification papers from non-Jewish people he had got friendly with. He gave them money in exchange for ID cards they would steal from their colleagues. So he would get ten identification papers from labourers (people who needed the money most) then ten from another profession, such as gardeners or shop workers and so on. Others were stolen by pickpockets. After a while the police got too many people coming in and saying they had lost their papers or had them stolen, so they made an investigation. It was not too difficult to find out where the central point was and so my father was arrested. He was sent to the "Oranje Hotel" in Scheveningen, which is close to The Hague, where political prisoners were kept and he stayed there for several weeks before the Jewish prisoners were transported to Westerbork.

His arrest is likely to have been January 1943. There is a list of prisoners, resistance people who have been in the Oranje Hotel. Unfortunately, however, Willem is not to be found on that list.

Miraculously he escaped. There was a truck outside the prison waiting to transport the prisoners to Westerbork. The prison was well known to everybody, as it was a political one so there were always people hanging around to see what was happening. So on this day there was the normal crowd when the prisoners were being loaded into the truck. My dad was not the type to be the first to get in the truck. Instead, he wanted to hang back until he was sure he had no means of escape, so he would rather be the last one. While the soldiers were helping a man who had only one leg he saw his chance. He decided to use the crowd and slowly he walked backwards towards them in such a way that the people understood what he wanted to do. They opened the circle so he could be in among them and enclosed him. In that way he could move to the outside of the crowd, where he simply came out and walked away. That was his escape.

I heard that from him the same evening. He came to Amsterdam and I don't know why he knew my address as it was a hidden address – perhaps I told him before that if something happens you can come there, or Mary might

Streekmuseum Jan Anderson (jananderson.nl).

have known it. He walked I think 50 minutes at least to arrive at that place. Now he could stay there of course – it was a good address, nice people – and the next morning I went to the Vechtstraat to find a hiding place for my dad, and Fré's mother opened her house so he could stay there for several days.

But meanwhile he was still meeting me and we walked the streets together looking for a possibility to get the family out of Westerbork. It was then that he decided to hire a lawyer and he made a declaration by swearing an affidavit that she was a Christian and that Kitty was not his child.

Imagine what Willem went through, having done all he could to make her Jewish and then because of good reasons, he had to try to reverse the whole thing in an attempt to save her and their children!

Later I learned from Sebastian van Lissum (the current owner of 15 Oudeschans who has carried out a lot of research into the Granaat family) that Louis, one of Willem's older brothers had also married out of the faith and this was kept secret. Louis' first wife Sipora Vigevano was Jewish and died in September 1935. His second wife whom he married in March 1940, was Margueritte Koffiard. Did he pretend she was the mother of his sons, David and Herman, in order to hide their four Jewish grandparents? Louis and both sons survived the war.]

Tootje

I think we heard about Father's arrest in a letter from Harry. He had still been free and working in The Hague when we were all arrested. He was caught some time after that and became a prisoner. For quite a while he was in Scheveningen Prison, near The Hague. It became known as the Oranje Hotel – because so many resistance prisoners were held there.

He was there perhaps a few weeks then escaped, imprisoned again and arrived at Westerbork while we were still there. At Westerbork we sometimes received food parcels from Amsterdam. My father would use the name "Vogel" (Dutch for bird) instead of "Granaat". On a label on one of the parcels he had written, "The bird has flown" [in Dutch]. We recognised his handwriting and we knew it meant that he was free. Afterwards we heard how he did that.

[In the spring of 1943, just before the mass deportations, the Germans began emptying old people's homes, hospitals, orphanages and other institutions such as Scheveningen Prison. Later we found out that 300 prisoners were "evacuated" and sent to Westerbork on 10 March. However, the deportations from the prison must have started in January and the transport from which Willem escape must have been several weeks earlier, as he was already in Westerbork on 6th March.]

My father told us how he escaped. He was among the prisoners who were having to climb up into a lorry and the German soldiers were helping a man who was invalid and there were a lot of people standing around watching, plus other German guards, nosy Dutch people and the rest of the prisoners. And my father just eased himself backwards and backwards and the Germans didn't notice and in the end he got away and he walked to Mary's house. By then he had shoulder-length curly grey hair, which was very unusual in those days, so she cut his hair short and he made his way back to Amsterdam. He probably took the train without any identity papers on him, using some money from Mary, and we heard then that he was free, via the message on the food label. But he went back to do the same work and of course somebody must have seen him and he was arrested again and this time he was beaten and his legs were put in chains. He was brought to Westerbork.

Harry

A few weeks after Willem's escape he went back to his address in The Hague and started to collect identification papers again. And no one is without faults.

He did it at just the same place and it was easy for him to be caught and after few weeks he was arrested again. This time he was tortured by his captors because they had been blamed for his earlier escape and so they took their revenge. He was sent directly to Westerbork as a punishment case and there he was put in special barracks and he had no chance to get out.

I knew his address in The Hague, so I went there and made a search of his room to see if some identification cards were still there. I didn't find any. I was wondering about a lot of newspapers I found there. Because in the evening he must have been reading all the things he could get his hands on [laughing] and they were all piled up. I had to unfold them all to make sure there was nothing hidden inside. I'm still wondering why the housekeeper let me in the room. So perhaps she knew a little bit of his business. So that was that.

The reason I went to search was because, on two previous occasions when people had been picked up, within a matter of days they had been visited and their house searched. Both times they found nothing. As a precaution Fré hid the false ID cards and other papers in Kari's cot (even before she was born). Fré also hid them down her corset.

At the time of one of these raids we were giving shelter to a non-Jewish German girl called Friedel, who was under a death sentence in Germany for resistance work. Friedel was a political refugee – a communist and a friend of Fré. They had been in the same left-wing organisation since the 1930s. She was in the house when the SS arrived. Thinking very quickly she put on an apron and picked up a rug and carpet beater and walked out of the house, bold as brass, past the men and managed not to be caught. Soon afterwards she was moved to a safe house in Limburg, where German accents were common.

Tootje

When my father was brought to Westerbork he had to go into the punishment barrack (number 66), which happened to be next to our one.

There was a whole lot of barracks, but I think only one for punishment at that time. He couldn't go out for a walk around like we could, just kept in there. But we could see him through the window as it was just a few metres away. Because we never knew when any of us would go, every time there was a transport he would put something in the window, a handkerchief or whatever, so we would know and see that he was still there and safe. We were allowed to go for walks but people in the punishment barracks were not allowed out.

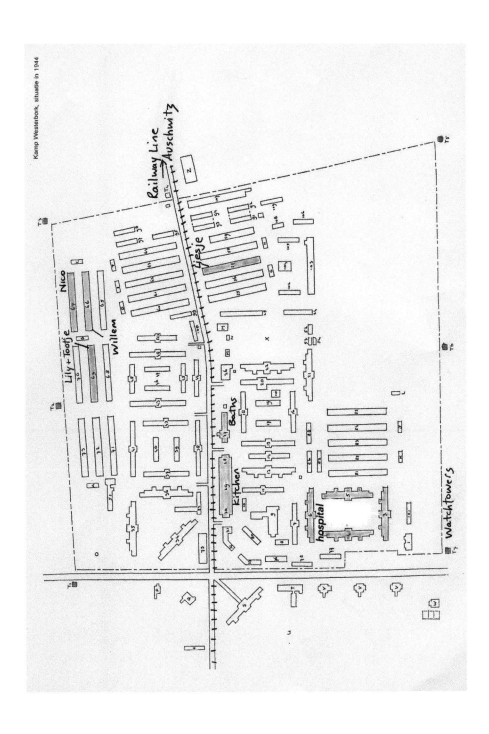

Kamp Westerbork, situatie in 1944

So Willem had been at Westerbork the same time as us but not for so long. During the day we could occasionally visit him and so talk to him. The last night we were there in April 1943 we were able to say goodbye to him before we were released. Mother wanted to know what the secret was that he had promised to tell her one day. But he wouldn't tell her and said it could wait for another time – so perhaps this meant he did not really think it was the end. Or alternatively that he wanted to give that impression to my mother so she would not give up hope. I remember being there and my mother being there. But not what was said. We went then.

I can't remember being told about being released, or how I felt or anything about the journey back – though I can remember all the details of the journey there.

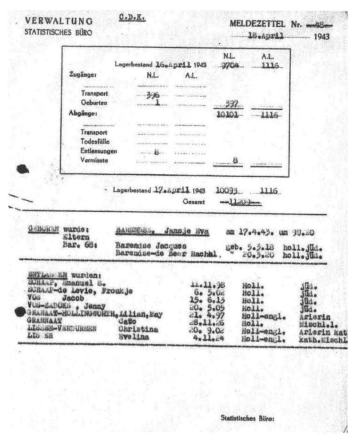

Lily and Tootje's release paper.

Although there is a statement signed by Lily after the war which says that Willem was arrested on 6th April 1943, our research suggests this is incorrect. Willem's record from Westerbork shows that he arrived there on 6th March. This fits in with Tootje's account of Willem giving them a signal to let them know he was not on the Tuesday transports. Their period in the camp together must have been several weeks, not just over one week (if the 6th April arrest was true) because Tootje and Lily left the camp on 28th April.

The sequence of events in 1943, subject to any further information from The Hague archives, Scheveningen or Dutch Red Cross, is thought to be:

- 11th January: first arrest in The Hague.
- 26th January: escape from outside Scheveningen Prison.
- 3rd March: second arrest in The Hague and interrogation.
- 6th March: arrival at Westerbork.
- 18th May: deported to Sobibor.
- 20th May: gassed in Sobibor.

CHAPTER 13

Trying to Free the Family

Harry

Before his arrest, my father and I had gone together to the lawyer, Mr Peridon. We found out there was not much progress with the case. He told me it would take months and months even *if* England answered. The letter was sent via the Red Cross to Switzerland and from Switzerland to England, but we didn't know for sure whether it had gone. Because it would take so long, he was doubtful that it would succeed. So, this was the first time I was involved in the case.

To make things thorough, I wanted to try every possible means to try to get the family free and to bring matters to a conclusion. At a certain point I felt time was running out. So I decided to go to The Hague together with Fré to put the case directly to the German authorities, without waiting any longer for the papers that were due to come from England. I used my false papers, of course, otherwise you couldn't travel. But I also took with me the identification card with the "J" on it and I went into the "Hollander Lion", in other words, in the mouth of the lion, the den or lair. It was the German office which controlled the deportations, the Reichskommissariat, and centre of the German civilian occupation regime. There were offices there specially made for people who claimed that they were not Jews. I was wondering at that time how many Jews' wives were "unfaithful" to their husbands because many claimed that their children came from the neighbourhood milkman or butcher in order that they were not deemed to be Jewish. Because, remember, to be Jewish you should have four Jewish grandparents. And, if you could prove that your child was from a non-Jewish man, he or she had only two Jewish grandparents and so that was okay. So everyone was looking for this kind of possibility. But there were other possibilities to get out of their hands, and that was to claim you were of English nationality or other foreign nationality, or you had the Iron Cross from Germany from the First World War. So all those cases were handled at that office, and they became very experienced. Before I entered the building I changed my papers so I had my identification papers with the "J" on once more.

I knew the name from the man who was handling our case, Dr Hans Calmeyer.[16] I learnt his name from Mary, who had also been in contact with him (in order to establish her own non-Jewish status). So I went there and met with him. I had to tell him who I was and I showed him my identification with the "J" on it. We talked about things and I showed him firstly the paper that my mother had when she arrived in Holland and was registered as belonging to the Church of England*. Secondly, I had the marriage certificate, which was in English.

That German man didn't understand English, but he was looking at it and one of the columns was "Status before marriage" and after my dad's name was written "bachelor" and after my mother's name was "spinster". But he couldn't have known what those words meant so he said "Oh "bachelor" is a baker – that's a Jewish profession – but the spinster?" – asking me, is it also a profession? But before I could answer he said "No – a spinster in Holland and Germany is a lady who is doing weaving of material" (on the spinning wheel). So he said a spinster is not a Jewish profession, so he believed that it was all right. He could see very clearly that Harry was genuine and spoke with conviction. He said he would look into it. Then a second man came in and asked Calmeyer what he was doing, and Calmeyer started to explain. He was another German man, of course, a very serious, dark-looking man. He said to me, "But you don't have a star on?"

I said, "That's right, because I cannot travel with the star – it is forbidden for Jewish people to travel, so sorry it was the only way I could get here." He said a few words to the first German man and went out. Then Calmeyer said to me, "I give you the advice to go as quickly as you can out of the building." So I got out as fast as I could and on the street we changed the papers again.

Fré walked on one side of the street and I went on the other side with my false papers. She had with her her own good papers but also took my identification card with the "J" on it and we went to Mary's house, because we were afraid to go to the station in case we got arrested.

[Calmeyer later reported that he would look for every possible loophole or reason to help people. When faced with Harry, with Lily and Willem's documents, he was probably more than happy to help. And probably Harry's audacious visit to The Hague was instrumental in the release of Lily and Tootje.]

Three weeks later everything was settled because we got the message that Tootje and Mum had got out of Westerbork. I got the notification that they accepted that I was half Jewish and there came the official new identification papers without the "J". That was in May 1943. So I could go back to my work.

Now I had got rid of the "J", I went back to the firm and they were glad to see me. From then on I was given all kind of papers that would protect me if I was picked up on the street by the Germans, who were always looking for people to go to Germany to work – not Jewish people. But you were not obliged to work in Germany as long as you worked for the German industries in the Netherlands. So I had good papers – I still have them – and life carried on.

* If Harry had possession of the Declaration signed by the Mayor dated 11th December 1942 (copy in Chapter 9) stating that Lilian May Hollingsworth came as a Christian to Amsterdam and therefore was not Jewish, he would not have waited so long to go to the Entscheidungsstelle. However, we think Harry had no reason to go the Oudeschans anymore. It would have been too risky with all the NSB neighbours who would have recognised him and reported him to get a reward. Therefore he was not aware of the paper. Harry is talking about a different paper she had "when she arrived in Holland".

Tootje

On my release from Westerbork I went back to the sewing school, although I had missed almost a year, being in IJmuiden and then the camp. I eventually got my diploma from the sewing school a year in July 1944, called a Diploma Kostuumnaaister from the Industrieschool voor Vrouwelijke Jeugd (female youth), Weteringschans 31.

My mother had her new ID card issued on 29th May 1943 to reflect her non-Jewish status. That summer of 1943 life carried on as "normal", with Jews being picked up every night, though by this stage there were not many Jews left. There were 20 students in my class. There was one Jewish boy and a Jewish teacher, who tried to become a Christian.

We would regularly make food parcels to send to Kitty. We had almost no contact with the other members of the Granaat family. By this stage most of them had gone into hiding or had been rounded up and sent to the camps. During this period we sometimes saw my uncle Jacob, who was a rather silly man. He never married but was friendly towards us. Occasionally he had meals with us and he seemed to know how to get hold of black market stuff, which was useful. I remember him bringing tea or cake. Though he was eventually deported. Probably in the last big offensive of 20 June, in which the bulk of Jews living in the East and South of Amsterdam were taken (source: Presser p202). Jacob was killed in Sobibor in July 1943.

> ### Jacob Granaat #26918
> Born 4 March 1886 Amsterdam, Noord-Holland, Netherlands (Family Card Amsterdam Hijman Granaat 24/11/1850) (source: birth certificate), died 2 July 1943, Sobibor, Poland, 57 years (source: War Grave Foundation). Occupation: waiter

Liesje

With so many Jews under threat of arrest and deportation, Liesje and Nico decided to try and go into hiding. They did not like the thought of being sent to work as labour for the Germans with a small daughter and baby son, Wim, who had been born on 20th January 1943.

Although heart-breaking to do, they agreed it would be safer to split the family up because it was easier to find safe addresses for the children. They also agreed that they did not want Netty and Wim to remain in Amsterdam, where the concentration of Nazis was greater. The risk of remaining together was that if one of them was found they would all be deported.

Liesje and Nico knew something of Harry and Fré's work helping children to go into hiding and so they approached them for help, which Harry and Fré were happy to do.

On 1st March 1943, when all the patients and staff of the Jewish Hospital were deported, Nico witnessed how brutally this was done. Even people who were blind or could not walk were beaten out of the door and taken away. Nevertheless the authorities (including the Jewish Council) said that they were being taken to Germany to work. Later, Nico connected this terrible event with the decision to have Netty and Wim go into hiding. He did not want to risk them being murdered. "When I saw this, all my doubts were gone. I did not know whether the rumours about many Jews being killed were true or not. But for the sake of my children I wanted to be on the safe side." He discussed his fears and the available options with Liesje, who in turn asked Harry to help find somewhere to take them. By then, Lily and Tootje had returned from Westerbork and would have been able to provide more information about the deportations. Having seen the weekly train, Lily would have had a strong opinion that going into hiding was the right thing to do. It turned out to be the best decision they made.

Netty was nearly three and Wim only three months old when they went into hiding at the end of April 1943. Fré took good care of both children before she found them safe places to live. She found a family in Friesland who were willing to take Netty and Wim also went to Friesland, but not to the same place. Netty was easy to hide. She was a beautiful child and with her blond hair and blue eyes she could easily pass as non-Jewish. Because Wim was a small baby they had a little tattoo put on one of his buttocks in order to be able to identify him later.

Fré took the children to Utrecht before passing them on to someone who would take them to their respective "in-hiding" addresses.

Tootje

At the end of April 1943, Netty was collected by Fré from the Oudeschans. At almost three years old she was an adorable girl with blonde Shirley Temple ringlets and vivid blue eyes. She had recently learnt to talk and, like all bright children of her age, her vocabulary was expanding by the day. She had already developed her mischievous sense of humour. An example comes from earlier, when we were still allowed to travel without the star. In private we used to refer to the Germans as "Rot Mof" (dirty German and still a Dutch swear word). I remember once we were on a tram and some Germans got on. Netty caught my eye and looked as if she was about to say "Rot Mof". I really thought she was going to and tried to look daggers at her so she wouldn't. She kept quiet but the twinkle in her eye told me she knew what she was doing!

I loved Netty so much that when she was due to leave for Friesland I went out for the day. I couldn't bear to see her go and did not want her to see my crying. When I got back Mum told me she had sat behind Fré's bicycle and went away laughing and waving.

Netty

Liesje

During the big raid of 26th May, which Kitty refers to in her story, Nico's parents, Isaac and Schoontje, were captured and taken to Westerbork. They were taken to Sobibor and gassed on 4th June. At this point the remaining Vuijsje family, including Nico and Liesje, started to go "underground". Before his arrest, Willem helped Nico and his brothers, Bram, Flip and Jaap, to obtain false identity passes. Like Fré and Harry, Willem was connected with the Groep Gerretsen, a resistance group of ex-members of the Independent Socialist Party.

Initially, Nico hid in a corner of an attic space in Amsterdam East and Liesje went to friends in Rotterdam. Going to different locations may have been a relief for there were now major tensions in their marriage. Liesje's happy-go-lucky personality had been suppressed by anger and fear. There must have been a huge amount of stress caused by the situation they found themselves in plus anxiety about Netty and Wim, who they missed terribly. Willem had insisted that she marry a Jew and now Liesje realised that, although she loved him, Nico had bound her and her children to people who were being systematically hunted down.

CHAPTER 14

Kitty in Westerbork

Kitty

At the camp, when I got the stamp to say that I was not Jewish, it was good for Maurice too. Being married to a non-Jewish woman, he would not be sent away. So we were quite happy about that. After some time we were not so much afraid. We were sleeping in separate barracks but could talk to each other during the day. At 10pm we had to go to bed. Maurice was one of the camp workers and was assigned to the food section, although not in the kitchen itself. His job was putting the food into large trays and then loading on to the barrels to be distributed in portions at the barracks. If a transport arrived during the night he also went out to help people, find them a bed and blankets. The camp workers were called Ordedienst.

I worked on farms and was in one of the large groups sent to work outside of the camp, to start with, in the winter, getting out the big bushels of hay, for animal feed, and weeding. Later on, in the summer, I was digging the potatoes out. Farmers had hired people from Westerbork as labour. Later, I went without a guard with a much smaller group of say two or three others, maybe two to three kilometres from the camp. Because security was much less tight doing farm work than it was inside the camp I could have escaped, but I would not have dared to with my family still inside. They would have been punished. Especially as I was still hopeful of release. Maybe it would be different if there was no chance.

There was a cousin in the camp who had also worked like I did on the farms – Abraham Pimontel. He escaped with the help of the resistance [see below]. But he didn't have the stamp like me. I knew that Mum had been released and I had just to wait until they gave me permission to leave. It took such a long time.

Some people did escape like that, but most did not. A lot of them came from a group of Jewish youngsters who came from Germany. In Holland there was a school for Jews who wanted to go to Palestine to be farmers. They were all taken to the camp and were very good at, say, milking. They stuck together and did not escape because they knew, if they did, the rest would be sent to Poland.

The Pimontels

The Pimontel family lived at Rozengracht 36, in the Jordaan area of Amsterdam. There was father Elias, an ironmonger, and mother Cato, whose maiden name was Granaat. She was my aunt and Tootje was named after her. They had two children, Abraham (born 19 November 1916) and Judith (born 13 April 1918). Judith worked as an office clerk.

In order to try to survive the war, they managed to get false papers. It is thought that Abraham was picked up in one of the raids in the late summer of 1942. He was taken to Westerbork and assigned to work as a farm labourer, like me.

Abraham was determined to try to escape and to survive the war. He did so just two weeks after his arrival in October 1942. Thus he avoided being transported. Somehow he made contact with the resistance – perhaps someone in the camp had given him the name of a contact. He moved to Cannes in the south of France, where he ran his own business and lived until 16 November 1999.

He married Marianna Trigallez. They had two children: Robert Alfred Pimontel (married Ellis Heek in Philadelphia) and Yvonne Martha (married Jean Michel Meyer in Strasbourg in 1975). Robert and Ellis have three children: Lisette, Renee Lindsay and Monique Ashley Pimontel. They are possibly all still alive. Their name could have the alternative spelling Pimentel.

My cousin Judith managed to evade arrest until one day when she was travelling by tram and somebody either recognised her or thought she had a Jewish look about her. This person then tipped off the NSB or a German soldier, who frequently rode on trams and would always be on the lookout for Jews trying to evade arrest. He demanded to see her papers. She was taken to the police station for a more thorough inspection of her ID card and for the record to be checked. The forged ID card at that stage of the war was unlikely to have passed this level of security, and of course the records did not match. She was arrested and sent to Westerbork in November 1942.

I cannot remember if Judith worked while in the camp. Unfortunately, when they did the big clear-out of Jews from Westerbork – at the same time I was transferred to Amersfoort and Willem went on transport – Judith was selected too. She was on the same train as my father and was killed in Sobibor on the same day – 21st May 1943. She was 25 years old.

Kitty

At the beginning of May 1943 my husband suddenly got ill and had a very high temperature. I was away for the whole day, so I never really knew what happened. I got back and they said he had a temperature over 38 degrees. After some days I thought he must be awfully ill. I asked the family – Uncle Simon and Aunt Lientje – for help, to see if he could be put into hospital. I kept asking but nobody did anything. In the end I managed to get him into the hospital which was within the camp. But he wouldn't take his tablets – he kept spitting them out. The orderly said for me to try to get him to take one, but he wouldn't. Back at the barracks, I spoke with a German couple, the man was a doctor – they were lovely people. I told him about Maurice. He said he knew what was wrong – inflammation of the lungs: pneumonia. He said the tablets were a new drug which he must take. But he just wouldn't swallow them and a few days later he died on 3 May. He was only 29.

Later I spoke to the sister of Maurice's mother. She told me his real mother had died from tuberculosis, and afterwards the children all had to go for regular medical examinations (check-ups). She told me one of the boys had a spot on his lung. Nothing happened; it didn't grow so they left it. But it could have been Maurice, especially as he got ill and died so suddenly. It developed so quickly and an inflammation of the lung wouldn't normally cause such a quick deterioration. Also, he did not have the correct treatment. If he had been in a proper hospital outside it might have been different. Nobody seemed to take it that seriously. They just said "He's got fever, he should stay in bed" and I didn't know it was so bad because he wasn't delirious. The whole day I was out working and only saw him in the evenings. I wasn't allowed to stay and look after him. Other people said they would look after him, give him a drink and aspirin, but of course that didn't help. Then for some days he went into a coma. He couldn't talk or communicate, just looked at me. Then one day I returned from work to find eight to ten men crowded round him, praying. I couldn't get near him and did not realise until afterwards that he was dead and then it was too late to say goodbye. It was horrible.

[On our trip to Westerbork in April 2015 we saw Maurice's record card, which stated that he had stayed in Barrack 67 and his cause of death was recorded as "TBC", which we were told meant "unknown/to be confirmed". However, TBC is also the medical abbreviation for tuberculosis, so perhaps Maurice's aunt was correct.]

Extract from ancestry of Dutch Jewish families relating to Kitty and Maurice (maxvandam.info)
Keetje (Kitty) Granaat born 4 October 1915 in London, UK. She married Mozes (Maurice) Tertaas on 29 January 1941 in Amsterdam, Son of Joseph Tertaas and Sophia Velleman, occupation diamond grinder; cycle repairer.

From the Jewish Monument:
Mozes Tertaas
Wingerdweg 19 Huis, bicycle restorer
Amsterdam, 2 February 1913
Reached the age of 30
Mozes Tertaas died on 3 May 1943 in Westerbork camp and he was cremated on 6 May 1943. The urn with his ashes was placed on the Jewish cemetery in Diemen on field U, row 4, grave number 28.

So I was alone but the small silver lining to this terrible black cloud was that I needn't be afraid anymore because I was no longer married to a Jew. So it had improved my chances of release, but it still took until October for me to get out.

[Kitty was seriously understating how she felt.]

At Westerbork I worked all day. At 8am we had to go on parade for the daily roll call. Then off to the land, from farm to farm. Back at about 5pm or so. The farmers always gave us food to eat – often potatoes in a milky sauce, sometimes with a few vegetables in it. When we came home to the camp, they also gave us some food. This is why we had rather a good life. The farmers were Dutch – most of them Nazis. They were not giving us food to help us. I suppose it was in their contract to give us a meal. We would stop working at 12 o'clock. The farmers would go to eat and that's when we had our meal. They wanted to keep us reasonably well because we were working their land and they were paying the Germans for our labour.

I made good friends at the camp. There were a lot of English people. Besides being half Jewish, I had an English birth certificate. So all the people like that, e.g. born in America or married to an American or, like me, born in England, were kept together and got to know each other. All these men and women were kept in the camp because the Germans thought perhaps they could exchange them for some German prisoners. I wasn't really English any more but I had the nationality.

In the end, the picking up of all these Jews went too slowly for the Germans. So they started big raids that summer. They sent us – the 100 to 150 or so with these papers – to a real concentration camp in Amersfoort. It was not a camp especially for Jews but for traitors, resistance workers and the like. This was to make room in Westerbork for all the Jews picked up in this big raid. Tootje could tell us more about that – she was nearly caught up in it.

Tootje

We returned home from Westerbork on 18th April. After we were home a couple of days we had a visit from a removal firm called Puls. They were quite well known in Holland, like Pickfords in England. And it became a verb later on – when something was "pulsed" it meant it had been pinched or taken by someone. When somebody took something they called it pulsing. The firm Puls were used by the Germans to remove the furniture out of the Jewish homes, when they had been taken out of their homes and sent to a camp. All the furniture and other belongings were sent to Germany to be used by the Germans.

And as I mentioned earlier, they take your keys away when you arrive at Westerbork and they had very good administration. The Germans, being very methodical, know where everybody is and everything is listed. But they made a mistake in our case. A couple of days after we got home they thought we had gone on to Poland and had come to take our furniture away. Luckily we happened to be home and we said "Oh, no, we are here, so go away." So that was all right.

I remember that afterwards the authorities sent us a bill. This was even sent for all the people who went to Auschwitz. I don't know who they sent the bill to – the leaders of the Jewish community, the Jewish Council? They sent bills to cover the cost of the train transport! Like a ticket. So the Dutch Railways collaborated with the Germans, who paid them to transport the Jews to the camps.

When we got back we discovered that our neighbours had come in after we had been gone awhile. They probably thought we would not be coming back, so they helped themselves to a few things. When we got back they did give a lot of it back, but not all of it. I had celebrated my birthday at the end of November, but I cannot remember anything except that all my presents were stolen. It was a lot worse for many others. The Dutch SS had forced their way into numerous Jewish houses and took everything remotely of value.

After a few weeks at home we heard that Maurice had got ill. He had got pneumonia and then he died. It must have been terrible for Kitty, being there all by herself and her husband dying. She loved him so much. So that was a pretty terrible time for us. I remember Maurice used to get so hot pushing the trolleys round the camp laden with food that he used to take his shirt off to cool down. I think he got really cold and this might have contributed to his illness.

After a while Kitty had to go to Amersfoort, where there was also a concentration camp. The day that she went to Amersfoort the transport also went to Sobibor. And my father went to Sobibor, which is a camp specially built for gassing people. There is no sorting out, no selections. It only existed for three or four months. And virtually all the people who went there were killed and that was that.

There is a film called *Shoah*, which is made by a French man Claude Lanzmann all about the Jews and what happened. One of the things he talked about was how methodical the Germans were. When people got off the trains they had to march, a nice quick march to the gas chambers – but they didn't know they were gas chambers of course – they thought they were going to have a shower. They were handed a little piece of soap to help with the illusion and the children were handed small toys. But some people who got off the train couldn't walk very fast because they were ill or were old. Oh dear, they would be looked after. You can go in lorries so you don't have to walk. But they went a little way to the woods, where they were shot there and then. And they only did that not to hinder the process of the people marching quickly to the gas chamber. It was all worked out in time and motion study. So many minutes for them to walk, so many minutes for them to be gassed, so many minutes for them to burn. Afterwards, the soap and the toys were taken from their hands to be given to the next group already waiting. It was a 24-hour operation, seven days a week. Somebody sat in his office and worked it all out, calculating how is the best way and what is the quickest way. While one train full of people was being processed, the next lot would 'shuntle' along the train and they would get out and march. Of all the atrocities in all the years of history and still happen… and we've all done it, the British and the Dutch; everybody is guilty of atrocities at some time in the past. There was nothing so methodical and so calculated (literally).

Pieter Scheffer, Kitty's son, if ever he had a job interview or something and he had to say what happened to his grandparents he always said, "My grandfather was murdered by the Germans."

Kitty

Before I left for Amersfoort I was able to say goodbye to Father and I wrote a letter home saying that I was going to the camp at Amersfoort, in case they wanted to send a parcel. I thought I would ask someone to take the letter for me. But when we walked through the streets the soldiers were really close. I saw a cart with apples or fruit on it. I just threw it on top of the cart and hoped that someone would post it – and they did because Mum got the letter.

Tootje still has this letter. It is two thirds in Dutch, largely for Tootje, and one third in English, for her mother. Her English was excellent.

Kitty's Letter
Written in Dutch and translated here:

Westerbork 17 May 1943
Dear All,
I've just received your parcel and it arrived just in time. In the first place we had run out of bread and in the second place we're both going away. Pa is going on transport and I'm going with all of the foreigners to Amersfoort.

The mixed marriages with children had to choose – be sterilised or go to Poland. Many chose the latter. But in the "S" barrack ("S" = straf (punishment)) there was no choice. Also the mixed marriages do not feel very safe. But whether father-in-law[a] *will have to go, we do not know yet. So, comfort mother with the thought that he [Willem] would have had to go as well.*

In Amersfoort the decision will be made whether we are interned or not. Some people say we will be back here (at Westerbork) in four weeks' time – so we will wait and see. If a parcel comes for me at Westerbork they will send it on to Amersfoort. Tomorrow I may be able to write with the address. Also, 100 people with special "red" permits[b] *have to go on transport. And also many others who never thought they would have to go. 2,500 people altogether are going tomorrow. Still you can never be sure whether he will have gone or not. So I will ask someone to send a thank-you card when father has gone – then you will know.*

Will you all please mind that mother should keep cheerful. Well cheerio darlings from Kippy[c] *and the old man (he is not here but of course it is also from him – cheerio).*

a Kitty's father-in-law had married for the second time, to a German Christian.
b People with red marks on their permits who thought they were in safe occupations.
c Kitty's nickname: Kippy means little chicken.

Witten in English:

Dear Mother,
I hope you are alright and still going strong. Don't be downhearted. You know that Dad will come through everything and you must be sure (as I am) that he will come back. Don't you write me, but cheery letters, for I will be very disappointed if you are not a brave girl. You always write to me that I shall (should) be brave, now I tell you to do just the same. Everybody goes away knowing how the war is going on and they are all in a good mood. Many greetings also from the family Jefferson and lots of kisses for you and dear little Tootje. You both have been so good in sending everything.

Goodbye and cheerio
Kitty.

We had gone by train from Westerbork and when we arrived at Amersfoort we were at the normal railway station. Because we were with German soldiers, the local people were really staring at us. I suppose because there were so many women, and prisoners were usually men. A lot of women started crying when they saw us. They were upset because they saw we were going to this awful camp where many were hanged and killed. They thought we were going to our deaths. At Amersfoort I was treated quite well because we were regarded as "precious people". We later found out the German Foreign Office wanted to protect these Jews in the hope of exchange with German prisoners. We did not work and had nothing to do there. It was for about two or three weeks and it was nice weather, being May.

After a few weeks I was sent back with the others to Westerbork and I returned to work on the farms. I received some more food parcels. Sometimes there was a loaf of bread. But it was becoming more difficult for the family to get much to send to me. You couldn't just go to the shops and buy what you wanted. But it wasn't the hunger winter; we were not starving. Sometimes we got a packet of tea or a cake. Mostly we did share the food. There was an English girl and an American who I liked very much. The three of us were always together so we shared.

We were in our own clothes at the camp, but working for the farmers we wore blue overalls and wooden clogs. They were terrible and gave us awful blisters. Our hands were blistered too, especially from digging furrows for the potatoes. It was very muddy and the ground was soft. I had to carry a big sack of potatoes. The man in front made the hole with a hoe and I had to put a potato in the hole. We walked up and down the huge field and when the sack was empty we filled it up and started again. It was exhausting and in the end all the skin on my feet was swollen and hard. I had to put on my husband's shoes. They were much too big but I couldn't wear my clogs any more.

The other work was binding the corn in sheaves, tying something around it and later stacking them up. We used pitchforks to get them onto the wagon. I remember one time when the whole thing fell to pieces. The farmer was standing on the cart and it just fell apart. He was swearing and couldn't see us laughing. I liked this work very much and could have done it all summer.

On another farm there were some very nice people. Some of the boys in my group had been preparing to go to Israel, so they knew more about what to do on the farm. They were able to catch rabbits, which they gave to the farmer.

Photo by W.R. Breslauer (4 July 1903 – 28 February 1945)

His wife gave us some rabbit stew the next day. Other than the calluses and blisters, I was very healthy and fit. Twice a day we had food and we benefitted from lots of exercise and fresh air. It was not a bad camp. We were not shouted at or hit.

There was even a little bit of entertainment in the evenings if you wanted it. There were some famous artists there from orchestras or who played as a hobby. (Among them Johnny and Jones, who arrived at Westerbork in September 1943.) There were people who sang opera or played a violin, and some comedians. Or if it was someone's birthday there would be a sort of party with a white sheet over the table and a candle.

By that stage I knew it was only a matter of time before I was released. My mother had written that Harry and Fré had been to The Hague to see the Nazi man who was handling it. In the end they said it won't be long before you are free. But in all I was ten months in the camp.

On the same day that I was sent to the camp at Amersfoort, Willem was put on transport to Poland. I can remember him saying, "We are all going to die. We are all going to be killed." Kitty said "Oh no" – what else could she say? Tootje thought no one knew what was going to happen. But Kitty says their father knew. He was astute.

CHAPTER 15

Willem's Deportation

Willem

This chapter is largely derived from the relevant sections of Jules Schelvis's book *Sobibor: A History of a Nazi Death Camp.* **From this account and his extensive research it has been possible to piece together what those last few days and hours would have been like for Willem. This provides the grim truth and stark details of Hitler's "final solution".**

Between 2nd March and 20th July 1943 there were 19 transports from the Netherlands, with between 964 and 3,107 people on each train, and one children's transport from Vught. From the total of 34,000 people Schelvis was one of only 18 Dutch Jews who survived by escaping from Sobibor.

The 22-year-old Schelvis, his wife Chel and her family were arrested in a raid in the centre of Amsterdam on 26 May 1943. They thought that going into hiding would be too problematical and like many others expected to be put to work in German camps. So they decided to let themselves be rounded up, with their rucksacks ready. They arrived at Westerbork on 1st June and after six days they left the barracks with their baggage and were put on a train to Sobibor.

Background to Sobibor

Sobibor, along with camps Bełżec and Treblinka, were the three extermination camps of Operation Reinhardt, the codename given to the secret Nazi plan to mass murder European Jews launched by Himmler and headed by Globocnik. Bełżec became operational just two months after the Wannsee conference in January 1942, Sobibor three months and Treblinka six months after.

In Amsterdam the name Sobibor was first mentioned at a Jewish Council meeting on 26th March 1943, when some recent transports went there rather than Auschwitz. "However the general situation with respect to employment remains as yet unclear." In all other respects the name Sobibor remained largely unknown for the duration of the war. Even in Poland only a few insiders knew of its existence.

So Willem would not have known where he was heading when he was selected for transport. He probably thought Auschwitz was likely. Did he guess the purpose was extermination? He was an astute man; he knew the sick, elderly and handicapped were indiscriminately being sent to "work"; and he would have known from his resistance and other contacts of the lack of news, communication or postcards from those who had already been deported. Plus, he had said to Kitty "We are all going to die".

Construction and Organisation

Even though the extermination camps were smaller and much further away, they could deal with incoming transports very quickly and thoroughly. There were no barracks for the victims, selecting prisoners for work was the exception rather than the rule and SS staffing requirements were minimal, all of which made them much more efficient in the eyes of the Nazis.

In the autumn of 1941, when the Germans were considering suitable locations for the Reinhardt camps, one of the most important criteria was secrecy. The camps should not be situated near densely populated areas, so that as few civilians as possible would find out what was going on.

Apart from the need for extensive camouflage, the following conditions also had to be met:

- The camp must be situated close to an existing railway line.
- The exterior of the camp must look completely innocent, so that victims arriving would not suspect anything.
- It must have a suitably large undressing area, as well as depots for the storage of confiscated property, insulated rooms containing a motor for producing the toxic gas; and areas where pits could be dug for the bodies.

Sobibor was 80 kilometres east of Lublin and Helm station was the last stop before Sobibor. It had a railway track and two sidings which could accommodate 50 freight wagons at a time. Another track was built to take trains behind the barbed wire up to the buffer inside the camp. Eventually a platform was built, which was 120 metres long and provided sufficient space for a locomotive and 11 wagons at a time.

The barracks built alongside the platform conveniently blocked most of the view from trains outside. This prevented Polish railway staff from seeing in and also the Jewish victims waiting in freight wagons outside from forming any sort of impressions of the nature or purpose of the camp.

Karl Frenzel, who became camp commandant, and nearly all of the people working for him had previously worked at the six T4 euthanasia establishments. The T4 programme was responsible for the murder of more than 50,000 Germans who were mentally sick, chronically sick or concentration camp prisoners deemed "unfit for work": politically undesirable elements, Jews and Gypsies. The Sobibor recruits, already sworn to secrecy, had the right credentials for the even bigger operation,

Sobibor model by survivor Jules Schelvis

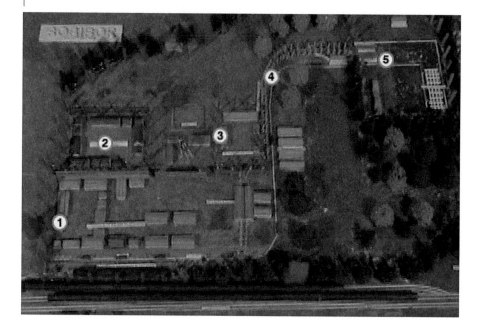

1. Officers' compound.
2. Accommodation and workshops for Jewish slave labourers.
3. Selection area where new arrivals had their belongings and clothing taken and new slave labourers were chosen.
4. The majority of arrivals were led naked at gunpoint down a path known as the Tube.
5. At the end of the Tube were the gas chambers, where they were killed.

(Source: Holocaust Research Project)

requiring not only the strictest confidence but also a complete lack of conscience when it came to murdering people on a massive scale.

A considerable number of men were used as guards; these were Soviet prisoners of war, mostly from the Ukraine. Armed with whips and confiscated Russian carbines, they took a very active role in the extermination process and often surpassed the Germans in cruelty.

Although Eichmann's office and the Reichsbahn would have kept records confirming the number of deportees, most were never unearthed. Therefore, the precise number of transports to Sobibor isn't known. However, the Statistical Office at Westerbork compiled lists of names for each transport. Willem's name is on line 22.

Willem's transport on 18th May 1943 was the third largest, with 2,511 people on board, of whom 1,180 were men. There were no survivors from this train. On the same train was Willem's niece, 25-year-old Judith Pimontel, mentioned earlier. It is very unlikely that they would have been in the same wagon.

Westerbork also filled out registration forms for each person. Willem's record from Westerbork is below. This shows his address, date of birth, barrack number (punishment barrack 66), his date of arrival at Westerbork (6 March 1943) and, scrawled in pencil, the date he was sent on transport (18 March 1943). This is the last piece of data recorded about Willem before his murder. When this was given to me at Westerbork it made me cry.

There was no point in registering people at any of the Operation Reinhardt camps, nor were there any roll calls. All the commandant wanted to know was the total number of victims, for statistical purpose, so he could report back to Berlin. There were no names, only numbers.

The lists of names at Westerbork were not intended to reassure those left behind. The Germans were much more interested in the property and assets of the deportees. Keys were handed over with names and addresses to make the process of looting more efficient when the person was sent on transport.

The Journey

Until March 1943 every transport from Westerbork went to Auschwitz, but from 2nd March 19 of the next 20 trains went to Sobibor. At that time Auschwitz was taken up with extermination of Jews from Salonika and was then ridden with typhus. Bob Moore explores why transports were switched to Sobibor when those from other Western European countries were suspended. The Dutch victims of Sobibor more or less account for the difference in mortality rates between the Netherlands and its neighbours. Before and after this period the levels of deportations were broadly comparable. An explanation is German satisfaction with the conduct of affairs in the Netherlands compared to the problems encountered in Belgium and France.

Shelvis's train consisted of a long line of freight wagons and carried 3,006 people. Conditions were extremely primitive, lacking even basic provisions, such as straw to lie upon. Apart from two barrels, one filled with water, the others for the waste, there were just a few bread parcels. The sick were wheeled to the wagons on trolleys. And all of this ostensibly to go to police-supervised labour camps in Germany, which is how it was put on the relevant forms. Gemmeker and his helpers stood by, watching the operation's progress.

Once everyone was aboard, the sliding doors were barred on the outside. There were 62 people and one pram in Schelvis's wagon. With all their luggage they were packed like sardines, wondering how long they could endure it. There was hardly any room to move and only one small, barred window, which was unglazed, to let some fresh air in.

The train left Westerbork at 10.30am. They did not know its destination: perhaps Auschwitz, which they had heard about. The train stopped countless times en route in order to let regular and military transports pass. Sometimes it stopped for hours for no discernible reason. Throughout the journey the doors were never opened and they had to relieve themselves in the little barrel, which soon caused an unbearable stench. Having finished the water from their own water bottles, by the first evening they were parched with thirst.

The journey lasted for three agonising days filled with despair and bickering. They travelled right across Germany via Bremen, Wittenberge, Berlin and Breslau and into Poland. The final destination was very close to what is now the Ukraine border.

Willem's train and journey would have been similar to Schelvis's, although perhaps with slightly fewer people per wagon. How would Willem have coped with the deprivations? We know he was a man of dignity; he was brave and went out of his way to help others, even at the expense of his own family. He had a clever and logical mind and would therefore have tried to explain to the others that there was no point in arguing as it just made the situation worse. He was a good conversationalist and perhaps would have encouraged his companions to talk about their lives, homes and loved ones in order to pass the time more pleasantly. Would he have shared his regret of not acting earlier to get his family out of danger by taking them to England? Probably not. More likely he would have spoken proudly of his wife and family, especially Harry and Kitty, who had gone to grammar school.

There would also have been lots of discussion and speculation about the war. By mid-May the tide had begun to turn against the Germans. The spring of 1943 had seen the German 6th Army surrender after the Battle of Stalingrad, the German and Italian surrender in North Africa, the Warsaw Ghetto uprising, the Bermuda Conference and the Dambuster raids. Willem had tried to reassure Lily and Tootje that he would see them again. At this stage of his Sobibor trip he may have been optimistically holding onto the hope that he would be selected for some sort of labour long enough to survive until they were liberated.

Arrival and Selection

During the delay in getting the first 11 wagons inside the camp the Ukrainian guards often exploited the situation by robbing the people still cooped up inside, who, having been locked up for days, were completely bewildered and unable to put up any resistance. They would demand the handover of treasured possessions, money and gold because, where they were going, they wouldn't be needing anything, because they were going to die. The people on the trains didn't believe it: "not in our wildest imagination did we think this would be at all possible".

Although the permanent staff at the camp all had clearly defined roles, when a Jewish transport arrived there was so much "work" to be done and everyone was required to help with some stage of the extermination procedure, especially during unloading. Victims were forcibly dragged or thrown out of the wagons, and some sustained broken bones as a result. The Ukrainians and SS could do the worst of which humans were capable, without fear. No one would ever find out what they were up to, or so they thought. They used whips, clubs and butt-ends of rifles. Men and women who could still walk were forced to join separate groups without a chance to say goodbye. Children under six had to stay with their mothers and any lone child would be pushed towards a woman.

Just a handful were picked for camp duties; others spent just a few hours there before being sent somewhere else. Willem's natural instinct for survival would have made him hold back in order to work out what was going on and to see if there was any opportunity to escape. It would have prompted him to try to join the younger men. Although his expertise in ironmongery may have been a useful skill in the camp, at 50 years of age and hair already grey, he would have been considered too old for selection.

Schelvis managed to get included in a group of young men chosen to work in a nearby camp. An SS officer told them they could return to their family and friends in Sobibor every night, to eat and relax.

As they walked the short distance from the platform to the place they had to leave all their luggage, the victims would have glimpsed the barracks housing the German and Ukrainian guards. First impressions of the camp itself aroused no suspicion, because the barracks looked rather like little Tyrolean cottages, with pretty curtains and geraniums on the window sills. They had red roofs and pebbled pathways and had names like "God's own home" and "Swallow's nest". This was deliberate deception, designed to put the prisoners at ease and prevent panic. In view of the whips and clubs he had seen used quite brutally, Willem was unlikely to have been fooled by this charade. He would have been so relieved to know that Lily and Tootje were back at home, confident that Kitty would be released too and that Harry through his ingenuity and guile would stay safe. He would have been more concerned about Liesje and Nico, frustrated that Liesje's latest pregnancy had caused them to dither about whether or not to go into hiding.

Those who were able then made their way towards Lager 2 – a deliberately planned process of "natural selection". As soon as the walking group were out of sight those left behind felt bewildered and completely isolated from the rest of the world, exactly as intended.

Once unloaded, the wagons would be cleaned thoroughly and minor repair work carried out. There should remain no tell-tale signs. With doors firmly shut for the whole journey, floorboards were sometime pulled up in attempted escapes.

When the victims reached the undressing area (Lager 2), an SS man would deliver a short speech explaining they would be taken to a place where they would prosper because in wartime they were needed for work. Children and the elderly would not have to work but would still be well fed. Before going there they must have showers. They were to undress and leave their clothes in a neat pile with shoes tied together. All valuables to be handed in at the counter and they should remember the number given. If any valuables were found on them afterward they would be punished. Soap and towels would be provided. They were ordered to undress and directed towards the bathhouse along the Schlauch (Tube). This was a three-metre-wide and 300-metre-long sand path along which Jews were herded to Lager 3, where the gas chambers were located. This was fenced off with barbed wire and interwoven with branches.

The naked women were then directed into a shed and found themselves in a large room surrounded by SS men and a few young Jewish boys, who would proceed to cut their hair. Whips were used on anyone not cooperating. Human hair was used to produce industrial filters and woven into yarn. The Reimann firm near Breslau paid half a Reichsmark per kilo of hair. Men's hair was only used if it was more than 20mm long. Fortunately, Willem's hair had been cut after his escape and in the intervening period (less than three months) it wouldn't have grown to 20cm.

The Killing

At the war crime court in Hagen in 1984 it was calculated that the maximum number of people in the undressing area at any one time was 600, which corresponded with the maximum capacity of the gas chambers. There were six gas chambers, about four by five metres each. There were showers installed, but only for deception. The internal walls and floors were covered in zinc up to a height of 1.1 metres. They were cleaned in between each use to remove any hint that they were in fact death chambers, so the victims were not aware of the purpose until the last moment.

There was a sign above the door saying "Bathing and Inhalation Rooms", as well as a large flower basket which made it look like a health spa. At this stage Willem, exhausted and weak from the ordeal of the journey and the disappointment of not being selected for work, probably guessed that his end was near. Deep down he had known since that day in IJmuiden. He recalled the kindness of the Porck family and was thankful. Without their generosity Tootje would have been arrested much earlier and would have faced this fate. With that in mind he is likely to have done his best to reassure those around him that they would come through. The Germans needed labour and why would they be taken all this way if the intention had only been to kill them? Above all, his mind would be occupied by his hatred of the Germans and love for his family.

The engine used to produce the carbon dioxide was from a Russian armoured vehicle or tank of at least 200 HP (V-engine, eight-cylinder, water-cooled). It used up to four cans of petrol a day and was installed on a concrete base with the exhaust connected to a pipeline which ran 10cm above the floor. At one end of each room a pipe was branched off at an angle at a metre above the floor; the end was open and pointed towards the middle of the room. The doors had rubber seals and once closed the chambers were completely dark. An initial trial gassing killed 30–40 women.

Following that, 50–60 people were put in each chamber. They were oblivious that they were about to die and there was hardly ever any resistance. They became suspicious only after they had entered the chamber and then there was no way back. They were packed in and the airtight doors were sealed. It took 20 minutes and then there was complete silence; the people had been gassed and were dead. After "improvements" were made in September 1942 the doors were enlarged and hinged like trapdoors to open outwards. These ran along the entire length of the external walls in a way that the dead bodies, often contorted and intertwined, could be easily removed and no longer blocked the doors. So, after the gassing, the doors did not open; the chamber was designed that the floor itself moved to tip the corpses out:

"just one more example of the resourcefulness of Germany's technologists and scientists" (Bob Moore).

The chambers were so crammed full of people that they were still upright when dead, leaning criss-cross into one another, others kneeling as space allowed. They were at least partly covered in excrement and urine. The bodies were dragged out two at a time, using belts tied round their wrists. Mouths were opened with a metal hook to check for gold teeth, which were then extracted by dentists using a small hammer or large tongs. Other body openings were checked for other valuables – money, diamonds, gold etc. Then the bodies were taken to mass graves that had been dug by machine.

Until September or October 1942 the bodies were buried but the mass graves filled up so fast it became a huge problem. The stench was so intense that it permeated Sobibor station even with the windows closed. It was decided to burn the bodies instead and a huge digger was used to excavate the decomposing victims and pile them into human pyramids. Then they were burnt. As many as 5,000 to 6,000 bodies were exhumed and burnt in a single day.

The glow from the fire was clearly visible from miles around, especially by night, and the foul stench of burning human flesh polluted the air over a wide area. So everyone in the surrounding area would then have realised what was going on.

The cremation of bodies, which already numbered over 100,000, required huge amounts of wood. Work parties were sent each day into the neighbouring forest.

Once the Germans started using the cremating pit, all the gassed bodies were taken straight there.

Estimates of the total death toll at Sobibor range from 170,000 (US Holocaust Memorial Museum) to 500,000 (the Holocaust Explained). Erich Bauer, known as 'the Gasmeister' after the war estimated that the number of Jews gassed at Sobibor "was about 350,000".

No wonder the final death toll of Jews from World War Two is such a round sum at six million. It could be several hundred thousand less (unlikely) or several hundred thousand more (more likely). What is certain is that a large number of the circa six million cannot be accounted for in any way. As well losing their individual lives and everything they owned, whole families were obliterated from history. There was no one left behind to report them missing, there was no longer any trace of their existence.

Jewish Camp Workers

The task of herding the victims into the gas chambers and digging burial pits fell to men of another labour command. Once inside the barbed wire of Lager 3, they would never re-emerge so what went on could never leak out. From time to time they would be liquidated in their entirety, except for those who had already committed suicide.

The circumstances under which the prisoners in Lager 3 were forced to work can only be surmised as none of the Jews survived and the SS were reluctant to reveal any information about this part of the camp.

Outside Lager 3 there were 600 Jewish workers required to keep the camp functioning, housed in Lager 1. They were not sure what went on in the gas chambers, though they would have heard the agonising cries and screams, caught glimpses of naked victims running through the "tube", the stench of decomposing bodies and later the sight of the fires.

The pyramid of human ash

The Uprising

A group of Jewish workers led by Leon Felhendler, a Polish Jew, plotted an escape in total secrecy. However, they lacked the strategic skills and resourcefulness to put the plan into action. In September 1943 2,000 Russian Jews arrived. Among the carpenters selected for work was Alexander Petsjerski, a Red Army lieutenant whose officer training had been geared to teaching soldiers how to fight and overcome extremely challenging circumstances. He joined the group and within three weeks prepared a detailed plan for the uprising. The subsequent revolt carries great significance, not only for the 300 men and women who broke out of the camp, of whom 47 managed to survive the war, and for their offspring; without these survivors there would have been no one to testify to what happened at Sobibor. There would have been no court proceedings and the crimes carried out in the strictest secrecy would never have been exposed. After the uprising Globocnik wrote to Himmler, "the evidence should be destroyed as quickly as possible, now that all else has been destroyed", and virtually all incriminating documentation was burnt.

The Trials

The SS prevented any form of contact between the Jews who worked in Lager 3, where the gas chambers and mass graves were situated, and the other camp prisoners. The killing was done in complete secrecy and no Jews who worked there managed to survive. Descriptions of the exterminations come from the SS men who were there. After the war they tried to play down their role. The trials and subsequent appeals took place between 1950 and 1985. Frenzel's retrial took place in 1985 in Hagen, when Schelvis acted as a public prosecutor. He was thus able to collect the information and was the first foreigner and non-jurist able to deliver an address to a jury in a German court of law.

Tootje

Although Willem was not considered by his family to be a good Jew, he did have high standards of ethics and behaviour. There were certain rituals and customs he always observed. For example, he would never be bareheaded in the street – I remember he always wore a trilby (not Jewish). And he would always kiss the prayer book before putting it away. So I imagine when it came to the end my father would have summoned up as much dignity as he could in that terrible situation. In the absence of anything else, he would have used his hand to cover his head. At least at the end of May it would not have been so bitterly cold.

Extract from the Jewish Monument
Willem Granaat was married. He and his wife had five children. The family lived in Amsterdam. Willem Granaat was a businessman. Because he had not transferred his business "appropriately" as a Jew, a warrant was issued for his arrest. As a member of the resistance, he arranged

about 120 identification cards with data adapted to the needs of the people requiring an identification card. He was caught but managed to escape during a deportation and continued his work with the resistance involving identification cards. On 6th April 1943 [date incorrect] he was arrested for the second time in The Hague and deported to Sobibor. Willem Granaat's wife survived the war.

He has an entry on the Roll of Honour (Erelijst Verzet en Koopvaardij). This is a list of names of Dutch citizens who died as members of the resistance, in merchant service, in the army, in the navy or at service in the Dutch East Indies.

It was much later we found out that Willem was sent to Sobibor. We heard that it was a new camp used for killing before it was even finished. In the beginning, because the ovens were not ready, when a train came in they just opened the door and machine-gunned the Jews. Harry learnt this from the Red Cross. So for year we didn't know whether he was shot or gassed. Gassing would be a slower death but when they shoot so many you might not be the first one. Whichever way it was, it was awful.

Sobibor was built just for killing, unlike Auschwitz, which was for killing and for working. It was only in existence for about 18 months then they broke it up again after the main purge. Some Jews would have been working there and survived, but very few. Some women and men managed to escape, working with the Polish resistance. There is a film I have seen called *Escape from Sobibor*. This has all the details of the camp, the uprising and escape.

The letter from Queen Wilhelmina says my father died on 20th May, perhaps a couple of days after Kitty went to Amersfoort, allowing for the travelling time to Sobibor. The actual date is not known. What the Red Cross did was add three days to the date of departure from Westerbork: 18 May plus three days comes to 21th May. In all, 14 members of the Granaat family (uncles, aunts, cousins and their spouses) were killed in Sobibor. The list of all 41 family victims is at the end of the book. Overleaf is the translated letter from the Queen:

Palace Het Loo 26th September 1947
To the widow L. M Granaat-Hollingsworth
Oudeschans 20 II

Because of his resistance work your husband Willem, who was so dear to you, was arrested and transported to Germany. From there he was taken to the camp Sobibor in Poland, where the enemy on 20th May 1943, in an abhorrent way, robbed him of his life.

With deepest feelings of sympathy I hereby send you and members of your family, my deepest condolences for your loss. May his memory give you strength in your further life.

Wilhelmina

PALEIS Het Loo, 26 September 1947.

Mevrouw de Wed. L.M.Granaat-Hollingsworth,
Oudeschans 20^{II},
A M S T E R D A M.

    Wegens zijn illegale werkzaamheden werd Uw echtgenoot Willem, die U zo dierbaar was, gearresteerd en naar Duitsland weggevoerd. Vandaar is hij naar het kamp te Sobibor in Polen overgebracht, alwaar de vijand hem op 20 Mei 1943 op laaghartige wijze van het leven heeft beroofd.

    Met diepe gevoelens van medeleven kom Ik U en de overige familieleden bij dit verlies alsnog Mijn hartelijke deelneming betuigen.

    Moge zijn nagedachtenis U een steun in het verdere leven blijven.

CHAPTER 16

Kitty's Release

Tootje

Kitty had been expected home for some time so in my lunch break I would often go to Central Station and meet the train from Westerbork in case she was on it. I roughly knew what time it would come. Occasionally one or two people would get off the train wearing a star. I knew they were from Westerbork because otherwise they would not have been allowed on the train. If Kitty wasn't there I would go back to school or go home. That went on for a while.

On one of the days (29th September) after a visit to the station I had walked back via Nieuwmarkt. There were German soldiers who would not let people on to the middle of the square. I didn't realise what was happening but, being inquisitive, I pushed my way through but then found I couldn't get out again! They had suddenly decided to close a big area of Amsterdam for the whole day and I was caught up in a Razzia [a raid]. The Germans had cordoned off the Nieuwmarkt square, looking for black marketeers and any remaining Jews, although there were very few Jews left in Amsterdam by then and if there were they wouldn't be so foolish to be there in broad daylight. I was there in the middle of it all. Luckily, Maurice's stepmother, who was a German non-Jewish woman, was there and she saw me and talked to one of the German soldiers, who then let me out. This was the big raid Kitty had referred to. It was the final clear-out. The Reinekking – cleansing.

On 4th October it was Kitty's birthday and a most important day for my mother. So she made a food parcel early in the morning and set off on the long train journey to Westerbork. She handed in the food parcel and asked to see Kitty, but they wouldn't let her. They took the food parcel from her but said, "No, you can't see her, go back." They didn't tell her that Kitty had been released that morning! So she went all the way back by train and arrived back in Amsterdam quite late in the evening, though luckily before curfew at ten o'clock.

On that day I went to the station as usual and there were one or two people with a star but no more.

Kitty

I went home on 4th October 1943. It was my twenty-eighth birthday. The boy courier came to my barracks again and I got a message that I had to go to the office. They told me I was released. I was to travel home by train and they gave me a ticket. The rest of the group that I had been with were sent to a place near the Bodensee (Lake Constance). The Zeppelin factory was also there. A camp was made there for them to be interned. They were a lucky group – the Germans thought they would be of some value and I suppose did not dare to kill American or British citizens.

Mother had thought on 4th October, "Poor Kitty still in the camp on her birthday". She made up a big parcel for me and took it to the camp. It was a long and terrible journey in those days. When she got there they would not allow her to give the parcel to me. The man at the office said "I'll take it, I'll give it to her", but of course they just kept it for themselves. No one told her I had been released. So when Mum came back late in the evening I was there. We all felt so sorry for her going all that way for nothing.

I travelled in a horse and cart to Westerbork station. There, I saw our cousin, Hijman Bromet (Uncle Simon and Aunt Carolina's son), a man very high up. I think he was also travelling to Amsterdam. We stood on the platform together and I told him I had been set free. He said, "Oh good." I told him I wanted to send a telegram home to say I'm coming home. I had some money for this. Hijman suggested I could have one sent from the station office. Unfortunately, while I was doing this the train came in and left again and the telegram was never received! I was very upset with my cousin, who was still at the platform. He told me not to worry: "There'll be another train before long." So that's why

Tootje missed me at Central Station. I had known that Tootje might be at the station to meet me as she had sent me a letter explaining that she often went to look.

Harry was in hiding in Amsterdam, but he came to the house for dinner because it was my birthday. He was now officially half Jewish so did not face the danger of being taken away, but he was doing resistance work and therefore still kept a very low profile.

Tootje

A while after we were home, the Jewish Quarter was just cordoned off and they just cleared out all the rest of the Jews. All the bridges were up and no one could go in or out the whole day. It took them the whole day to get the rest of the Jews and take them to Westerbork. I suppose soon after that they closed Westerbork as well, but I can't remember much about that. I've got books about it but I haven't read them really. Although the last train left Westerbork, on 3rd September 1944, there were still people there when the camp was liberated in April 1945. I don't know when the last Jews from Amsterdam arrived.

We must have been aware of the huge risk Liesje and Nico were facing, but I don't remember talking to anyone about it or how this felt.

At our house in the Oudeschans, Nico was living with us together with another friend called Teun, a man who Harry had brought to our house because he needed shelter. They had been with us for several months, in hiding. "Teun" is a very Dutch name. His real name was Salomon Schrijver. He was a very careful man. They had to be very quiet when they were on their own not to flush the toilet or walk on the creaky floorboards because the neighbours in the flat below could not be trusted. Teun had a non-Jewish woman friend and later on she managed to hire a flat somewhere and he went to live with her. So that was a bit of luck for him considering what happened later.

I used to go to the library for Nico and he used to read such a lot because being in hiding – he was with us a long time, perhaps six months in all – there was nothing much else to do. So he liked to read, mainly cowboy books or detective books. Years after he would say how pleased he was with me because I never got the same book twice. How that happened I don't know – I didn't take that much notice of them.

When Kitty got home after being released from Westerbork she rang the doorbell and no one replied. I was at school and my mother was on her way to the camp to try to deliver the parcel. The woman who lived one floor below them (Mrs Boekelman) opened the front door and told Kitty where her mother had gone. Kitty couldn't get inside the flat, so she just left her suitcase outside the door. Nico padded across the floor carefully, avoiding the creaks. He whispered something to her at the door, but he couldn't let her in because that would let the neighbours know there was someone inside.

So Kitty went wandering about the street of Amsterdam for a few hours (which must have been marvellous after being imprisoned for so many months) until she knew I would be back home to let her in. When I got back I was thrilled to be told Kitty had been there and I waited for her to return with great excitement.

Later, because it was her birthday, Kitty's best friend, Miep, arrived with her husband, Frans. (Later, Frans became Kitty's second husband.) So we were all reunited and sat round waiting for my mother to come home. In the end it turned out to be was quite a gathering with Miep, Frans, Liesje, Nico, Teun, Harry and our mother.

The next day Kitty found out that their home in the Wingerdweg had been taken over (by Nazi sympathisers) and all their furniture, papers, jewellery and clothes had been taken away. Everything gone, even her wedding dress. Of course, they had lovely furniture and other belongings – they had not been married that long when they were arrested. So all that was lost.

When the Jews were "picked up", the contents of their houses were given to Dutch Nazis or they left some things there for a German or Dutch Nazi who would move into the house. In a way the Jewish Council were at fault – they decided who had to go.

When I look back at that time and knowing what happened afterwards I have often thought about what was going on between my two sisters. There seemed to be a lot of misunderstanding between them and very little empathy. Even sisters who love each other dearly can, at times, be envious of each other's circumstances. Putting myself in their shoes I can understand them both and this is what I imagine was going through their heads during the period between Kitty's release and Liesje's capture.

In Kitty's view, she had suffered horribly by being arrested and taken to Westerbork. Terrified by German soldiers with dogs and guns, she'd had to undertake forced labour and had spent ten months away from home. She'd endured a bitterly cold winter in a desolate part of the country and with the continued threat of being deported. Maurice had died tragically and suddenly and on returning to Amsterdam she found she had lost all their possessions and her home too. She was 28 years old with no husband, no children and no home. Her younger sister, on the other hand, had an adoring husband and two lovely children who were now safely in hiding. She was looking as beautiful as ever and still attracted all the male attention.

I think Liesje's point of view was very different. She saw Kitty's circumstances as good fortune. Even though she was only 13 months older, it had been established that she was not Jewish. Liesje knew this to be untrue, but thought it typical of her mother to go out of her way to protect Kitty, who, it was obvious to all, was her favourite child. This meant Kitty was now free to spend the rest of the war in safety, without living in constant fear of being discovered and arrested. Kitty didn't seem to understand how unbearable it was to be separated from her children who needed their mother, especially Wim, who was only a baby.

CHAPTER 17

Harry and Fré's Resistance Work

Harry

Much of our resistance work was to find safe addresses for people to be able to go into hiding. This was very difficult. Even though the majority of the Dutch people were against Germany, they were scared to do such active things which were forbidden. The reason for this was that, if they were discovered to have hidden a Jewish person in their house, they would also be arrested. Apart from that, if they had children, there was a greater risk because they were not sure if the children would talk, for example say "Oh we have an uncle staying in our house" or something like that. So it was hard to find places, especially in the bigger towns because in a town it is more difficult to hide people when you have neighbours both down and up who might hear somebody walking about or using the toilet, if there is normally nobody at home. So it was difficult and most addresses we found were in the country, where it was much easier for people to hide. There are endless stories about that.

Another part of the work arose because when people were hidden they still needed their rations – food and so on. So we were collecting ration papers from the distribution office. Every month we got a sheet of ration coupons. The danger was that the basic ration cards were blocked, so there were people who had the possibility to check up on you. If the numbers were blocked you had to throw the card away and find another way of obtaining rations. The resistance succeeded in printing the same cards, more or less. If I wanted to get hold of this paper I had to go to the large printers who made the originals in Zaandam. They had the big format of paper and then they were cut by machine. But the resistance had only small ones.

So every month I went to get a certain amount of these distribution sheets and brought them to the people who were hidden. Often we gave them two instead of one so they had double rations. Not for their own use but to provide extra food for the families where they were hidden. This was to help create a positive climate. It is understandable if you have hidden people who can't go out they get nervous, and they sometimes got nasty. So it was sometimes challenging to keep a positive relationship between the hidden people and the people willing to hide them. So, to make that situation a little bit better, we often gave them more.

One of the nice things that happened once was when we decided to make extra stamps, or rations, used for smoking. Because once a month we could get just one packet of cigarettes. So we thought if we could make extra rations we would give them to these people too and that will also make a better climate. To do that, I remember I had a colleague in Werkspoor [the name of the factory where Harry worked] who lived in Zaandam. And in Zaandam there was a big paper mill which made the paper specially for the distribution of ration coupons. So I asked him if there was a possibility that he could get some sheets of that paper. He succeeded and I had to collect them from Zaandam. We ended up with about five square metres of that paper and each coupon is only 1 cm × 2 cm, so we could make thousands from those sheets [25,000!]. They were printed and then sent back to me and we had to cut them using scissors. You can't cut them with a machine because it was too straight. But everyone got together at home to cut them.

I remember I gave them to a family that were hidden to do some of the cutting. They had their own house with false names etc. And when the man gave me the results of his work there were thousands of coupons. And he said that it cost him his trousers: from kneeling on the floor to do all the cutting his trousers had worn out! Anyway, it was very successful and everyone who was in our group had stamps for extra cigarettes for the hidden people and it did improve the climate. This is just an example – we did so many things like this.

Tootje

Occasionally Harry asked for us to get a bed ready for an Allied pilot whose plane had been shot down, but Harry always managed to get another address for them. He really didn't want my mother involved with that.

Gerard, Harry's friend and work colleague (from Werkspoor), had been living at the Vechtstraat for a while, not because he was hiding but because he did not have a place of his own. Gerard was a Christian boy, an abandoned child, or foundling, brought up by a very poor Jewish family. When this family was taken away, he was suddenly all on his own.

He and Harry would eat with me and my mother once a week – this was after Westerbork. I remember me bringing some thin runny yogurt and something about a bolt of cloth, which was used to conceal things, perhaps the ration card paper. As he was not Jewish, Gerard would have been ideal for transporting things in this way. Harry used to hide cigarettes under my sewing machine.

Mary was living in The Hague and I went to stay with her sometimes after my release from Westerbork. Mary's work at that time was selling grapes, which she did from a large basket over her arm. When she had to collect more from the market she would sometimes leave her son, Aby, a little boy of five years old, on his own in the house.

One day Aby had to come home from school at lunchtime, I don't know the reason why. Mary and I were both out. At that time the Germans were out hunting down any remaining Jews and I am not sure why it happened, but somebody told them there was a Jewish boy living there and he was taken away. When we got back home, Mary and I were told by a neighbour what had happened. We were beside ourselves with worry. We went as quickly as possible to the big castle in The Hague which had been taken over as the Gestapo headquarters. We managed to get him out by explaining that he was not Jewish. So that was a near miss for Aby.

Of course, the war was full of incidents. One which I can never forget was when one of the resistance groups shot a German officer. As a reprisal the Germans took a number of men, I think it was six, out of the prison, which was the on Weteringschans, and shot them by firing squad. Girls from my school, which was also on the Weteringschans, had to stand there and watch. They were on their way to the school, about nine o'clock time, and they were forced to stand there and see them being killed. Luckily I didn't walk that way from school or I would have had to see it too.

Fré

While Harry was busy with his resistance work, Fré was also an active member of another resistance group or cell. Even though she was not Jewish, she had many active friends, including Miep, who was her best friend.

Fré's resistance work involved helping Jewish people escape from arrest, helping them to find safe places to live "in hiding". She was particularly active in helping children. In many cases her network was the only means to escape from arrest and almost certain death. It was easier to find a safe place for a child than it was for a whole family. More people were willing to help a child, especially if they had a young

Fré in 1939

family or if they could not have children. They could pretend that a nephew or niece had come to stay to escape from the dangers of Amsterdam life, though some of the hidden children stayed in Amsterdam too during the war. Children under the age of six did not have to carry an identity card.

For many parents, their last desperate act to save their children's lives was literally to give them away, often to a complete stranger, either at their point of arrest or after their arrest, ideally with the aid of fraudulent papers and help to have their child's name deleted from a list.

Fré was one of the women to rescue such children. She was active in the area of the Hollandse Schouwburg, the large theatre where the arrested Jews were usually kept before being transported to Westerbork. Opposite the Schouwburg was the crèche, especially for the little children, because the Germans did not want babies in the theatre. Fré and other young women, who were mostly students, saved a lot of those children by taking them away from the crèche. They were simply handed over through a window at the back of the building and then the women took them, mostly by train, to some person waiting for them on a station in a small town, from where they were brought to an address. Fré would probably have taken them via Utrecht.

Sometimes, to make them go, the parents would feign anger with their children as they pushed them away, perhaps with a few small treasured possessions or

Photograph taken in the Schouwburg museum

mementos. It must have broken their hearts.

When small babies were given to Fré, she would pretend to be their mother and already have with her a pram, a feeding bottle and some powdered milk, spare nappies and other items of baby equipment, in order to be able to convince someone, if stopped, that she was the rightful guardian of the child. Being non-Jewish it was easier for her to do this work and she was much less likely to be challenged. The records state that she helped at least 30 young children. All their descendants can be grateful for her brave actions.

The house belonging to Fré and Harry de Vries was 27 Vechtstraat. Fré used her home there to help many people who needed somewhere to stay, some for only a few hours and others for some days. The people who were hiding there were then taken from this address to other places, mostly in the country far from Amsterdam. Usually a person or some persons just turned up at Fré's door and she let them in. She knew that after a short while somebody else from her "group" (who she did not know, of course) would arrive to take them away.

Harry's role in the resistance was not so important that he was written about. He did what many others in Amsterdam did. But he, as well as Fré, are mentioned in a book about the Gerretsen resistance group, connected to a rather left-wing organisation (OSP), of which Fré was a member before the occupation.

Miep, Fré's friend, was in hiding. Although she married a non-Jewish man, she was not very sure about it, so she stayed in hiding in a little village near Amsterdam (Sloterdijk) during the war. I have never heard about any resistance activities. In fact, Miep divorced Bram (her non-Jewish husband) solely for reasons that had to do with the persecution. Later they remarried, of course.

Harry

A very sad episode concerned two elderly people. Looking back, they were not very old but, when you are young, everyone over the age of 50 is considered elderly. I think they were 60 or 65. There came a point in time when these two couldn't stand being hidden any longer. They said they wanted to go out but were afraid to get into the hands of the Germans. They said, "The Germans will press us to tell them where we have been living and we are not heroes enough to give you a guarantee that we won't tell them the address. So please help us and give us a means to commit suicide." At the house in Vechtstraat we had some pots of poison powder. It was cyanide, the most lethal poison. It was enough to kill like that [he clicked his fingers]. So we supplied them with poison and they went out and died together in the park.

This is to illustrate that helping out was not only done in a positive way. It was also helping, let's say in a negative way, by helping them to die.

There were other problems. Hidden couples were normal people and therefore, of course, they had sexual contact but sometimes the protection failed and the woman became pregnant. There was a sad plan in place when that happened. The woman asked us to help and we had to arrange for a doctor to come to perform an abortion. This was also part of the resistance. And so you will understand all the discussion about what has happened after the war. If people are desperate, if people don't know what to do with a child that they don't want – or they can't have – an abortion is the most straightforward solution. But during the war there was normally no choice; it had nothing to do with murder or anything like that. In most situations, having a baby while in hiding was very difficult for many practical reasons, and the risk of someone hearing a baby cry was just too great. It happened in several cases, I don't remember the number. Not every day, of course, perhaps three or four times a year. My involvement with this was nothing to do with my conscience. It was necessary so you arranged it. You knew your friends, you knew the doctors and you knew which side they were on. They also understood why, so there was always a way to find a solution. This gives you a brief idea about the resistance work. There were many more people who did much more of that work. We were only on the passive side of the resistance.

Because it was forbidden to have a radio, all our "permitted" sources of news were controlled by the Germans so we mostly didn't know what was happening outside of Holland. Of course, there were some people who still had a kind of radio, and they heard bits and pieces, but the reception had terrible interference. These illegal radio stations were subject to a high level of disruption by the Germans, but even so some messages came through. There were still some people in Holland who had official, but secret, radio contact with the Dutch government in England. There were a number of senders and receivers who went to a different address each week in case they were tracked down by the Germans.

But our resistance was not enough. It was not the sort of resistance you would see in films. There were many people who did other, more dangerous work, and many died... That is all I want to say about my resistance. If you ask me why did you do it? Was it dangerous? I will say we never thought about the dangers. Of course we were careful and took precautions. But we were not heroes. It was something that we were able to do and we were glad to have the possibility to do it. I was glad to be active and not just hidden and doing nothing. And we did it for the whole group that we were in. Most of the time they were doing something and you never really knew what. There was a group of three or four who were just making false papers – all the things I described. Other ones did other work, but we didn't talk to each other about what we were doing. Because if you were captured it was best not to know too much. No one could be certain that they would not tell the enemy if they are tortured. So, if somebody out of our group was picked up and arrested, the others always went to clean up the house. Not clean up in the way of tidy up but to be sure that all the kinds of papers and stamps, or anything incriminating was taken away.

I remember that, sometimes, because we did our resistance work every day, it became normal work. And as it becomes routine you get less careful. At a certain moment there was a special stamp that should be fixed on the distribution card to get rid of the false ones of the people who were going to be deported. And we had to go to an office and they put it on. Fré once got to the office, opened her card and four or five

Photograph © V. Cornelius / Nederlands Fotomuseum

of the forged stamps fell out. These were copies of the stamps to put on the cards of the hidden people. Her heart must have been in her mouth but the man said to her, "Ah, I left them on the table by accident," and he just put them in his box with the rest of his stock of those stamps. He said, "My fault," and took them away. We think that in that way we were really lucky people. I don't mean happy, but really lucky people.

We had two occasions when the Germans came to our house to search. But both times we were warned beforehand and the house was cleaned so they couldn't find anything wrong.

Now we stop about the resistance.

Tootje

I always seem to have done the shopping, even as a small child. In January 1944, I remember reading in the newspaper, as usual, on a Friday evening what would be available to buy with our coupons for the coming week. Rationing was not too bad at that time, not like it was after September 1944. I used to try and get hold of more or less everything I could. I would queue at the two shops that were next to each other on the Nieuwmarkt called Simon de Wit and De Gruyter [like Tesco and Waitrose]. The reason I did this was because a customer could buy something extra, not rationed but in short supply, like a packet of biscuits or a small ontbijtkoek [breakfast cake]. On that Saturday I could buy a bottle of "wine" – it was alcohol-free, more a sort of fruit juice. When I got home I heard that the Allies had landed at Anzio (22nd January), their first foothold in Europe, so I said I would keep the wine to celebrate the end of the war. I can't remember now when we did drink it but it was a happy feeling at the time.

In June 1944 there was D-Day – the invasion of France at long last. We had been waiting for this for so long. Much earlier, even when we were in Westerbork, when we arrived all the people asked "Is there any news? Is there any news?" People hoped the war would be over any day and right from the beginning we thought that the misery would soon be over. And of course there was never any news for them like that, but they were so interested in war news. All radios had been handed in early on in the war. But Willy's parents still had our old radio taped under their dining table. So they listened to the news. And of course the resistance had radios and they typed little news sheets and handed them round and put them in letter boxes of people they knew. So we knew a little bit of what was happening. The Germans only gave you one-sided news of course. I wonder, what did German or Dutch newspapers report 7–9 June?

We were happy about the D-Day landings, and we all had new hopes that the war would be over soon. The invasion seemed to go quite fast for a little while and then it sort of stopped and was very slow. That was in the early summer. It went from June up until late July/early August and the Allies suddenly made a push through and they liberated part of Holland, below the Rhine. We heard rumours that they were as far as The Hague and people went on the road out to welcome them, but it was only rumours. They didn't get as far as that.

CHAPTER 18

Liesje's Abduction

Liesje

In 1942, special groups were formed within the Dutch police with a sole purpose of tracking down Jews in hiding. They roamed the streets and checked passes of anyone who looked Jewish and responded to information from the public. There were thousands of denunciations, mostly anonymous, and many Jews were betrayed by neighbours. Even so, in the spring of 1943 it was estimated that there were between 10,000 and 15,000 Jews still in hiding.

With the last phase of deportations, the Germans drafted in more Jew hunters and enhanced the bounty, which had stood at fl5 per head. By the summer of 1944 it stood at fl40 per head. The most notorious group was led by Henneicke, a former car mechanic turned black marketeer and police informer. He had a "column" of 35 men who between them arrested 3,400 people. Henneicke was assassinated by a resistance group at the end of 1944. Although we knew nothing of these Jew hunters at the time, one in particular was to play a significant role in the family history.

Harry

After the events which led to Mum, Kitty and Tootje being released, the next thing that occurred to have a big impact on the family was to do with Liesje, because she was married to a Jewish man. And if you are half Jewish married to a Jew, you could not get protection. So she still had to have the "J" on the front of her clothes and on her identity card. By this stage the Germans had stepped up their campaign to find remaining Jews in hiding, so Liesje and Nico were in great danger.

The world Fré and I lived in was almost unknown to the family. Not completely unknown, but certain details were hidden. So neither our mother, Tootje, Liesje or Kitty knew what we were doing. Apart from *Het Parool*, which was written on the walls, we did not advertise our activities – it was too dangerous. But, even though we were careful, sometimes the family would pick up the vibes and if someone came in we would ask them to go to another room. So they knew that there was something going on, without knowing the facts. Therefore there was danger. The family knew our friends and they knew many of their names. If there was a birthday, the whole group was there and also the relatives. So there was always the danger that, if they were captured, one of the outsiders without being aware of the implications would give all sorts of information, if asked.

Tootje

This happened in the summer of 1944, after D-Day and before the hunger winter. Liesje had a false ID card and never wore a star, easily passing for a non-Jew with her fair hair. Interestingly, Nico's hair was also fair and he had blue eyes, though he looked more Jewish. Even so, it became increasingly difficult to find safe addresses and we found out later that less than half of those in hiding managed to evade capture. Many of them had to move several times. Liesje had been living in Rotterdam, but she had some trouble with the man she was in hiding with and had to find somewhere else to live. Initially she stayed with Harry and Fré and then Kitty hired an attic bedsit. Although this was very risky for Kitty, the two sisters lived together. Kitty got a job in a chic café/restaurant in the Kalverstraat. All the black market people frequented it; they were the only ones who had any money. Later she got a job in the office of the milk distribution board.

Kitty had to go to an official place to get her ID card changed to reflect her non-Jewish status. At the office she met a Dutch Nazi and he and Kitty became quite friendly. Without really thinking this through, Kitty introduced him to Liesje. Not long after, he introduced the sisters to his friend and police colleague, who was fair-haired and very good-looking. But he was also a Nazi, a member of the Dutch SS, and made extra money by hunting out hidden Jews! Liesje was very attractive to men – very sexy with her thick fair hair. This blond Nazi took an immediate fancy to Liesje but instead of arresting her he took her to his house.

The Nazi policeman's house was in Biesboschstraat, and he forced her to live with him there, more or less as his hostage. If she didn't go along with what he wanted, he threatened to arrest her and take her to the police station. I imagine she resisted this fiercely as she loved Nico.

He was involved in black market trade and used her to help him. This put Liesje in grave danger. She had to pretend to be a hidden Jew that he had just arrested. He made her go out with him with a large trunk which contained his black market goods. In this way they could go around Amsterdam quite freely. I remember how worried we all were about her safety. I used to "shadow" Liesje to see if she was all right. A few times I waited outside where he lived and when they came out I would follow at a distance to see if she was okay. I made sure they didn't see me. Liesje couldn't go out on her own, and when he was out she had to stay locked in his apartment. Liesje could not see how her predicament would end and was worried he would murder her. Like many others, she thought that the war would soon be over.

He kept a gun under his pillow. Harry suggested to Liesje that she should take the gun when he was asleep and shoot him. I don't know how Harry communicated with her or how we knew where she was living. Perhaps Harry had followed them or got the information from Kitty's friend. Anyway, I think he waited until the man went out to communicate through the locked door. Liesje couldn't contemplate shooting her captor – she was far too frightened. Even if she could do it, what would have happened to her then?

Liesje

The Nazi wanted to find out where Nico was hiding, and pressured her to tell him, but she wouldn't. He tried to persuade her by saying how much better her chances of survival would be if she was no longer married to a Jew. Perhaps he was looking for the financial reward from finding another hidden Jew. It was more likely that he wanted to get rid of Nico because he knew she loved her husband and was jealous. He told her that he loved her and therefore wanted Nico out of the equation so she would stop trying to resist him. Or perhaps he was just an evil man!

Liesje certainly did not want to give this man any information, but then things got worse and he blackmailed her by threatening to find out where her children were and have them deported. He might have guessed Nico was at 20 Oudeschans because that was the address on Liesje's ID card, and perhaps he threatened to arrest her mother and Tootje again. Liesje believed he had the motivation and means to find out where Netty and Wim were hidden and do them real harm. In the end, faced with an impossible dilemma, she caved in and told him what he wanted to know. She made him promise not to harm her children and not have her mother and Tootje arrested for hiding Nico.

Poor Liesje! As well as anger, fear and guilt, what emotions must she have been going through? Having been trailed around Amsterdam with this man, playing the role of captured Jew and seeing all the non-Jews going about their normal daily routines, she desperately wanted her life back and longed for her freedom. Mothers with crying babies and laughing toddlers would have tugged hard at Liesje's heartstrings.

Remembering all the things she used to take for granted, she vowed to live life to the full if she ever got out of there. There would have been guilt and anxiety for Nico, resentment towards her parents and envy for her brother and sisters' new status. Plus absolute loathing for the Nazis, especially this man, for using her, abusing her and trapping her into betrayal. And, above all, the yearning for her children.

The term "being caught between a rock and a hard place" doesn't even begin to describe the situation she was in. As far as options were concerned, she'd reached a dead end.

CHAPTER 19

Nico's Arrest

When the Allies successfully landed on the French coast, Liesje like everyone else thought they would soon be free. But then in July or early August 1944 came news that the BBC had reported the existence of extermination camps in Poland, which were different from the concentration camps in Germany, Austria and the occupied countries. The BBC named the victims as Jews, Gypsies, Polish intellectuals, Slavs, Jehovah's Witnesses and homosexuals. The extermination camps were working day and night with the sole purpose of gassing prisoners and cremating their bodies. Auschwitz and its sub-camp, Birkenau, were known of and had the most sophisticated methods. It was estimated that two million Jews had been killed by then. Otto Frank's diary states "We knew about deportation to Poland, after all. And we also knew what was happening in Auschwitz, Treblinka and Madjanek. But then were not the Russians already deep in Poland?"

It is likely that Harry would have heard this news from his resistance network. Would he have passed this on to his sisters? More likely Liesje would have been told this by her blond Nazi captor, who could have used this information to exert more pressure on her to relinquish the whereabouts of Nico. Tootje said she knew nothing of the death camps until 1945.

It was 20th July that an attempt on Hitler's life was made and this was reported in the Guardian newspaper two days later. But did this generate more interest and news about what was going on in the Nazi regime? And were questions asked about what was happening to the tens of thousands of Jews being transported east? It seems not nearly enough.

Liesje

So, having told her captor what he wanted to know, the Nazi went to arrest Nico on 6th August 1944, taking with him his friend and colleague, whom he could trust not to harm Tootje or Lily. It wouldn't have been in the interest of either man to arrest or punish Tootje and Lily for hiding a Jew, given one was in love with Liesje and the other was a friend of Kitty. Afterwards, Kitty wondered if Liesje may have told them where Nico was. But, on Liesje's false ID card, Harry had put her address as Oudeschans 20, so it was thought that this is what led them there. Liesje said it was silly of Harry to have put that address on the card.

Tootje

It was 6th August 1944 when Nico was arrested. My mother was washing down the wooden stairs and she was on the first floor near our front door. So there she was cleaning the stairs with a bucket of water. I happened to be looking out of the window and I saw a motorbike draw up with two chaps on, one with dark hair and one blond. Although they were not wearing uniform one was dressed all in black leather and was clearly a Dutch Nazi. They looked on the doorpost, where everybody in Holland always has their names, and I thought they were looking at next door because there were Nazis living there on the second floor. So I didn't take a lot of notice and they were able to walk straight in and go up the stairs past my mother and through our door, which had been left ajar because my mother was cleaning.

We had a false wall built into a cupboard in the back bedroom, so that Nico could go in there and hide, but these men came up with their guns in their hand trained directly on me and Nico. My mother came up, of course, straight after them, but there was no chance for Nico to hide or to escape.

So that was another memory for me – being threatened by somebody pointing a gun at me. The dark haired man had gone with my mother and Nico to get his stuff together. But while that gun was trained on me there is something I remember. This Nazi looked at the big paper map I had on the wall showing the fighting on the Russian front and the Allied front, which

I had marked out with pieces of woollen thread and drawing pins. I had cut out a picture of Felix the cat from a cardboard box of cat food and had it poised as if it was ready to pounce on Germany. And he said, "Oh, it looks bad for us."

I was aware that I was showing off to him – I have always been a show-off. This was quite a long time after D-Day – or else there wouldn't have been two fronts. I found out afterwards that the reason we were not arrested for hiding someone was because the two men who came to our house were the blond Nazi who had taken Liesje and the other who was Kitty's friend. [Tootje added later: I can't understand how Kitty could go out with this Nazi.]

They took Nico away. Before handing him in at the police station, we can only speculate about what unpleasant things the blond Nazi said to Nico about his relationship with Liesje.

Liesje

Harry had a serious dilemma. He discussed at length with Kitty the problem of Liesje being with the SS man. He must have been at his wits' end because this man was clearly very dangerous and Liesje knew so much about the underground resistance work. When days turned into weeks, he told Kitty, "We must get Liesje away from him because she knows so much about the group." Because she had stayed with Harry for at least a week, she had met many of the resistance workers and knew all of their names. Harry weighed up his options, which were limited to say the least. It is hard to imagine how Harry felt as he reached his terrible conclusion about what he should do.

It was after Nico's arrest that Harry believed that the situation had become untenable. They could not be sure that the man keeping her would not coerce more information from Liesje using more threats. Harry rationalised that, even though she was his sister, the safety of the whole group was at stake and they should not be put at risk. They knew they had to get her out of there one way or another. Afterwards,

Harry said that it was the toughest decision he had ever had to make. Kitty therefore agreed to speak to the Nazi man that she was friendly with and say that her sister was in the hands of this other man. She said, "Can't you get her away from him?" He said he could manage to do this and Kitty asked what he would do. He said Liesje would be let go as they wanted to arrest the man who was keeping her captive. Because of the black marketeering and living with a Jewish woman, he was more important to them than Liesje. Harry and Kitty believed this but it was not true. When they discovered that Liesje had been arrested they realised that they had both been betrayed.

So, ten days after Nico was arrested, Liesje was also taken away. We think the man holding her was punished, but we don't know. At this stage of the war, records were not as meticulously kept as they had been earlier and it has been difficult to find information about the Dutch Nazi, verify his arrest or find any details of what happened to him.

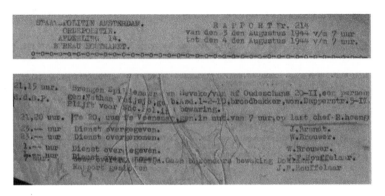

The extracts above are from the police report about the arrest of Nico. The paragraph beginning 21,15 states, "Nathan Vuijsje, born in Amsterdam on 1st February 1910, bread baker by profession living Dapperstraat 5 II was brought in by two policemen, named Spillenaar and Seveke, taken from Oudeschans 20-II and to be kept in prison for the time being." So we know the identity of the two men who were Liesje's captor and Kitty's friend, though we have been unable to find out for certain which was which, although our further research leads us to believe that Liesje's captor was Spillenaar and that after the war both men were prosecuted and lost their jobs as policemen. More details are in the Appendices.[17]

There has been much debate within the family about this sequence of events and, of course, it is only with hindsight that we know the consequences. In trying to understand the dilemma Harry faced at the time, there are a number of factors to consider.

Not least, he believed the war would be over soon. At that stage the Allies were making great progress. They had liberated Paris on 25th August and were advancing rapidly. Harry could not have foreseen that there would be such serious setbacks in the form of Operation Market Garden. By 27th September the Allies north of Arnhem ceased fighting and retreated back across the Rhine.

Secondly, there was the real risk that more information would be extracted from Liesje in order for the Dutch Nazi to find more hidden Jews as well as members of the Dutch resistance – it was how he made his living.

Finally, in Harry's view there was the awful realisation that now Liesje was in this man's hands it was extremely unlikely that there could be a happy ending. Ultimately, either the Nazi would hand her in and she would be deported to a camp or he would murder her. At Westerbork, the risk to her safety would be less.

My uncle Harry was an extremely logical man. He would have considered this emotional and ethical dilemma from every angle, weighing up the different options endlessly and knowing that no course of action would be likely to have a positive outcome. In the end, though, he showed courage too in not shying away from making a decision, knowing that he would then have to live with it.

Harry maintains that he made a pact with the Nazis that Liesje would be treated well. Liesje remarked to Tootje later that it was strange that she was never beaten or hit or shouted at, though she had witnessed lots of others getting bad treatment. Tootje believes this to have been true and not that Liesje was trying to hide unpleasant events. There were, later, some harrowing experiences that she did recount to Tootje. However, it's very unlikely that a request from Harry would have helped Liesje in the time that followed her arrest. At Westerbork, Gemmeker would not give a damn, and at Auschwitz there was no idea at all about the names, origin or anything whatsoever of the people kept there. So there had to have been other reasons why she was treated well.

Kitty

Liesje was the prettiest sister – she had lots of sex appeal. I remember going out sometimes after high school. If Liesje came with me, say to the park, she got all the attention and nobody looked at me. I never realised – she was my sister and I always took her with me. The men just fell for her, of course.

I never told Liesje about Harry's fears. After the war, Liesje was always talking about it to my son, Pieter, and his wife Marianne until they did not want to hear any more. She blamed me for being sent away. I never told her it was really Harry who was so afraid his group would be betrayed. So, it was very complicated. I just forgot all about it and don't want to be reminded of it. Liesje and Nico were both very lucky to come back.

CHAPTER 20

Liesje and Nico in Westerbork

Details of what happened to Liesje from this point onwards have been largely derived from piecing together the testimony of other survivors. These are the accounts of women who shared similar experiences in Westerbork, Auschwitz-Birkenau and Kratzau. This is supplemented by the snippets of information which Liesje herself told Tootje on her return and from the information Liesje told Nico, which was later researched and recounted by his daughter, from his second marriage, Marja Vuijsje. Marja's beautifully written account of what happened to the Vuijsje family during the twentieth century includes a chapter on the war years. Her book, written in Dutch, is called *Ons Camp*. Marja Vuijsje is the half-sister of Netty and Wim and is an established author living in Amsterdam.

When Marja visited Auschwitz as part of her research for her book, she travelled with a group of Dutch women. They were part of the Dutch Auschwitz Committee, which organises trips to Poland. When introduced to them, one of the women, Leny Boeken-Velleman, said, "Vuijsje, I knew a Vuijsje in the war. Her name was Liesje Vuijsje." This was such a fortunate coincidence as Marja was able to find out valuable information about what happened to Liesje.

Leny was part of the same group of Dutch women at Birkenau and then transported to Kratzau. She told Marja how Liesje was treated by the Russian soldiers. Liesje did not play a central role in Marja's book and so information about Liesje was not of great interest to Marja at that time. Until recently, Leny was still helping in the family haberdashery shop in Amsterdam's Nieuwe Hoogstraat. Marja has since told me what she knew and sought to contact Leny for any further details. Unfortunately, Leny was then over 90 years old and not well enough to be able to remember anything further.

This account is based on the following sources from women who survived Kratzau:

- Leny Boeken-Velleman, who made the same "journey" as Liesje and wrote a book about her experiences in her book, *Breekbaar, maar niet gebroken* (*Fragile, but not broken*).
- Helen Waterford's oral history (US Holocaust Memorial Museum) and book, *Commitment to the Dead*.
- Two reports obtained from NIOD (the Netherlands Institute for War, Holocaust and Genocide Studies).

The first of the NIOD reports is a statement from two sisters from The Hague: Betje Rachel Boektje (born 24/3/21) and Sera Sophia Boektje (born 24/3/26). This was recorded in The Hague in 1947.

The second report was made by two witnesses, one of whom was an agronomist, born in 1913 and taken prisoner in Paris, from where she was sent on to Auschwitz via the French transit camp, Drancy, the same as her companion, a dental assistant, born in 1909. The report was made in November 1944. The women were sent from Auschwitz to Kratzau and managed to escape from there.

Further details have been taken from the biography of Otto Frank (Anne's father), written by Carol Ann Lee. From these various sources I believe we now have a reasonably reliable account of Liesje's experiences.

Liesje

Anne Frank and her family were arrested from their hiding place in Prinsengracht on 4th August 1944. They spent a night in the Euterpestraat (the Gestapo headquarters) and two nights in the Weteringschans Prison. Nico was taken away on 6th August and within ten days Liesje had been arrested too.

Liesje may have spent a couple of nights in the Amsterdam city prison, as did Helen Waterford and the Frank family, who were interrogated in the Euterpestraat and slept in its basement cells. Helen was questioned separately from her husband and, like Liesje, she was not physically harmed.

Liesje's journey to Westerbork, probably on 18th August, would have been similar to that of Lily, Kitty and Tootje. It would have been late in the evening when she was put onto a tram, with its windows painted out, and taken through the dark streets of Amsterdam's wartime blackout to Central Station and, from there, put on the train to Westerbork.

On arrival at Westerbork, men and women were separated. Because they had been in hiding, both Liesje and Nico were placed in punishment barracks. Liesje was in Barrack 57, the same as Anne Frank and her sister and mother. Nico, who had arrived a week earlier, was in Barrack 67. They were treated as criminals and not allowed out during the day. Unlike the other prisoners they had to wear a uniform and clogs rather than their own clothes. The men had their heads shaved and the women's hair was cut very short. Rations were less and work detail was greater. Most worked doing unpleasant and dirty battery dismantling. It is not known if Liesje and Nico had any contact while at Westerbork or afterwards, though from other accounts it seems that men and women could mix during the day.

During this period plans had been made in London to order the Dutch railway workers to go on strike to coincide with the Allied plans to attack the southern flank of Holland. German intelligence was aware of the preparations and had picked up radio messages about the strike. As a consequence, it became a top priority for the Germans to deport as many Jews as possible from Westerbork to the east, while the trains were still running.

There were three final trains from Westerbork and in the early hours of Sunday, 3rd September, Liesje and Nico's names were among those read out over the barrack loudspeaker. They had to report to the train station in the morning. This last transport left with over 1,000 people, of whom 127 survived.

In three days the camp was almost emptied, apart from the 300 who remained. I wonder, in that last period, who held the power to decide the few that would stay?

When the camp was eventually liberated by the Canadian 2nd Infantry on 12th April 1945, it was noted that several of the survivors had been there since the beginning of the war. Many were of German origin, who had been in a good position to help with the various administrative and other roles in running the camp and were probably preferred (over Dutch Jews) by the German army in charge.

Being in the punishment barrack, Liesje and Nico stood no chance, nor did the Frank family, who travelled on the same train to Auschwitz-Birkenau. Helen Waterford and her husband were also on this train.

blad 3   GER:PATRI ERDE JODEN

<u>T r e i n: 5 September 1944</u>

Lakmaker, Rachel	van Lennepkade 61 den Haag
van Leeuwen-Bartels, Estella	1e Boerhavestraat 12 Amsterdam
Levee, R.	Overtoom 572''' Amsterdam
de Leima, Sally Bernard de Liemspv.Gelder, Roosje	Spui 227
Meyer, L.V.R.	Stadionkade 4 Amsterdam
Meijers, Clara M.	Roelof Hartplein 4 Amsterdam
Muller, L.M.	Statenweg 111b Rotterdam
Muller- de Jonge, F.	Noorderhagen 34 Enschede
Vuyaje, N. Vuyaje, Granaat Elisabeth	Buiten Visscherstraat 3'' Amsterdam
Roos, Anita	Ringbaan-Ooost 19c Tilburg
Sealtiel, R.	Julianalaan 320 Haarlem
Simons, S. (kinderarts) Simons-Vlessing, B.	Utenbroekestraat 35 den Haag
Thaler, Felly	Biesboschstraat 63 Amsterdam
Vitstein, Sonja F.	Brigittenstraat 22 Utrecht
Zadick, Benjamin Berendt	Singel 295 Amsterdam
Noach, Siegfried	Uiterwaardenstraat 142 Amsterdam
Slager- de Levie, J.	Scholestraat 15 Steenwijk
Verdoner-Cohen, Julie	Parsifalstraat 45 den Haag
Israël, B. Israël-Schaap, S	Kastanjelaan 37 Apeldoorn

Liesje and Nico's transport list

CHAPTER 21

The Later Stages of the War

Kitty

Towards the end of 1944 and after Liesje's arrest, Kitty fell in love with Frans. "I had known Frans a long time. He was married to my best friend, Miep." But Miep left Frans to be with her lover, and Frans and Miep divorced. At first he was a good friend and then became more than a friend. Kitty went to live with him while the war was still on, during the hunger winter: "We were hungry but happy." Kitty and Frans married in November 1946.

Kitty and Frans

Kitty and Frans's wedding. From the left – Abe, Mary, Ies, Lily, Frans's brother, Frans, Kitty, Harry, Fré, Tootje and Liesje

Miep was my very best friend since the age of 14. Even when we were both married, as couples we visited each other very often. We were not allowed out after eight in the evening, but they could come to visit Maurice and me. Frans's parents also lived on the other side of the IJ.

Later, at the time when Arnhem started, I remember Miep and Frans both coming to my mother's house. This was probably for my birthday on 4th October 1944. Miep whispered to me, "I've told him, I've told him," because she was crazily in love with her dentist, who was much older. Even when we were at school he was Miep's dentist and even then I looked on him as an old man! I remember he was always joking with her. She was a very pretty girl, tall, with very fine hair. He was also tall. When I came home from Westerbork she told me she was so much in love with him and they had begun an affair. Frans must have suspected. Having lost my own husband and then finding out she was doing that to her husband, I would say, "How can you do this?" When the truth was known, Frans made her leave him. It was after this that Frans and I began our relationship, which was to last 50 years, until his death in 1994.

I used to visit Miep and all the time she talked about this man. Miep used to ask a neighbour on the other side of the canal if she could use their telephone to call him; very few people had a telephone in those days. But the neighbour had a housekeeper who took a very dim view of what was going on so she always made out she could not use it. I can never understand why she was crazy about this old man. She was just besotted. If I was with her for 24 hours in the day she would be talking about him for 24!

We found out later that he was a high-up Nazi and a very rich man. He lived in a beautiful big villa in the Konninginnweg near the Valeriusplein. After the war, he was put in prison in Harlem. He threw himself off the roof of a building and killed himself. So she had nothing, no husband. It was sad for her, but later she did marry again, had children and became a schoolteacher.

Harry

Life was going on and, although there were terrible things happening around us, at times we had a lot of fun. If you are with good friends it is always the same. We had plenty of ideas about what should be done. Fré was operating with another resistance group that I was not involved with, and was travelling to various places in Holland. We were able to create such a nice a climate and we laughed a great deal. We even had a cabaret, though of course this was illegal. One man made the music and another wrote the scripts. And it was always during the night when there was the curfew and what we called "spare time". The Dutch word for this is "spertijd", or "sperrzeit" in German. From 1944 there was a curfew every day from eight o'clock in the evening until five o'clock the next morning. You couldn't go outdoors so we made the most of it and all the trusted people were invited to come to the cabaret. It was always at the homes of the people who had the largest houses. So perhaps there were 15 or 20 visitors and they played during those forbidden hours, and then they went home again. I remember a brilliant concert with two top violin soloists playing on a staircase.

We had another friend – a fat lady whose father was a butcher in Friesland. She used to smuggle in joints of meat, which we roasted and shared with our friends.

So the war did not feel like the worst time of our lives. Afterwards, looking back, it was the worst time of your life. We had missed our youth. Normally if you are 20 to 25 years old you are out and about; you are developing your personality. We had no time to develop our personalities. We just had what was there. This gave us characteristics which were not helpful in later life. It made us opposite – contra to many things in life. But the only thing that mattered

Fré and Harry in 1944

then was to work together in that small group who were all good friends. We regarded all the others as enemies. Even if they were good Dutch people, you couldn't tell, you could never know if he is good or if he is not good. So we didn't make new contacts or new friends. We lived in a closed world which was not really good to develop our social skills and so on.

Normally we were not afraid – why should anyone be arrested? Why should the Nazis make a link? But, for certain people, we were afraid that if they were captured, that they would talk – to save their own lives. And, without mentioning names, in what I call the second circle, there were some contacts we couldn't be sure about. Sometimes we had cases where a man or woman from the second circle was captured or, even voluntarily, was a spy. And sometimes we got to hear that they had contact with the Germans and we could trace that only that person can have told certain information. In this situation there was a process in place. This was a special meeting of the inner circle, who would discuss the facts, weigh up the risks and then agree what to do. In some cases the judgement was that the person causing the threat should be killed. Don't think this was done every day; of course it was not. But perhaps ten times a year or so, for the safety of the whole resistance group, they had to kill people. There is only one example known to me personally that turned out to be the wrong decision. They made the judgement without realising that the man was a double agent: he had given all kinds of information on a higher level to the resistance. But there is a price to get that information. All of the other cases are in the literature. Most of them are mentioned in the book by Dutch historian Louis de Jong. Most of them were justified.

As time went on more people became certain that the Germans were losing the war, and more people then wanted to join the Dutch resistance. But they were all refused. Put simply, they were too late and we didn't trust them. "We don't know you and we don't know if you are sent by the enemy or not." And that's all I want to say about the whole thing.

There was a nice incident during the latter stages of the war. Fré and I were on holiday and Tootje was with us, somewhere on the Veluwe, which is now a National Park in the province of Gelderland. This was in September 1944. Tootje remembers being there for about a week. Harry and Fré stayed for two or three weeks. There came a message that Antwerp had been liberated and also the province of South Holland. The British troops had arrived in Belgium, though at that moment they had not reached the south of Holland, but the Germans believed that they had. The Dutch called it Mad Tuesday: "Dolle Dinsdag". All the German officers rushed to leave and quickly put all their stuff – possessions and loot – into lorries and drove off east towards Germany as fast as they could.

Source: unknown

So we were, for a short time, liberated. We believed it too [much laughing]. And you saw all the people with their radios, which had been hidden, on the streets. The Germans believed it and the NSB believed it because they ran away to Germany too. It was, indeed, crazy Tuesday. We also heard the Allies were at The Hague, but perhaps there was just one tank or something like that and it got exaggerated. So typical, a real panic and all the Germans were fast boys and had to get away. It was only one day and in 24 hours it was over. I also took the radio from my hidden address to the Vechtstraat. Although the euphoria was short-lived, it was one of the funniest things in the war.

[This was in stark contrast to what was happening to Nico and Liesje, who on that day, Tuesday 5 September, arrived at Auschwitz.]

That was the beginning of the hunger winter. One or two weeks later Market Garden started, which is the code name for the attack at Arnhem. This had the end result of the famous "bridge too far" and it was a big setback for the Allies and a huge disappointment for us. Then the period of hunger came, but Fré and I had a little extra food because we were still helping all the hidden people with extra food ration stamps. In Holland we say, the man who is transporting apples is eating apples. So we were also having extra rations. But at the end of the hunger winter, let's say a month before the end of the war, even if we had 10 or 20 of those stamps, we could only get half a loaf of bread or so to eat, or some sugar beet. So we were fairly hungry and very thin too by then. Towards the end there was a relief organisation accepted by the Germans, who brought big ships from the province of Holland to the province of Friesland, where the farmers lived, and they brought back and distributed potatoes or cheese. It was the Interchurch organisation.

For the people we were looking after we got potatoes, pieces of cheese and apples. So we also had cheese and potatoes. We were very fortunate never to have had real hunger or starvation. We were also eating some meals from the central kitchen which had been set up. But they were preparing terrible food and it was poorly organised; you had to go there one day to get it at nine o'clock for one group and the next day at ten o'clock and so on until five o'clock. This all depended on the letter you had on your card. So, knowing how to handle cards [laughing], you could always succeed to get there in the right queue. So if you have five cards you put the right number on the top. Simple things like that made a big difference. So we had no real problems except for the last few weeks of the war.

To keep the people on the street informed about what was really happening, there was a weekly, and later daily, bulletin fixed on the walls by the resistance people. This was called *Het Parool*. This is still the name of an Amsterdam daily newspaper. One of our jobs was to help write it. For a certain period every evening, other members of the resistance brought us what had come through on the forbidden radio programme. We wrote it down and then made several handwritten copies. Of course, they were all handwritten because we had no other option. We made them out with quite large lettering so people didn't have to stand too close to them to read and so be a bit more discreet. So at 11 o'clock or something like that they came to collect them. We made 10 to 15 copies of them, the three of us – Fré, me and my friend Gerard, who in the hunger winter was also living in Vechtstraat. I remember on one occasion we were so fatigued that we made all kind of stupid letters and spelling mistakes. But it was a nice thing to do and the next morning you could see the paper you had written pinned to a tree with the news. Of course, they hung there for only a few hours before the Germans came and took them away.

I don't know if I have emotion enough for the next thing I remember. It goes back to the beginning. I told you about the strike in February 1941 and I told you a little bit about the communists who organised their resistance very well and that strike also. I have to add that the strike was not only in Amsterdam, but also in Zaandam… it was more likely there than in Amsterdam. The population there had a number of prominent Jews. And a few weeks after that the resistance was already started the day after we were captured – after Holland capitulated and surrendered. And it was started by Christian people: people from the Church. Not the Catholic Church, but the Protestant Church (and not the special groups who were very strict bible followers). So they started and they were the first ones who were captured. A very good group. Very strong people who did it out of their belief and out of their religion. They did very good work. So it was not only the left party but also some other ones.

So, for 18 men who were captured and held in the Orange Hotel, there was a process (a judgement). Nobody thought they should be killed but three of them got life sentences, so there were 15 left and, to the 15, three others were added and these were the strike leaders. The three who had "a pardon" got life sentences, meaning prison for life. They were sent to Germany to camps and were probably gassed. So three got a pardon and instead of death punishment a life sentence. But they wanted to have 18 so three others joined them and they were all killed. We heard it in the afternoon. Shot down by a firing squad (13 March 1941). They were all highly religious so they passed their crucifixes to their priests and they wrote letters to their families. They were given the opportunity that their family could visit them. A young boy refused. He didn't want them to see him. To be that desperate. And so it came to pass that they killed 18 people… It was the first one, except for one special case there was before. And the 18 were fully publicised, to the German people, of course.

And there is a very good poem about it that was published called "The 18 Dead". It's only in Dutch. But it starts with "My cell is three yards long and two yards wide, that small little place".[18]

[Harry was very upset at this point and found it hard to continue. Have a rest. Tape stops.]

Well, that is what I have to tell about my experience in the war. It is only a few stories there are so many more. But you can find them in all the books about the war. What if the name was Harry, or the name was Johnson or Pete, it doesn't matter. They all did what they thought they should do. They all did it their own way and according to their own conscience. The only thing that I want to add is this: the number of people who were in the resistance was a very low percentage of the population. Sometimes history gives the impression that in Holland we had a big resistance – it is not true. There were only a few people and that was one of the dangers too, because we had to do so much work. Really too much work, because if you are working in one circle and then also in another circle – the group making false papers, or the group which did sabotage or the group who tried to get prisoners out of prison or make robberies of the town halls to get official papers. If you are involved in too many of those groups, the contacts are not safe anymore. Ideally you should know only one person from another group. So that's the only remark I want to make and I know it was similar in France.

CHAPTER 22

Liesje's Deportation

Liesje

Helen Waterford, her husband, Siegfried, Anne Frank and her family and the Boektje sisters were all on the same train as Liesje and Nico from Westerbork to Auschwitz[19] on 3rd September 1944. In total there were 498 men, 442 women and 79 children on this train. This was the last train to leave Westerbork.

Also among them were Max and Nol the singing duo, Johnny and Jones. They had been in Westerbork for 12 months. During their imprisonment they continued to sing and several times they went to Amsterdam to record their songs. Coincidently they were transported from Westerbork in the same train as Liesje. They died in the concentration camp Bergen-Belsen during the last days of the war. Max was 28 when he died. My mother still has a Johnny and Jones record and several recordings can be found on YouTube, including "Westerbork Serenade". They have their own display in the Amsterdam Historical Museum.

The train, made up of completely empty cattle cars, was very long – about 20 wagons. People were loaded indiscriminately: young, old, children, babies and the sick were crammed in, about 70 to 80 in each car. They had to stand against each other and there was no room to sit on the floor. Luggage took up badly needed room, it was dark and there was very little air as there were no windows and no openings in the doors. There was a small bucket available as a toilet, though it was difficult to find the room to squeeze a way to use it. Much earlier, in 1943, the Jewish leaders at

Westerbork had sought to make the journey more comfortable by providing benches. However, this was pointless because after just one journey the train returned from Poland empty.

For many who survived the war, this journey was one of their most painful and unforgettable experiences. On the way to the train everyone was given a piece of bread and there was some jam to share. Once this was gone there was no more food provided or any water. On the journey of 3 September the train often stopped and three times the doors were opened by German soldiers. The first time was to collect fountain pens, the second time watches and the third time money. The Jews were told that Dutch money was worthless and must be handed over.

Helen Waterford and her husband gave up the money in their pockets and when the train left again they tore into tiny pieces all their remaining money, which they had hidden. "How hard it was physically and mentally to destroy the money for which we had worked and saved for years. It was Siegfried's idea, for which I am forever grateful."

During the journey, Liesje, who had always got on so well with children, made friends with a little girl who had lost both her parents. Liesje would have done her best to comfort her, telling her stories and passing the time by talking about her family and her home in Amsterdam. Like others, Liesje hoped that the stories about the existence of family camps were true and that this little girl would be looked after there.

They arrived in the middle of the third night, the very early hours of Tuesday 5 September (Dolle Dinsdag!). The doors were opened to reveal a brightly lit platform and prisoners in blue and white uniforms whose job it was to unload the trains, getting everyone off, taking out the dead bodies and piling up all the luggage and rucksacks. This was distressful for those who had brought precious belongings with them. Although reassured that they would get them back, they did not.

The new arrivals would have been completely disorientated and confused about what was going on amid lots of shouting, beatings, shooting and screaming.

Men were again separated from women and children and they formed two long columns, which moved slowly towards the end of the platform. A well-dressed, handsome German officer with shiny boots stood in charge. This was Dr Mengele, known later as Dr Death. Liesje, still looking after the little girl, observed what was going on. Although weak, she was on alert and had a natural instinct to survive. She noted that the older women, the sick and women with children were directed towards the left. Compared to many of the other women, Liesje was in very good shape. Mengele would have noticed her and her lovely fair hair. Mengele asked her if the little girl was her daughter. Liesje hesitated, but in that instant she thought of Netty and baby Wim.

She shook her head and Mengele indicated with his thumb that she should go to the right. Liesje briefly kissed the girl and tried to gently move away from her. But the girl did not want to leave her new friend and started crying, clinging on to Liesje so she had to push her towards the women on the left, which was very painful. She told Tootje this after the war. Liesje joined the smaller line of younger women on the right, who were told to go down a path into an open siding. They could hear voices, dogs barking and in the distance some music playing. They briefly met up with some of the men from the train. They were then marched to Birkenau, a distance of three kilometres. After their ordeal of the journey, with no food or water, this must have been exhausting.

The old and sick, along with all children under 15 years, were among more than half the people from the train who were gassed immediately on arrival.

After a while the women were told to go into a large single-storey building. They were lined up to be registered. All their details, including their occupations, were recorded. Many women seemed to have a useful profession – would Liesje have said she was a shop assistant? Each was given a number, first written in a book and then tattooed on their left forearm. At 90 years of age Tootje still dwells on how painful and humiliating this would have been for Liesje. This number had to be quickly memorised as it was used in place of their names. Betje and Sera Boektje were given numbers A25265 and A25266. We don't know Liesje's number – she had it removed as soon as possible after the war and it is difficult to find out because the Germans destroyed nearly all of their records before the Russians came.

These registration tasks were carried out by women each wearing a different dress of silky black material. They had attractive hair and looked more like civilian employees than prisoners.

Liesje and the women she was with were told to enter a large circle of German soldiers with Alsatian dogs. They were ordered to strip completely naked and were bodily searched by the women in the black dresses for any remaining jewellery or other hidden valuables. They were allowed to keep only their shoes.

They then had the hair on their heads cut very short and other body hair shaved before being pushed under cold showers. By this stage it was evening and becoming cooler. Each woman was given just a dress, without regard to size or fabric. There was no underwear. Fortunately for most of the women, menstruation had stopped.

They then walked in rows of five to a barrack. There was still no food or water and they had not been able to use a toilet. The barracks were former stables. There were no windows, no toilet facilities and no water. Bunks were in rows of three, each meant for six people. Because there were so many women on that first night, ten had to share each bunk, but they were so exhausted they slept.

CHAPTER 23

Auschwitz-Birkenau

Liesje

On their first morning in the camp it was still dark when the lights came on and they were ordered to get up for roll call (appel). Appel was how every day at Auschwitz-Birkenau began. The women had to get up, run outside and then stand in rows of five for hours on end. "Breakfast" was hot black liquid carried in a barrel by four women who supported it with wooden sticks. Appel was held again in the evening and there was always a discrepancy in the counting of the women present and the official number who were supposed to be there. They then had to wait while an SS soldier came to check the figures. The missing numbers were usually those too sick to get up or they were found dead in their bunks. Even so they

© Sheetal Chadha

were all carried out and laid on the ground to be counted. Sometimes there were too many present, caused by women who did not belong to the barrack. Each barrack held about 1,000 women.

©Tom Bartel, travelpast50.com

The latrine accommodated up to 64 people and became a social meeting place. It could only be used at set times and there was no toilet paper. Another barrack had iron washtubs on high metal legs. There was only cold water, no soap or anything to dry themselves with.

Jamie's picture from his school trip to Auschwitz April 2015

No German guards were in evidence and there was not a tree or blade of grass in sight. Just many thousands of women surrounded by high barbed wire fences and wooden watchtowers.

Liesje found out she was in Birkenau, one of the 40 sub-camps of Auschwitz. She was told that the smaller building in the distance next to a large chimney was the gas chamber and crematorium. She saw first-hand the truth of the earlier stories – that the chimney was constantly letting out a stream of smoke and people, mainly Jews, were being gassed 24 hours a day. It was known as the only way out. Hence the title of Presser's book, *Ashes in the Wind*.

One woman survivor could not get out of her mind the image of dark grey wisps of smoke, "just as they used to rise up day and night from the chimneys, our only way out of the camp. The burning of the corpses never ceased, night or day. Always the sky was fouled by an oily cloud that filled the whole horizon, covering the sorrow-stricken barracks that were our whole world."

It was said that Poles and Russians, coming from harsher climates and lower standards of living, were able to endure the conditions, being more able to endure hardship, taking care of themselves. Not much less adaptable were the Greeks, followed by the Slovaks, the Germans and Czechs. The Dutch were at the bottom of the list.

During the day they were not allowed into the barracks so they sat on the ground talking to other Dutch women and waiting for food. Like Liesje, many of the women were physically well from being in hiding and comparatively well fed. They tried to remain optimistic and hoped the war would soon be over. Liesje thought constantly about her family and was determined to do all she could to survive and to see her children. Above all, she missed baby Wim and hoped he was okay.

Each barrack had a KAPO, an acronym for camp police. KAPOs were described by Helen Waterford as cold, hard women. Always Jewish and mostly Polish, they were each responsible for the supervision of approximately 1,000 prisoners, making sure they were quiet and "clean" and did not enter the barrack during the day or leave it during the night. They wore the same silky black dress and were allowed to grow their hair. Liesje told Tootje afterwards that her barrack KAPO was an old school friend of Tootje's called Lena Lierens. Tootje remembers her as a kind girl, but Liesje did not have a good thing to say about her; she was quite vicious. She would have been a lot younger than Liesje, perhaps 18 or 19 years old. This was not unusual as other KAPOs were as young as 15.

Helen Waterford's survival instinct led her to try not to stand out in any way. She felt it safer to try to be "invisible" and to avoid being selected for special work parties or anything else. This might have been more difficult for Liesje, with her attractive personality and looks. There were various punishments meted out, often for no apparent reason. They once witnessed a woman hanged, though they did not know why. Sometimes if roll call went particularly badly the women were made to kneel on the gravel for hours on their bare knees. According to Liesje she was never beaten.

We know from survivor testimonies that, while it was strictly forbidden, and that Polish prostitutes were provided for the guards, some German soldiers raped Jewish women in Auschwitz. According to the historian Bob Moore, they would do so whenever they could get away with it. There are no accounts of rape in Westerbork.

Before long the women were covered with lice, which was uncomfortable and potentially dangerous, because some lice carried typhus. Occasionally they had to visit a delousing station in another camp, an event which took all day. Each woman brought a blanket, which was put with her clothes into a huge drum of hot liquid. Meanwhile, the women were able to wash themselves with warm water provided in buckets but without soap. Afterwards they might find just a dress to put on but all their previous clothing was gone. Also gone were any valuable items they had managed to collect such as rags, a piece of paper or string. It must have been very annoying for the women to lose everything again, and pointless too, because within a short time the lice were back just the same.

The most terrifying events were Mengele's selections for the gas chambers. After her arrival Liesje probably would have gone through at least two more of these during her period in Birkenau. There were constant rumours about selections and when they occurred, without warning, the women were shut into the barracks. The barrack leaders received a signal that a selection was about to take place and the women were then ordered to take off their dresses, put them over their outstretched arms and walk nude past Mengele. As at their arrival, he would signal with his thumb to the left or right. Those selected had to go into a separate room, while those spared could return to their barrack. By now everyone knew what selection meant so it was extremely stressful, especially when family members were separated.

On 7th October 1944, during Liesje's time in Birkenau, one of the four gas chambers was destroyed. Four women had smuggled gunpowder from the Union-Werke armaments factory where they worked and given it to the Jewish Sonderkommando – the Special Work Unit, selected to undertake the most terrible work, processing and disposing of the bodies in the gas chambers. The Sonderkommando used the explosives to set fire to the crematoria and then cut through the fence. In all, 250 Jews attempted to escape but the SS surrounded them and all of them were gunned down. In the fight, three SS guards were killed and ten wounded. The four women taking the explosives were hanged. This was the largest uprising at Auschwitz.

One of the few details Liesje recounted to Tootje after the war was her own little piece of sabotage. She was involved in making artillery shells, probably in the same factory mentioned above. She had to pick up the incomplete shell from a pile, undertake some process with it and then put her completed work into another box. When the overseers were not watching she would take a handful of shells from her completed box and return them to the first pile, and then pretend to be working on them again. She liked to think of the Allies approaching as she attempted to slow down the manufacturing of these deadly shells.

CHAPTER 24

The Hunger Winter

Tootje

When the Allies landed on D-Day it was a long time before they came. They got to the South of Holland by August and we thought "that's it". They got to Eindhoven and we heard rumours that they had got as far as The Hague, but it was not true. We were waiting for them, but then all progress stopped when they got to Arnhem.

We've all heard about Arnhem and the attack which should have been our liberation but it went all wrong. Traitors again, Dutch traitors. The Dutch government from London on Radio Orange told the train workers to halt all the trains so the Germans couldn't ferry their troops around. So they did but then the operation at Arnhem was a disaster. The drivers and other railway workers couldn't go back because they would have been punished for being on strike. So there were no more trains running after 17th September. The Germans used this as an excuse to take all the food away from us and said, "Well, you can't have any food because there are no trains to transport it." And that is when our hunger winter started. If you couldn't get anything on the black market you were just stuck.

We had about 1lb of potatoes per week but they were mostly unobtainable and you got half a loaf of bread per person per week, which was a small flat brown loaf. I remember we got one loaf between us and I used to have to queue for hours for that. I went to different places including the bakers in the Prinsengracht, on the corner of Leidsestraat. I remember once a piece of black market goat's meat.

There was no heating, no gas and no electricity. We had water and that was about all. Fortunately we still had the piped radio from the flat below and I remember listening to this, sitting in the dark during the hunger winter with tiny candles floating in ½ inch of cod liver oil.

By now the curfew was at 8pm for everybody. It was a very miserable time. People were so hungry that some would just die and their bodies would be lying in the streets. And small children had big tummies like you see in the Third World when there is a famine. That's how they were in Holland. People with jewellery in the beginning of that happening would go to try to barter it in exchange for food. This included Kitty and my mother. But, for most people, towards the end of the winter they had nothing left to barter and food became more and more scarce. This was when the whole of the Dutch population suffered, not just the Jews, and Amsterdam suffered the worst shortages. By this time the pursuit of the Jews had slowed right down as very few remained unless they were in hiding. The Nazis were trying to capture resistance workers and were looking for labour to work for the German war effort.

Kitty went on her bike a long way away – Friesland or somewhere – and "bought" a pillowcase of oats for us. For this she bartered my mother's wedding ring and other jewellery – my grandfather's gold chain that his watch hung on, as well as his watch. This had been inherited by my father from my grandfather. We had bought it for him as a present in our better-off days. That was the only thing he had inherited. All these precious things we had all went for some food. We also got some wheat that we could grind in the coffee mill.

We used a sort of stove which had been invented. This consisted of a large container such as a two-gallon paint tin and a smaller one-pint tin which was hanging inside the big one. We would put little pieces of wood about the size of matchsticks and burn them. The heat went up and around and it was quite effective. You had to keep lifting off the saucepan to add more pieces of wood.

I used to cook the sugar beet in the saucepan with water. It took a lot of cooking to make it tender enough to eat. That made the water sweet and we would use that to boil the oats, which in turn made them more palatable.

For my mother's birthday on 21st March 1945 I ingeniously made some "cakes". I used the ground-up wheat to make flour and I managed to buy some yellow and red food colouring. Nobody else in the family did any cooking apart from my mother and me, and nobody did any baking. I made some shallow rounds, like little tarts, and baked these in the Dutch oven. I put them together with some jelly (having collected gelatine) to form little cakes. They were so successful that Harry asked me to make some more for his birthday on 30th March. People used to eat tulip bulbs and crocus bulbs, but the only time I ate some was on Harry's birthday, when we ate crocus bulbs. So whatever happened we still celebrated birthdays!

On 20th March, Mary and I went to the south side of Amsterdam, where there were smallholdings. It was a long walk. We took with us an empty milk bottle and we tried to get some milk and a few vegetables for my mother's birthday. We tried several doors and asked the people, but got nothing so walked all the way back empty-handed.

As far as food goes, Harry and Fré had a different life than us. Harry and Fré had lots of false ration cards, so they were better-off, just until there wasn't really anything left to get. Kitty got oats for us but she and Frans also lived their lives apart. It was my mother and myself who were the worst affected.

Once we had a bit of bread and sardines from Sweden. This was as a result of the Dutch government-in-exile asking neutral Sweden to send food supplies. So food parcels came by plane – but this was in April, right near the end of the war – but still not many. Another time I remember we fetched bread from the central food kitchen, supplied from the Swedish Red Cross. I couldn't believe the loaf was so high and white.

During the hunger winter doors and windows were taken from the empty Jewish houses, chopped up and used for fire wood. Then they took away the floorboards and in the end very many of the houses had to be demolished. We went to visit the Weesperstraat area in 2003 and I could not recognise it. This is where the Vuijsje bakery used to be and where the monument is now.

Kitty

My husband, Frans's job during the war was working for the council. Normally he was a building inspector, but no buildings were built during the war, so he did other duties. Mainly he was in the food department working on distribution, for example when the English came with food parcels, which they dropped from planes. During the hunger winter he went out to farms to see how much milk they could send to the towns or how many beetroots or beans.

Sacks of beans came in from the farms. They had to be cleaned by machine so all the muck came off. Frans would supervise the machine and make sure nothing was stolen. He went with other men to pick up the food parcels, which were flown in and dropped with parachutes at Schiphol. He collected them in a horse and cart as there was no fuel. We lived in Sanderijnstraat, a district to the west of Amsterdam. Again, he had to make sure none were stolen. Some of the parcels had

Operation Manna – "Many Thanks" for food dropped by the RAF written in tulips, Holland, May 1945. Source: wikipedia.org/wiki/ Dutch_famine_of_1944

broken open and he would share these out with the others. For example, if a tin of spam had split open, it had to be eaten. So we did get a little extra food. It was difficult to make something out of all these different things that came down. A sort of wartime "Ready Steady Cook".

I used to say to him, "As soon as I see an English soldier, the first thing I'm going to ask is 'Have you got any Cadbury's please?'" One night he came home from Schiphol and said, "Look what I've got"! There had been some Cadbury's in the drop!

During that winter we were rationed to only half a loaf per person per week and we had to queue a long time for it. Also one kilo of potatoes per person per week. But often we just couldn't get them; they were not being dug up because the ground was frozen. So mostly we just had the bread. We couldn't grow anything because we had no garden. Sometimes there was sugar beet, but I couldn't eat it and would rather be hungry.

We had to go into the country to barter with farmers. In February 1945 I went with a friend on a five-day journey on my mother's bike looking for food. It was snowing. One evening I got a flat tyre just before the eight o'clock curfew. In all I had five flat tyres on that trip! I knew of a place where Frans had relations living, although I had never met them. We pushed our bikes into the village and found them. They said to come in and gave us some food. In the country there was much more food. We ate a lovely meal that evening and the next day they repaired my bike so I could go on, further north.

The girl who came with me on the trip lived nearby in Amsterdam and also had a bike. She had brought with her some money and a tablecloth. But of course the farmers did not want tablecloths – they had plenty of that kind of stuff. I had my father's gold watch, a lovely new hammer from the shop and a whole packet of nails – which couldn't be bought except on the black market. The farmers gave me a piece of lard for the hammer and nails, and a sack of rye for the watch, as well as some bread.

On our way back to Amsterdam we wanted to return to the family who had helped us on the way up. But we only got as far as the next village when it was nearly eight o'clock and a man shouted to us "Oh, it's eight o'clock and you can't be in the street any longer. You must go in." He sent us in to a church and we spent the whole night there sitting on the wooden pews. We had the big loaf of dry bread so we broke some off and ate that, but nothing else.

Tootje

The Germans had invented their deadly flying bomb, V1 and V2 rockets. These were unmanned missiles which could fly at supersonic speed. They were launched towards London from the back of lorries, from various points along the coast, including The Hague. Sometimes the launch didn't go according to plan and the bombs fell on residential areas in The Hague, not far from where Mary was living. The launch sites became a major target for RAF bombs. At that point Mary decided it would be much safer for her and Aby to relocate to Amsterdam and she and Aby walked all the way to the Oudeschans to live with us (57 kilometres!). They stayed with us a while then found their own place on the Oudeschans, the other end from the tower.

Towards the end of the war I remember walking in Thorbeckeplein near the Rembrandtplein. It was a beautiful day. As I walked along I looked through a big glass window and saw some German soldiers in a café. There were two officers sitting on either side of the table with two girls enjoying themselves. There was an officer's peaked cap lying by the window with two pairs of gloves in it. I always remember that image of the cap and their beautiful leather gloves. These two men looked so smug and well fed in their smart uniforms. This made a big impression on me I don't know why. I suppose there was such a stark contrast: the sun was shining and everything looked perfect except for the fact that all the people of Amsterdam were nearly starved to death.

CHAPTER 25

Kratzau

Liesje

The final selection Liesje was involved in at Birkenau was very different from the earlier ones. On 27th October 1944 she was among 300 of the more healthy women who were counted and taken to another barrack. The counting was a positive sign because those selected for the gas chamber were never counted.

Anne Frank and her mother were part of this selection for Kratzau. However, because Anne's sister, Margot, was in the infirmary, they hid from the guards in order not to be separated from her.

Sera Boektje was also selected for Kratzau and recounts that they were told to choose shoes, socks, a vest, trousers, a dress and a coat.

The following day, those selected were given some bread, margarine and sausage and were loaded onto a cattle train. It was a relief to be leaving the chimneys. Each wagon had two SS guards and a latrine bucket, which was emptied regularly. Unlike their earlier journey, the doors were kept open and they could enjoy the lovely autumn scenery. The train travelled west, which they saw as another positive sign. In the evening they arrived at a small town high in some beautiful hills. This was Kratzau (now called Chrastava), in Czechoslovakia, part of the Sudetenland. It was a revelation for the women to see people walking round freely and mothers pushing prams.

They walked through some woods along a stream to the camp, which was housed in an old castle – a three-storey building surrounded by fences and a large wooden gate. The camp was a sub-camp of the concentration camp Gross-Rosen near Breslau. A young woman in uniform introduced herself as the commandant. She was 23 years old and had been a hairdresser in civilian life. She welcomed them, said that as long as they worked hard there was nothing to be afraid of and she reassured them that there were no gas chambers. The stone building to the right of the castle was to be their home for the rest of the war and had been converted from an old factory with one very large room on each floor. It was clean and empty, apart from approximately 100 three-tier single bunks, each with a clean blanket, a pillow and a straw mattress. Such luxury compared to Birkenau. In total there were about 1,000 women. To begin with, each was allocated a bunk, but when the camp became overcrowded they were two to a bunk.

On the ground floor lived the German and Polish prisoners. The Dutch women were on the first floor, together with the Belgian and French girls, on the second floor, the remaining Polish girls, and on the third floor the other nationalities were put as well as the hospital ward. The first floor was absolutely full with 250 prisoners, of which about 150 were Dutch. They were not allowed any contact with the Belgian or French.

To the left of the building there was a garage for the cars of the officers and there was a central kitchen. At the back was an open space where about every two weeks the women had their heads shaved and were checked for lice. The officers were afraid to get ill. The courtyard used for roll call had cobblestones, which made walking difficult and painful.

The camp was ruled by the SS, which had both male and female guards. The commandant's assistant (SS-Unterscharführer) was a male medical services officer who was also responsible for the kitchen. On the first morning they were greeted by a friendly SS sergeant. But most of the guards were really nasty and liked to push the women around. For example, they would sometimes stand on someone's foot, or near the stairs they would give a really hard push or suddenly scream in the ears of a woman who did not obey quickly enough. The female guards at Kratzau hated the location and the 12-hour shifts having to watch the prisoners working in the factory. Sometimes there were beatings. The women still felt like prisoners and could not answer back. They could see in the faces of the guards that they enjoyed making them feel bad.

The munitions factory had been converted from a former textile works in the village of Weiskirehel. This was quite a long way and took an hour to walk. The roads were not good; it was hilly, muddy and slippery when wet. Some women still had no shoes and lagged behind. Along the way some tried to pull up moist grass to chew in order to get some water. The two regular guards went with them and the "dame" in charge walked behind them with her stick in order to beat stragglers. The guards were to prevent any talking among the women and to keep them in line. This was difficult as it was always dark. The guards would shout so loudly that the locals complained about the noise. Much further behind were two German soldiers in military uniforms with boots and each carrying a gun in a holster. They were frightening and important at the same time.

The work of the factory completely controlled the life of the camp. Inside there was an overseer in every hall and a German engineer who made sure that there was no talking between the prisoners and the other workers. The overseers were not too bad and some were even sympathetic to the plight of the women and declared their condition scandalous. However, the commandant and her deputy did everything they could to make camp life as unpleasant as possible. Camp police who showed any accommodation or solidarity with the women were replaced immediately.

The factory produced stick hand grenades out of lightweight metal. The insides had to be worked with a delicate knife on an electric bench. As in Auschwitz, when no one was looking Liesje would pick up a handful which were already complete and put them back onto her bench – so that she would do less of this work than they thought. The women did not know what they were making but realised they must be important because production was 24 hours a day, for six days a week. Helen Waterford chose the night shift from 6pm to 6am as this came with the promise of an extra portion of food on Sunday afternoon, which was free time for everyone.

Occasionally, as they walked through the town of Kratzau, there stood a mug with water or milk on a window sill, and sometimes a piece of bread, left by one of the locals. A small gesture, but an act of human kindness which was much appreciated.

To begin with, the women did not mind their walk to work. It gave them lots of fresh air and the scenery was pretty beside the stream and through some woods, then into the town. But then it became too cold. Helen described the winter as "Beautiful to see but gruesome to experience". Kratzau is situated at a height of 300 metres and, at the beginning of November 1944, there was already snowfall. In their summer clothes, they suffered terribly as it was a bitterly cold winter throughout Europe.

To get the food the women had to remember their number. This could be a problem because they had nothing to write it down on and it was different from the number which had been tattooed on their arm at Auschwitz. Food consisted of "dinner", which was soup or a few potatoes cooked in their skins. Rations became smaller as time went on. The women had no knife, cup or any sort of container and no pockets. So their bread was eaten straight away. In the barrack everyone tried to hide their blanket, but it was difficult to guard against theft. As one shift returned the other shift had already set off. This was another snippet which Liesje told Tootje. Sometimes she managed to switch lines – set off on the day shift and move across to the night shift just returning and thus be able to spend a whole day resting in the barrack. Motivated partly by sabotage and partly to improve her chance of survival, she seemed to get away with this.

Although the Dutch women were often kind to each other, they competed every evening for the best place to sleep and wanted to be together with their group of friends for comfort. Leny thought they behaved just like children. They slept in bunk beds, two singles together and three storeys high, just the same as at Westerbork. Everyone liked to sleep in the top bunk so that nobody was above them. Lots of girls, because of the lack of nourishment had ailments and could not contain their urine, so the top bunk was the safest place.

At the camp, there was a Jewish female doctor and two nurses, but they only had limited medicines. For two weeks, there was no medication for diarrhoea, which caused considerable devastation. The infirmary had 12 beds, but the commandant would only allow eight people to be admitted at a time.

The toilets were in the hallway and were not much better than the latrines at Auschwitz: a hole in the ground with a thick pole across it to sit on. Between the toilets was a wooden partition that gave some privacy. They were not cleaned often enough, so stank terribly. Everybody was troubled with flies, rats and other nasty things. There were two sorts of flies: those that sat on the wall and others that got into their clothes. It was a nuisance that every day there were places on their bodies that were bleeding and because the women were so weak their wounds would not heal properly. To make things worse, the shaving of different parts of their bodies did not always go well and resulted in more wounds. This was an ordeal not only due to the shaving apparatus but also the nasty manner of the men who did it. Leny thought that having men in a women's camp was done because the Germans wanted them to feel degraded. The male guards had dogs and sticks and seemed to be real women-haters. Some were just as nasty as their dogs. Outside was their domain but they came inside, where the women lived. These men had families and could sometimes be heard talking lovingly about their wives and children. So it was hard to understand why they could be so horrible and sadistic. The dogs were used to frighten the women and it worked because they were always afraid of them, scared to death of the dogs' foaming mouths and vicious teeth. The guards laughed when someone, or a whole group, were chased by the dogs and reacting as if they were going to be killed. They used their sticks frequently, though could not be too rough with the women because they knew they were needed for the work. Leny managed to keep out of the way of the dogs and the guards as much as possible by keeping herself busy. She looked ahead, kept her head down and did as she was told. Perhaps this was Liesje's tactic too or did she stand out too much?

The condition of the women's clothes was the main reason why hygiene in the camp was so terrible. When they left Auschwitz in October, they each had one set of clothes. They did not possess a handkerchief, towel or any change of clothing. If they wanted to wash anything (always without soap), then they would have to be content with just their dress in the meantime. After two weeks of working in the factory and being outside, the women were in an indescribably dirty state. When they were given rags to clean the machines, the women would make them disappear in order to make head scarves.

Shoes were another big problem. The road from the camp to the factory was a muddy country road. After about ten days, their shoes were in such a state that they would often arrive at the factory with completely soaked feet. By the end of November, some women already had to walk barefoot. They were promised wooden slippers because the overseers would complain daily that they could not get the women to walk in line. These so-called slippers were wooden, open at the back, making it even more difficult to walk through the snow.

Some clever women managed to make underwear out of the blankets. Since no one ever undressed before going to sleep it took a while for the others to realise why the blankets had disappeared. Tootje imagines Liesje being able to do this as she was quite good at sewing.

During their time at the camp it was important for the women to know what day it was. To remember who they were and what they were doing helped to put their thoughts in order, to retain their identity and to know who they were as a person. Leny recounted, "We knew every day the date and we said it: 'Today is...'". On Saturday, 4th November 1944, Liesje "celebrated" her twenty-eighth birthday. And on Tuesday 28th November Liesje would have said, "Happy eighteenth birthday, Tootje." She never forgot her little sister's birthday.

At Christmas there was horsemeat, potatoes and peas, which must have tasted delicious. This and the "coffee" were for once served in brown plastic bowls.

There were many nationalities in the camp so it was inevitable that the Dutch women became friends. During their free Sunday afternoons they would talk. Most were married with children in hiding so often they were in the same boat, of similar age, sharing the same language and the same hardship. One day a question arose, "What would be harder to endure when the war is over, if our husbands did not return or a life without our children?" The women were honest and shared their deepest thoughts with each other. Nearly all the women came to the same conclusion: while they longed to see their husbands, they could not bear the thought of losing their children; it was part of their flesh and blood that would be lost forever. It's easy to imagine Liesje taking part in this discussion and agreeing with the majority.

A large shower installation was built, which caused some excitement and hope among the women. But before they could be used a new commandant arrived with different ideas on how to treat the women and the showers were made out of bounds. Instead, they were taken to another camp with saunas and a delousing station. This trip took two days by freight train. Everyone went, even the sick, who were given nothing but aspirin and dressings made of paper. On the journey the freight cars remained open, so it must have been very cold and there was hardly any food. On their return they found all the windows in their living quarters had been left open so it was bitterly cold. Everything had been thoroughly cleaned, but the blankets and any bits of hoarded paper or rags were gone, just the straw mattresses were left, which they had to use as cover. The lice returned and the showers remained closed. Their captors did not seem to realise that the filth and vermin came from the women not ever being able to wash themselves or their clothing.

Then there were rumours about food parcels from the International Red Cross. One Sunday they were given a handful of white sugar, which they had to eat from their hands. Also a can of sardines, but these were far too rich and made them all ill. The next day there was no work and after roll call a car arrived. In it were women from the Red Cross, wearing green uniforms, sent to inspect the prisoners. They were appalled by what they saw. The commandant spoke to them in German, "Look at those pigs, how filthy they are, and be aware of the strong stench of these Jews. We have the most beautiful showers here, which I will show you, but nobody takes the trouble to use them." The Red Cross took this at face value, shook their heads and walked away without asking a single question. They were told that the prisoners were ordinary criminals taken by the Germans from occupied countries. They were satisfied with the explanation and pleased to leave. Helen Waterford spoke perfect German so could understand every word.

A few days later a shipment of clothes arrived. Some got a heavier jacket. There was a patch sewn onto the back with their prisoner number on – in case they tried to escape. Also shoes, although there was not one matching pair.

One woman managed to escape but she was recaptured and sent to Gross-Rosen, the "mother camp". This was a large concentration camp with many satellite camps like Kratzau.

The early spring of 1945 was the hardest time. The cold weather and shrinking rations made it difficult and many gave up hope. Several women died within a couple of days of that state of mind setting in. Liesje managed to cling on to her need to survive, which had so far not let her down.

By this stage things were grim for Germany. Food was in short supply for them, so even more scarce for the prisoners. The women who were fluent in German could overhear the guards talking. They heard that the Allies were already in the middle of Germany and the guards were increasingly worried about their families. On 25th January Auschwitz was liberated by Russian troops. The Allies were not aware of more than 12,000 concentration and labour camps of various sizes.

At Kratzau there was another delousing trip. By then the women had distended bellies from being near starvation. This time the camp was not cleaned even though there had been almost constant diarrhoea.

Nico

The Granaat family always believed that on arrival at the concentration camp they asked Nico what his occupation was and instead of saying "baker" he said "musician" and that was how he survived: by playing the trombone in the camp orchestra. But this isn't accurate. Nico, being a young man and, like Liesje, in reasonably good health, was selected for work at Auschwitz. During his first weeks this was the awful job of digging graves. He was often beaten. In October 1944, all the Polish non-Jewish prisoners who were undertaking various roles at Auschwitz were moved to other camps, which left a number of vacancies in the camp orchestra. This was when playing the trombone was very helpful to Nico and from then until January 1945 he played the trombone in the orchestra.

In January 1945, the Russians had advanced so far into Poland that the Germans decided to dismantle Auschwitz. On 18th January, all the prisoners who could still walk from the camp were removed. Only the seriously ill were left behind. Nico was one of the 60,000 who started the so-called Death March. In his striped suit, and wearing mittens given to him by his niece, Janny, and broken shoes with no socks, he walked through the snow, ice and frozen mud. On the way they could hear gunshots.

Anyone who fainted or fell was shot. Nico saw around him one after another fall or faint from being cold or from illness. Sometimes the march was stopped and the ones who lived were transported by goods trains to the west. At one point Nico was pushed into a cattle wagon with people who were nearly dead. When the train stopped the dead bodies were thrown out. Through all of this the living used the remains of the dead as chairs or beds. Nico thought that sitting on the bodies of his fellow prisoners was one of the worst things he had done and he felt guilty. That he was tired, hungry and bewildered he found to be no excuse.

On 28th January they stopped at the concentration camp, Gross-Rosen, and, after a few more days, further into Germany. Through snow and ice, Nico walked without a break: five days and five nights without food or water. All they could eat was snow.

At this point in his story it was clear to Nico that being in Auschwitz was nothing compared to the awful events that followed. For this last period it is so difficult to understand where Nico got the strength to carry on. Why did he want to live while around him people went to rest forever? Nico said, as they all said, "Because I wanted to see my children again."

On 4th February the Death March arrived in the concentration camp Dachau. There the prisoners were registered. They were given another set of camp clothes, but they were the just as filthy as the ones they were wearing when they left Auschwitz.

In the spring of 1945 Dachau was one of the last Nazi camps to be dismantled. Nearly all of the survivors of the Polish camps were placed with those already there. Many thousands of ill and forsaken prisoners put together; everywhere lay corpses of people who died of typhus or from hunger. More and more were brought to the crematorium, which because of the shortage of fuel was no longer in use. The smell must have been awful.

CHAPTER 26

Liberation

Harry

The last copy of *Het Parool* that we made, I think it was three or four days before the end of the war and we wrote the news that Hitler had died. [Hitler committed suicide in his bunker in Berlin on Monday 30th April, but the news did not leak out until the following day.] And we put them out in broad daylight – I think it was a Sunday and Frans and Kitty were visiting us in Vechtstraat and they brought also some of their copies. I remember that Frans was so proud that when he went home at five o'clock in the afternoon or so they were already put up and being read by jubilant crowds of people and he could recognise his own handwriting.

I remember that on one of the final days rumours came that our liberators, Canadians or Americans, would arrive during the night. So we assembled on the route we thought they would take and stood there to wait for them. We didn't have flags but we were singing heroic songs all about the brave people. They didn't arrive for ages and then they came at last and we saw the tanks and stood there to welcome them. We didn't climb on the tanks or anything like that but it was a great feeling.

Just before then I have to tell that the previous Friday night on the radio it was announced that Germany was captured and had capitulated. Although it was forbidden to be out after eight o'clock on the street, everyone went out. And that evening about five hidden people came to join us. We had no idea that they were hidden – they did not belong to our resistance group – but after the news they just turned up. It was quite lovely of course. But suddenly German cars started patrolling on the street, so everyone had to go in. That was Friday. On Saturday everyone was singing and relaxed. There was a big celebration on the Dam Square, but the Germans still had machine guns and 19 people were killed. [Harry became very choked-up again]

Kitty

On 5th May the war ended with the German surrender. They left on 8th May. In Amsterdam we all thought the English would be there right away, or the Canadians, but they didn't come – it took some days. In the meantime we all thought we were free and could do what we liked. The Germans hated seeing us celebrating. It drove them mad to change from being boss of the world. Each day on the 5th 6th and 7th, Mum, Tootje and Mary went out to wait to welcome the English.

One of the days, the 7th May, Tootje got separated from the others and went home. The Dam Square was absolutely packed with people, singing and dancing. The Germans had taken over a big hotel on the corner of Kalverstraat and Paleisstraat, and members of the German navy watched from a balcony high up. Soon after Tootje had gone, the Dutch began shouting up, "Oh it's all over for you now," and things like that and laughing and jeering at them. The Germans still had guns – they opened fire with machine guns and a lot of people died or were wounded. Kitty has a book with pictures.

Tootje

On 4th May we were tidying the house, because the next day was Mary's birthday and we would expect visitors. We knew things were looking up. There were reports that Hitler was dead and the Allies were getting nearer. Mary decided to clean some mats with the "matterklopper" on the railings opposite our house. It was a lovely warm evening. Trouble was it was five past eight (curfew at eight) and I was worrying that she would be arrested; you know what I am like! Suddenly, as I was looking out of the window, I saw lots of people coming out of their houses; they were cheering because they had just heard on Radio Orange that the war was over! Kitty and Frans came to see us, also Teun and his wife-to-be. Everybody was so happy. I

7th May, German navy shoot into festive crowd in Dam Square; 19 killed, 117 injured
© W.F. Leijns / Nederlands Fotomuseum

wrote about a lot of horrible things, but writing about the evening of 4th May makes me cry.

The next day my mother, Mary, Aby and I all went to see if we could see the Allied soldiers coming. We didn't know if they would be British or American but they turned out to be Canadian. But nothing happened on the 6th or 7th. At one point I got separated from the rest so I went to the Dam Square, which was full of people. Then I walked somewhere else before turning to home. There were Dutch resistance people who wore armbands and they were like police for a while. They stopped me and said I couldn't go through a certain street. But being nosey I did go through it and I saw several big carts, like the backs of lorries. They had the dead people lying on them covered with tarpaulin. I could see their feet sticking out. I had only left the Dam Square area shortly before this happened.

By the end of the war all the family were very thin. But food supplies arrived quickly after liberation.

Liesje

At the time of their liberation from Kratzau Leny had been very ill and was laid up in bed. One morning the overseer came into the ward and with a sweet-sounding voice she said "Meine liebe mädchen, bitte aufstehen. Betten bauwen" – "My dear girls, please stand up and make your beds". They did not know how to react and looked at each other thinking, "Are we crazy or is she?" Later the women could see in the distance the Russians coming. Hundreds of them were near the village and would soon reach the castle. Leny was too ill to walk downstairs, where the only window was, but one of the girls looked outside surprised and happy. She shouted, "These are the soldiers, our liberators, hooray. We were free!"

Soon after, the Russian soldiers arrived and the guards ran away. Everyone who could do so walked outside, not knowing what to expect. And then they knew, for among the liberators were Mongol soldiers, rough men who were just on the hunt for women. Some of the girls and women were raped. They pleaded with them not to do it, to leave them alone. They did not do anything to Leny. She said "Because I was terribly skinny and did not look good. At that moment my illness was my good luck." Unfortunately, Liesje, according to Leny, "was one of the women the soldiers would not leave alone."

It is likely that local women in the town were also raped. Reports are that this was indiscriminate – from young girls to very old women – the Russian soldiers did not care.

Liesje herself told Tootje that she was eventually liberated by Russians and raped. Also that one of the men took her out looting in his car. He gave her fur coats and all sorts of stuff but as they got back to the camp she threw it all back in the car.

Helen Waterford's account simply states that on 9th May the guards had left during the night. The women were on their own and did not know what to do. The following day the Russians set up a soup kitchen. The director of the factory thanked the women for their work and told them the International Red Cross would be arranging transport home for all the different nationalities.

Nico

American soldiers who arrived at the camp would probably never forget what they saw. For Nico's story the passage about Dachau was the introduction of his return to Amsterdam. It was a terrible camp, but there were no gas chambers.

How he spent his time in Dachau he did not know. He was with a man called Lex van Weren and together with another four Jewish prisoners on 25th April they suddenly had to leave the camp, a few days before Dachau was liberated by the Americans.

By train they went to Mittenwald, a winter sports resort near Munich. They were there for some time and did not know what was going to happen. Although the guards were not so strict as they had been, Nico and the others thought that the survivors from German camps would not be allowed to live. "We had seen too much" was Nico's opinion and he was sure they would be killed.

In Mittenwald the six of them tried to run away. Nico stumbled over a piece of barbed wire and could not stand up. He thought that was it. His knee was cut open and he could not walk. But then with the others in front of him he saw the soldiers arrive. They were Americans. They were appalled by what they saw and took him to a hospital nearby, where there were more ex-prisoners. On the way they gave him so much chocolate that it made him feel sick.

On 1st May Nico arrived in Beiren, the birthplace of the Nazis. He weighed less than 45 kilos. He was taken care of for several months before he was allowed to return to Holland. In a hospital in Paris his knee was operated on. On 12th July he went home by train. It wasn't until he saw the station sign "Amsterdam Centraal" that he really felt free.

The Liberation of the "Lost Train" near Tröbitz

Transports leaving Concentration Camp Bergen-Belsen on 23rd April 1945

The last of the three transports leaving Bergen-Belsen between 6th and 11th April 1945, carrying about 6,700 people, went down in the annals of history as the "lost train".

The passengers were "Jews on exchange", who had been accommodated in special sections at Bergen-Belsen and among them were a large number of Dutch Jews, including three Granaat family members. The Nazis had contrived plans for these Jews to be exchanged for merchandise, foreign currency or captured Germans.

The first of the transports bound for Theresienstadt left Bergen-Belsen on 6th April, its route running through Uelzen, Salzwedel and Stendal. On 13th April that transport was freed by American troops near Farsleben, not far from Magdeburg.

The second train, which held a large number of Hungarian Jews, started out from Bergen-Belsen on 7th April and arrived on 21st April at Theresienstadt, which was liberated on 8th May.

On 11th April, the third train departed and moved across Germany for two weeks – passing Soltau, Lüneburg, Büchen, Berlin-Spandau and Neukölln. The train stopped

Source: Peter Lande, US Holocaust Memorial Museum and
www.hagalil.com/archiv/2008/10/troebitz.htm

off near the Berlin–Dresden highway, then went on heading for Finsterwalde and Falkenberg. On board were Jews from more than 12 countries, and among the Dutch were a distant cousin, Simon Granaat, and his two sons, Maurice and Joseph. The almost incessant moving back and forth and the trail of devastation stretching along the city of Berlin made this route excruciatingly long. It lasted until 23rd April 1945, when the Red Army freed the Jews near Tröbitz. More than 200 of them failed to survive. Whoever had died en route was buried hastily and superficially near the railway lines. Illness and emaciation claimed the lives of another 320 people after liberation.

The small community of Tröbitz came face to face with about 2,000 survivors of the Holocaust. The Red Army opened a commandant's office in the place, and a sort of self-government was established for the survivors of the train. They were put up in a former camp for forced labourers and were given their own cemetery ground to bury their deceased.

In 1947, France demanded that the mortal remains of 43 deceased should be exhumed from the the Jewish cemetery at Tröbitz and transferred to burial places in their native lands, among them the Granaat family members. The remaining graves were marked by memorial slabs with the names and dates of the dead victims. Over the years, memorial stones and slabs were placed or erected along the route the transport train had taken at the time.

I don't know what Simon Granaat did to be on the lost train as an exchange prisoner. Perhaps he had bought false foreign passports.

*Headstones of the Granaat family at the Jewish cemetery in
Diemen Simon Granaat and his family
Source: Peter Lande, US Holocaust Memorial Museum and
www.hagalil.com/archiv/2008/10/troebitz.htm*

Simon Granaat and his family
Cronjéstraat 6, Amsterdam
Simon Granaat (Head of family)
London, 13 September 1905 – Tröbitz, 30 May 1945
Maurice Granaat (son)
Amsterdam, 22 July 1928 – Tröbitz, 23 May 1945
Joseph Alexander Granaat (son)
Rotterdam, 24 April 1936 – Tröbitz, 28 May 1945
Wife and two children survived the war

(Source: Jewish Monument)

CHAPTER 27

After the War

Tootje

I remember after the war there were weekly reports on the radio about the progress of renewing the railway lines and stock which had been taken away by the Germans when the railway strike happened in September 1944. The strike had not just had an impact on food and fuel. The man would say something like, "the line from Hilversum to Utrecht is now in operation." The following week some more etc.

I remember getting a postcard from Liesje – it was addressed to me because she was bitterly angry with the rest of the family. She said on the postcard she was coming home, which was wonderful news. I don't remember when in 1945 this was.

We found out that in the camp band Nico had to play every morning when the prisoners marched to work and again in the evening when they came back. This is what saved his life. When Nico was liberated he was so happy that he ran towards the American soldiers who had entered the camp. But he was so frail he fell over and broke his knee. He had to go to hospital in Paris to recuperate before he could come home.

The family in Friesland grew to love Netty and when Liesje returned from Kratzau they didn't want to give her back. Liesje went to Friesland twice to visit Netty before bringing her home and the first time I went with her. This

Lily, Kitty, Frans and Mary with two Canadian soldiers in the Dam Square,
June 1945

was in the summer of 1945 across the Zuiderzee [nowadays called IJsselmeer].
There was probably some official paperwork to be completed before she could
collect her. So we could not take her away that day; it was just a visit. It took
several months – resisted by the woman who wanted to legally adopt Netty
– by this stage she would have loved Netty as if she were her own daughter. I
remember the woman saying, "I wish you had died."

At one point in 1945 I was dismayed to find I had nits in my hair. My
solution was to go to the hairdresser for a perm which would kill them all
off. There was still no power in Amsterdam but the hairdresser had its own
generator. It was run by a tandem in the room above. It was ingenious but also
amusing as I sat there under the big hairdryers thinking of the two people sat
upstairs pedalling to make the power for my perm.

Mary's husband, Ies, called himself Jack in Canada. He came back after
the war – so changed in the way he looked that I was the only one who
recognised him straight away. He had put on weight and looked very smart in
his merchant navy uniform. He wanted to divorce Mary because he had met
someone in Canada. Mary was happy to divorce him because coincidently she
had met and fallen in love with a Canadian soldier, Ronnie. Though in the end
neither of them married their Canadian loves. I remember we all went out one
evening and I danced the Hokey Cokey with him. While we were dancing all
the others stood aside and it was just him and me dancing. Fancy that!

Ies went to work in Rotterdam at the docks. He tragically died in an accident – a crane fell on him – in 1959. Most of all this was a tragedy for Aby, by then 21 years old.

Liesje

Liesje, Nico, Netty and Wim all survived the war. Probably a family of four were more likely to survive separately than if they had stayed together. In November 1945 the family started living together again. They were given a small space in a former Jewish home for the elderly in the Plantage area. In 1945, hundreds of returned Jews were given shelter there. It's now where the Hotel Lancaster is situated.

With the endurance with which they survived the camps, Liesje and Nico tried to rebuild their lives, but it was not a happy family reunion. Netty and Wim were estranged from each other and from their parents and almost six months living in a temporary shelter did not help. They needed a proper home and Nico needed a job.

The Dutch authorities decided that Jews would not be given priority over other Dutch war victims, the idea being that all the misery started when the Germans segregated the Jews and they thought it wise not to repeat that mistake. They also thought that making special allowances for Jews would fuel anti-Semitism. This was not unfounded: in the first couple of years after the war, there were all sorts of anti-Semitic feelings, which had barely existed before the war.

In contrast to the heart-warming reactions of some Amsterdam people who were especially kind when they saw their Jewish neighbours and colleagues again, there were heartless remarks such as "you were lucky not to have been here; we had to go through the hunger winter" and even "they forgot to gas you." Opinions about Jews being rude and money-grasping human beings were openly aired.

This period was called "the little Shoah" by historian Isaac Lipschits, who also initiated the Digital Monument to the Jewish Community in the Netherlands.

Nico and his brothers planned to revitalise the luxury brand Vuysje and together they tried to get back the bakery in the Weesperstraat. They did not stand a chance. The civil servant in charge said: "You can bring in your whole family, but this business was registered in the name of Isaac Vuijsje and, if he doesn't show up, then you may just as well forget it." Isaac had been gassed in Sobibor in 1943.

One possession which was not lost as a result of the war was Nico's treasured trombone. This had been left at the house in the Oudeschans and looked after by Lily and Tootje.

So Nico went back to playing the trombone and played in the Dutch Airforce orchestra. The family lived in the Buiten Visscherstraat and tried their best for a while to make it work. In the camp, while Liesje had wanted more than anything to see her children again – especially Wim – Nico desperately missed his beautiful daughter. But after the war, although she had missed him so much, Liesje found Wim difficult. Had the mother–son bond broken from being apart for so long? By contrast, Netty was her natural charming self and perhaps found it easier to adjust to life with her parents.

Although Nico and Liesje still loved each other, they had big cultural and religious differences. Liesje didn't want to speak about anything that happened to her or to be reminded of it. For her it must have been an ordeal that Nico couldn't stop himself from talking about his camp history. Whereas Liesje soon had the number tattooed on her arm removed, Nico kept his and was always happy to show it to people.

The couple argued a lot and eventually divorced in 1948, taking one of the children each. Liesje took Netty, which Wim found difficult to come to terms with. Later, Wim went to live in Israel, where he married and had two children.

When Harry and Fré attended Nico's funeral in 1996, they recounted the story to Wim of his escape from the Germans. He seemed not to believe them, but his eyes widened in surprise when Fré mentioned the tattoo. But he didn't want to acknowledge it.

Bob remembers seeing Liesje and Nico in June 1947. The whole family were together in a flat provided for them quite near Central Station. He made them steak and kidney pie.

Tootje

After we were liberated, English and Canadian soldiers were sometimes billeted to stay with us. I went out with a Canadian one, but he touched me up, which I didn't like. He wanted me to go upstairs with him, but I didn't want to.

When Liesje and Nico came back they were allocated a flat, after the Germans or Dutch Nazi were booted out. There I saw two small porcelain dishes with lattice edges that I liked. Liesje gave them to me, which was so typical of her. Years ago Dad bought a larger dish, same make, same pattern. I still have them.

In August 1945, Bob's ship, the minesweeper *1034*, was stationed in Amsterdam. They were on a community visit – sort of PR. Unusually this was close to the Oudeschans, probably because the main part of the harbour was so full with other ships.

One day, Aby, who was eight years old, came running in excitedly and told his grandmother he had seen a British ship! She didn't really believe him but said she would go with him to look. Bob was on watch and when she saw him she called up, "Hello, sailor! Good afternoon." Bob, surprised, said hello and remarked that her English was very good. Lily responded "That's because I am English!"

They were allowed to invite local people on the boat so he asked if they would both like to come and look round. When they got to the mess and stores he gave her lots of things. The conversation went something like:

Bob: "Do you like biscuits?"

Lily: "Yes, of course."

Bob: "Good, please have these. Would you like some English tea? [Gives her a packet of tea] Would you like some sugar and powdered milk to go with that? What about a jar of jam?"

Lily: "Yes please."

Bob: "Do you smoke? I can give you plenty of cigarettes because I don't smoke."

Lily: "That would be wonderful! We don't smoke either but we can us them to barter for top-quality food. Cigarettes are better than money!"

Bob: "If you don't mind me saying so, you both look very thin. What about some Cadbury's chocolate?"

In the end there were too many things for Lily and Aby to carry so Bob offered to bring them round to her house when he came off duty. Lily thanked him for his kindness and said when he came later she would make him a cup of tea. She explained where they lived.

Later, my mother, who had the habit of looking out of the second-floor window, remembers that the first she saw of Bob was the top of his head and his sailor's hat.

Bob

It was the first Monday in August 1945 – 6th August – and also the day the atom bomb was dropped on Hiroshima, but of course we knew nothing about that! In England it was bank holiday weekend and the four minesweepers which were sweeping out of IJmuiden went on a courtesy visit up the North Sea canal to Amsterdam.

When we met Lily we thought, "This lady is English so we should make a fuss of her." I took her into the mess and introduced her to the crew. After Lily and Aby had been on the ship ("I'm sorry it's a bit of a mess!"), it was about 8.30 in the evening when I got off duty and went to Lily's house on the Oudeschans for the first time, to deliver the food I'd given them. I went with Cornell, a friend of mine, and we were introduced to Tootje. We had a cup of tea and a chat in English. They told me what had happened to them during the war. We felt we had made friends and decided to visit them again next time. I said, "When we come back I will come and see you."

So in between visits I bartered my cigarettes for more food for them because I knew they were short. We had an issue of 200 cigarettes a month for five shillings; I was the only man on the boat who didn't smoke. I remember giving them a basket of 24 eggs and lots of packets of biscuits.

So several times I went to visit, taking the train from IJmuiden to Amsterdam. We were sweeping out of IJmuiden from just after the war ended.

To start with we had been based in Calais in early 1945 and then moved up to sweep out of Ostend when that became free. We were in IJmuiden from May 1945 for quite a while. I heard all of the story about the camp and her father and I found it very interesting.

One time I stayed the night and Tootje had to help me pull my shirt off. Sailors' shirts were very fitted and tight. Normally we asked a friend to help, but that evening…

It got to close to Christmas and I had leave. Half the crew had Christmas off and half had New Year. Down in the engine room we had an oil-fired heater, which we used to heat water for the showers. One time the tray caught alight and there was quite a serious fire in the engine room. We were not sure if the boat would be scrapped or repaired but they decided to replace the timbers and so the ship had to go into dry dock to be refitted, probably in Lowestoft. So we all had some extended leave. Eventually, in March 1946, we went back sweeping in IJmuiden, but it had been a long time between visits so they were very pleased when I came back to the Oudeschans again. During those visits I met Kitty and Liesje and I got to know the family quite well. I was also introduced to Tootje's best friend, Willy. I remember meeting Uncle Simon too; he was very elegant.

I remember a concert at the Concertgebouw, a trip to the opera to see *La Traviata*, and I went to the cinema with Tootje. One time she came to IJmuiden to look around the boat. I was really attracted by her beautiful eyes – she has always had lovely eyes. There was also a sense of vulnerability about her, mixed with an inner strength which drew me to her. We liked the same things, especially classical music. She was intelligent and made good conversation. Later as her health improved she had thick, glossy hair.

[Tootje: "I liked his eyes too and his lovely curly hair."]

It was quite a fun time to be in Amsterdam at that time. I remember amphibious DUKWs (nicknamed ducks) were giving people rides up and down Prins Hendrikkade. It was a very lively place in the evenings, especially in 1945. People made the most of rejoicing and there were street parties every night while it was light in the evening, until it got dark.

The relationship between Tootje and I grew into a close friendship and then more. At the end of 1946 Lily and Tootje came to stay in Olwen Cottage. Lily went to Ware to visit her family, who she had not seen since 1938. Tootje stayed with Nanny Martin (Bob's mother, Florence), perhaps for two weeks while I had Christmas leave. For their journey home I went with them to

Liverpool Street Station, where they would catch the boat train. On the way to the station Lily wanted to visit her father, who lived near to University College London in Gower Street. He was living with a Swiss woman and Tootje and I sat on a bench outside the house while she went in. Tootje thought her mother was ashamed of her and didn't want them to meet. I think it was more likely that she was ashamed of her father and didn't want us to see him. Anyway, we waited on a park bench. It was quite cold so I shared my coat with Tootje. This was when we first got close as a couple. After that we wrote to each other more often. And then we got closer still. I used to go and meet her from school in the late afternoon. I was writing poetry and very much in love. I still have the poems.

Poem IV

I am I. And you are you.
But together we could do,
All sorts of wonderful things.
With a little luck we'd have a house,
And you my dear would be my spouse.
Then in a year or two or three,
There would not be just you and me.
But four or five, or six or seven.
Which of course would be just heaven.

Later Poem

For every hour in every day
I love you more in every way
And every day in every week
I'll lay a kiss upon your cheek
And every week in every year
I'll walk beside you never fear
Through every year in my life
You will be my only wife.

After completing its duties as a minesweeper, the ship was converted to RNVR tender *Kilmory* and was eventually sold in 1955. I purchased the oil painting of the ship in IJmuiden using my cigarette ration, from the Dutch artist Haaike Abraham Jaarsma (1881–1970).

In 1947, at the end of May, I left the navy in my demob suit. After being demobbed I went to stay in the Oudeschans for almost a month.

I think I proposed by letter. Tootje wrote to me to say she didn't think we should get married because our children might have a lip problem. But I would have none of that. I loved her just how she was, but I also knew that there were people who could help her and that she would be able to feel much happier with the way that she looked. The first doctor she had seen in Holland was not very good.

I have always been interested in medicine and if there had not been a war I wanted to be a doctor. I knew about Mr Archibald McIndoe, a plastic surgeon in East Grinstead, who helped a lot of injured pilots. I wrote to him personally to ask for his help rather than go through the family doctor. I took Tootje to an appointment with him in East Grinstead. He referred Tootje to someone in Holland for the first operation. She had this first operation in Amsterdam before we were married, but it was not a success. So then we were referred to the Professor Kilner, a very nice man, at the Churchill Hospital in Oxford. It was a Dr Kalman who did the final operation, which was very good.

Tootje only weighed seven stone when she got to England. So she must have weighed even less than this by the end of the hunger winter, when I first met her.

Ours was a double wedding with my sister Rene and my best friend, Ted Palmer. Rene and I had come up with the idea for a double wedding. Ted got married in my demob suit. I think he had opted for a sports jacket and trousers when he came out of the navy, which was a while after me. I had been demobbed in June and I left Ted ready and waiting for his demob number to come up. He had been on the HMS *Illustrious* for a large part of the war. But was then sent to India on HMS *Nubian*, a destroyer, until the end of September.

I didn't like the demob suit so was happy for Ted to have it. Instead, I bought a smart dark navy pinstripe suit from the Fifty Shilling Tailors in Reading. They were a chain of shops. I cycled to Reading to get it. I had some money saved and when I came out we had £28 discharge pay. At the farm I earned £6 a week, so £28 was quite a lot of money. I also wore a lovely pair of shoes with buckles on, which I had bought earlier from Elliot's in Northbrook Street, Newbury, for three guineas.

Mum made her wedding dress in Amsterdam. She had seen some beautiful ivory satin, but when she went back the next day to buy it there was none left, so she had to settle for a pale icy blue colour, which she didn't like nearly as much.

We got married at 11am on 17th April 1948 in Saint Mary's Parish Church in Thatcham. The vicar was called Rev Thackeray – he had a strange hump on his chest and an old-fashioned box hearing aid.

There were quite a few guests, including Harry and Fré; Kitty and Frans, who travelled from Amsterdam on their bikes; and Kitty Boekelman, who was Tootje's neighbour from the Oudeschans. Then there was Ted's family – his brothers and Ted's sister Emmie as bridesmaid. Our neighbour, Mrs Lane's daughter and Pat were also bridesmaids. My best man was my brother Tommy. Ted's best man was probably his brother Charlie (he was married to the beautiful Vera, who had been "Miss Newbury"). There was a reception at Olwen Cottage – we did it all ourselves. Mrs Lane made the cake. At the reception, Tootje was left on her own to greet everyone, who she mostly didn't know, while I went up to change my clothes. It had been a lovely morning so Ted and I walked to church but half way there it bucketed down and we got soaked. The rest of the family and the bridal party had cars.

The weather turned out nice so we were able to overflow from the house into the back and front, which we needed to with so many people in such a small house. We had our honeymoon at Binstead Manor hotel on the Isle of Wight. It's where Queen Victoria stayed when Osborne House was being built.

We caught the four o'clock train from Newbury to Portsmouth and then the ferry to Ryde. We spent a week there. It's where I first saw camellias and that was love at first sight. You could walk through the garden, which went right down to the beach.

Tootje

After I had met Bob for the first time of course I liked him very much, although I knew only a few words of English. You could say I wouldn't have dreamt that he would want to marry me. But the odd thing was that I did have a dream about his shoes. In Amsterdam we used to have a big cupboard with shelves. The only part of the dream I remember was seeing Bob's shoes next to mine in a very homely and comforting sort of way. I woke up with a sense of wonderment but disbelief – how could I dream such a thing?! My father said I would never marry because of the way I looked. Harry said the relationship wouldn't last!

Before we got married I stayed with Bob's mother at Olwen Cottage and worked for a while at the Ministry of Defence depot in Thatcham, dismantling gas masks. I was friendly with one of the men who worked there and we both enjoyed listening to the music. Later he moved to a different section but we still caught each other's eyes and smile when a song came on that we liked, for example Mario Lanza.

Lily and Tootje in Newbury in 1955 with my brothers and sisters,
Moira, Robert, Bill and Vicky

Harry

After the war I used to look at the photographs to see if I could recognise any members of Kiki's family or other friends of ours who might have come through, but there were so many who did not come through. Out of 100 only ten or 15 and all the others were killed. One of the fortunate ones who made it was one of my school teachers, a lovely lady who taught history. I learnt so much from her. The first half year she only talked about Greek mythology. It was so nice; just after the war I heard that she had been in hiding and I visited her. She was very pleased to see me. Oh yes. Her name was Caroline Eitje, a very popular teacher.

It was in the 1960s that I finally accepted that Willem had been killed in a gas chamber. Up until then I thought my father might one day come back and believed he could be living in Poland or Germany, ashamed that he had not protected his family and put them all at such risk.

Lily tried to reopen the shop in the Oudeschans after the war was over, but it was too difficult and she gave up after a few months. Eventually she was awarded a form of war widow's pension.

Kitty

In 1977 Frans and I travelled to Israel to visit Nico. While we were there I visited Yad Vashem, The World Holocaust Remembrance Centre in Jerusalem and made a testimony for my father.[20]

Roll Call for the 41 Dead

Below is a list of the 41 Granaat family members who lost their lives as prisoners, in chronological order of date of death. Their names can be found in the Digital Monument.[21] Their average age was 35 years. The names in blue are from the Simon Granaat branch of the family.

Family member	Place of death	Date of death	Age at death
Elisabeth Granaat	Auschwitz	27/07/1942	56
Elias Granaat	Monowitz	15/10/1942	49
Hanna Granaat	Auschwitz	15/10/1942	49
Michiel Granaat	Auschwitz	05/11/1942	59
Rebecca Granaat	Auschwitz	05/11/1942	42
Selina Granaat	Auschwitz	05/11/1942	16
Theresia Granaat	Auschwitz	05/11/1942	14
Helena Granaat	Auschwitz	05/02/1943	23
Maurits Granaat	Sobibor	20/03/1943	65
Sara Granaat	Sobibor	20/03/1943	64
Louis Granaat	Sobibor	20/03/1943	64
Samuel Granaat	Sobibor	20/03/1943	54
Marianne Granaat	Sobibor	20/03/1943	24
Carla Granaat	Sobibor	20/03/1943	14
Maurice Tertaas	Westerbork	03/05/1943	30
Willem Granaat	Sobibor	21/05/1943	51
Judith Pimontel	Sobibor	21/05/1943	25
Jacob Granaat	Sobibor	02/07/1943	57
Mietje Granaat	Sobibor	09/07/1943	68
Hanna Legerman	Sobibor	09/07/1943	42
Barend Legerman	Sobibor	09/07/1943	43
Henrietta Granaat	Sobibor	23/07/1943	25
Hijman Granaat	Sobibor	23/07/1943	27
Jacob Granaat	Auschwitz	10/09/1943	33
Aleida Granaat	Auschwitz	10/09/1943	35
Hetty Granaat	Auschwitz	30/11/1943	22
Renee de Jong	Auschwitz	30/11/1943	18
Benjamin de Jong	Auschwitz	31/03/1944	26

Carolina Bromet	Theresienstadt	24/09/1944	68
Carla Bromet	Auschwitz	06/10/1944	11
Emanuel Bromet	Auschwitz	06/10/1944	6
Alice Bromet	Auschwitz	08/12/1944	39
Yvonne Bromet	Auschwitz	08/12/1944	12
Madeleine Bromet	Auschwitz	08/12/1944	10
Philip Bromet	Auschwitz	08/12/1944	2
Hijman Bromet	Grünberg	31/12/1944	40
Joseph Bromet	Middle Europe	28/02/1945	38
Maurice Granaat	Tröbitz	23/05/1945	16
Joseph Granaat	Tröbitz	28/05/1945	9
Simon Granaat	Tröbitz	30/05/1945	39
Flora Bromet	unknown	unknown	35

Appendices

1. Jewish Populations in Selected European Countries

Country	Pre-war Jews	Holocaust Deaths	% of Jewish population killed	Post-war Jews
Poland	3,300,000	3,000,000	90%	45,000
Germany	525,000	138,000	26%	119,000
Austria	191,000	57,000	30%	9,000
France	260,000	76,000	29%	475,000
Netherlands	140,000	105,000	75%	30,000
Belgium	60,000	24,000	45%	30,000
Italy	45,000	7,500	16%	28,000

2. Family Trees

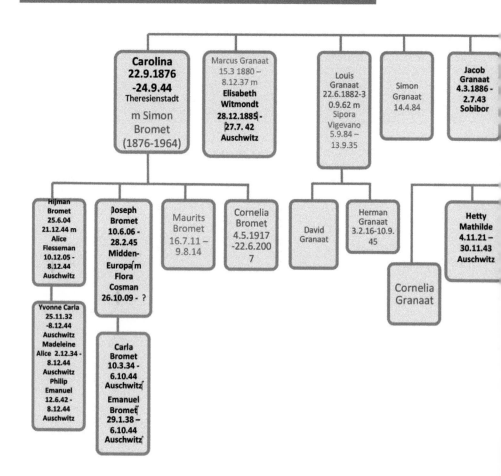

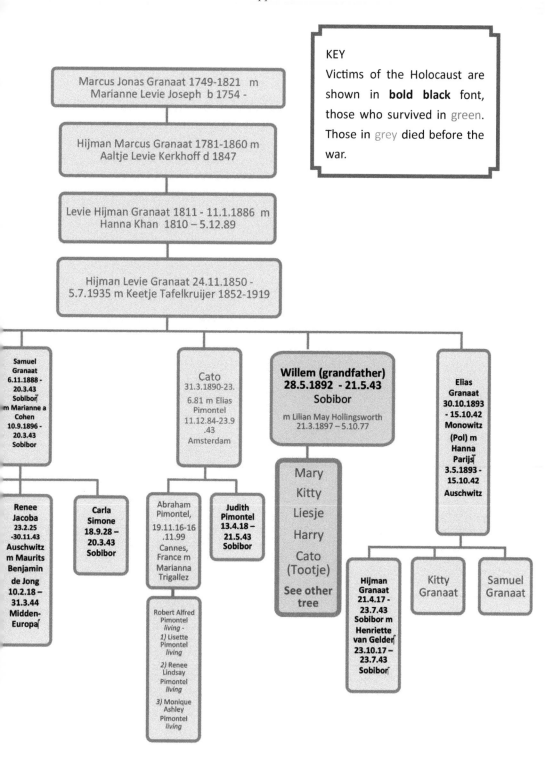

KEY
Victims of the Holocaust are shown in **bold black** font, those who survived in green. Those in grey died before the war.

Marcus Jonas Granaat 1749-1821 m Marianne Levie Joseph b 1754 -

Hijman Marcus Granaat 1781-1860 m Aaltje Levie Kerkhoff d 1847

Levie Hijman Granaat 1811 - 11.1.1886 m Hanna Khan 1810 – 5.12.89

Hijman Levie Granaat 24.11.1850 - 5.7.1935 m Keetje Tafelkruijer 1852-1919

Samuel Granaat 6.11.1888 - 20.3.43 Sobibor m Marianne a Cohen 10.9.1896 - 20.3.43 Sobibor

Cato 31.3.1890-23. 6.81 m Elias Pimontel 11.12.84-23.9 .43 Amsterdam

Willem (grandfather) 28.5.1892 - 21.5.43 Sobibor m Lilian May Hollingsworth 21.3.1897 – 5.10.77

Elias Granaat 30.10.1893 - 15.10.42 Monowitz (Pol) m Hanna Parijs 3.5.1893 - 15.10.42 Auschwitz

Renee Jacoba 23.2.25 -30.11.43 Auschwitz m Maurits Benjamin de Jong 10.2.18 – 31.3.44 Midden-Europa

Carla Simone 18.9.28 – 20.3.43 Sobibor

Abraham Pimontel, 19.11.16-16 .11.99 Cannes, France m Marianna Trigallez

Judith Pimontel 13.4.18 – 21.5.43 Sobibor

Mary
Kitty
Liesje
Harry
Cato (Tootje)
See other tree

Hijman Granaat 21.4.17 - 23.7.43 Sobibor m Henriette van Gelder 23.10.17 – 23.7.43 Sobibor

Kitty Granaat

Samuel Granaat

Robert Alfred Pimontel *living* - 1) Lisette Pimontel *living* 2) Renee Lindsay Pimontel *living* 3) Monique Ashley Pimontel *living*

Simon Granaat's Family

KEY

Victims of the Holocaust are shown in **bold black** font, those who survived in green. Those in grey died before the war.

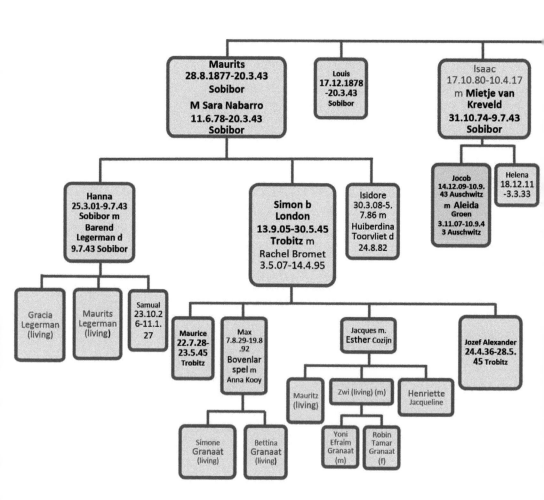

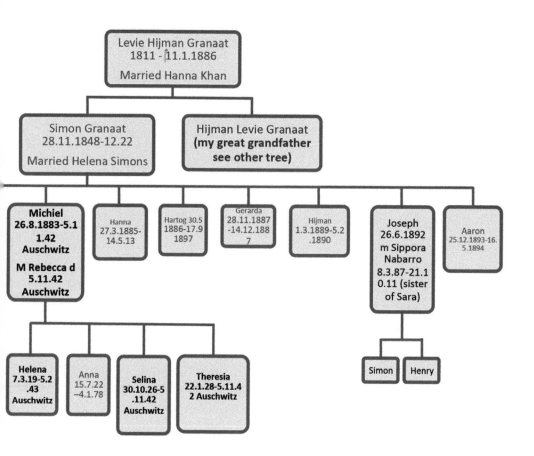

Levie Hijman Granaat
1811 - 11.1.1886

Married Hanna Khan

Simon Granaat
28.11.1848-12.22

Married Helena Simons

Hijman Levie Granaat
(my great grandfather see other tree)

Michiel
**26.8.1883-5.1
1.42
Auschwitz**

**M Rebecca d
5.11.42
Auschwitz**

Hanna
27.3.1885-
14.5.13

Hartog 30.5
1886-17.9
1897

Gerarda
28.11.1887
-14.12.188
7

Hijman
1.3.1889-5.2
.1890

Joseph
26.6.1892
m Sippora
Nabarro
8.3.87-21.1
0.11 (sister
of Sara)

Aaron
25.12.1893-16.
5.1894

Helena
7.3.19-5.2
.43
Auschwitz

Anna
15.7.22
—4.1.78

Selina
**30.10.26-5
.11.42
Auschwitz**

Theresia
**22.1.28-5.11.4
2 Auschwitz**

Simon   Henry

Willem and Lilian's Family Tree

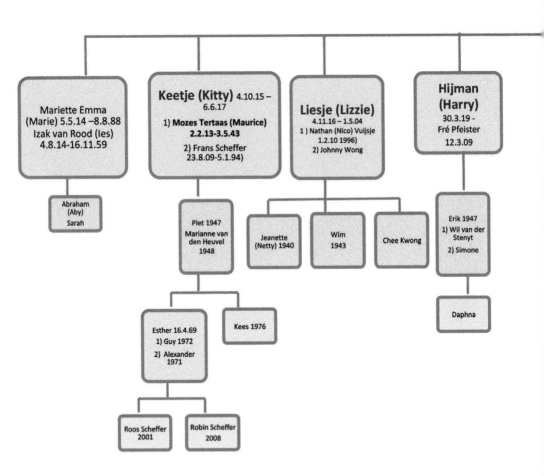

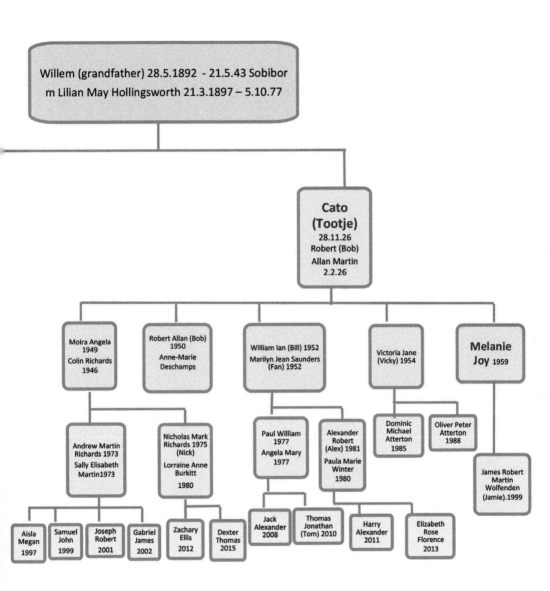

3. Background to the Final Solution (the Destruction of the Jewish Race)

Only three weeks after the September 1939 invasion, Heydrich issued orders to his chiefs of security police outlining the stages and methods involved in working towards the "ultimate aim":

> *"The planned measures, and also the ultimate aim, should be kept strictly secret. A distinction should be made between 1) the ultimate aim, which will require a longer period, and 2) the stages involved in achieving the ultimate aim, which are of a short term nature. The first precondition for achieving the ultimate aim is to move the Jews living in the countryside to concentration points within the larger cities. It is a matter of urgency that this is accomplished. In order to facilitate future measures there should be a few of these concentrations as possible, and they should be located either by a major railway junction, or at least on a railway line. In principle all Jewish communities of fewer than 500 heads should be disbanded and relocated to the nearest concentration area. The establishment of Jewish concentrations in the cities is to be justified by their substantial participation in terrorist attacks and looting".*

In his letter of 31 July 1941 Goring wrote to Heydrich and used for the first time the phrase "Endlösung der Judenfrage" (final solution to the Jewish question).

TRANSLATION OF DOCUMENT No. NG-2586-(E)
OFFICE OF CHIEF OF COUNSEL FOR WAR CRIMES

The Reichsmarschall of the Greater   Berlin, 31 July 1941
        German Reich
Plenipotentiary for the Four-Year Plan
        Chairman
of the Ministerial Council for the
        Defense of the Reich

                To
                the Chief of the Security Police
                        and the SD
                SS-Gruppenfuehrer HEYDRICH

                                    B E R L I N

        As supplement to the task which was entrusted to
you in the decree dated 24 January 1939, namely to solve
the Jewish question by emigration and evacuation in a way
which is the most favorable in connection with the
conditions prevailing at present, I herewith commission
you to carry out all preparations with regard to or-
ganization, the material side and financial viewpoints
for a final solution of the Jewish question in these
territories in Europe which are under German influence.

        If the competency of other central organizations is
touched in this connection, these organizations are to
participate.

        I furthermore commission you to submit to me as soon
as possible a draft showing the administrative material
and financial measures already taken for the execution
of the intended final solution of the Jewish question.

                            (signed) GOERING.

            CERTIFICATE OF TRANSLATION

        I, Wolfgang Von Eckardt, hereby certify that
I am thoroughly conversant with the English and German
languages and that the above is a true and correct
translation of the Document No. NG-3945.

                    Signature: W. Von Eckardt
                                 U.S.Civ.A.165634.
                    - END -

At the Wannsee conference in January 1942, Heydrich quoted from this letter.
He went on to say:

"From now on, with the express permission of the Führer, the solution will be to evacuate the Jews to the East. Under authorised leadership the Jews will, within the context of the Endlösung, be sent to work in the East as appropriate. Those who are able to work will be transported in labour convoys to these areas, they will be segregated by sex, and deployed on the construction of roads, which will undoubtedly result in a large number of natural losses. Those who potentially survive, i.e. those with the highest resistance levels, will be treated accordingly. Otherwise, if they were ever to be freed, they might form a natural elite and become the seeds from which new generations of Jews would germinate. Within the context of the practical execution of the Endlösung, Europe will be combed from west to east. The Reich, including the protectorate, Bohemia and Moravia, must, in view of the housing issue and other political implications, take first priority. Each and every Jew who is evacuated will first be transferred to so-called transport ghetto, and from there be transported further east. There are around 11 million eligible Jews."

(source: from Sobibor by Jules Schelvis)

4. Amsterdam showing Waterlooplein, the Oudeschans and part of the Jewish Quarter

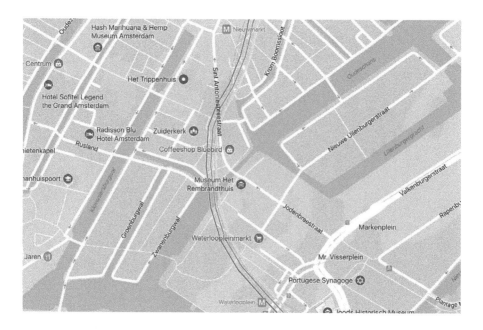

5. Mauthausen

Although officially a concentration camp in Austria, Mauthausen functioned as extermination camp. Many prisoners died from total exhaustion caused by the gruelling conditions and from their brutal treatment. The majority died in the camp's notorious rock quarries where they had been put to work. One nickname for Mauthausen was Moordhausen – "house of murder". When Dutch Jews in the occupied Netherlands were ordered to sign up for work in "the east", the occupiers threatened them with deportation to Mauthausen if they didn't comply. The JewishGen.org/database for Mauthausen provides details of the "Death Book" and the history of the camp. It estimates that, between May 1938 and liberation on 5th May 1945, 150,000 out of 195,000 prisoners perished. It provides a gruesome translation of the 60 different "causes of death" recorded in the books. This includes "sub-cranial fracture as a result of burying" and eight different forms of suicide. An eminent US news reporter, Fred Friendly, said, "Mauthausen was built with a half-million rocks which 150,000 prisoners (18,000 was the capacity) carried up on their backs from a quarry 800 feet below. They carried it up steps so steep that a Captain and I walked it once and were winded, without a load. They carried granite and made 8 trips a day... and if they stumbled, the S.S. men pushed them into the quarry. There are 285 steps, covered with blood. They called it the steps of death."

There were very few Mauthausen survivors and no Dutch survivors, according to www.hollandscheschouwburg.nl.

6. All the measures taken by the Germans can be found at

http://www.verzetsmuseum.org/museum/nl/tweede-wereldoorlog/achtergrond/ achtergrond,jodenvervolging/overzicht_1940_1945.

7. The Dutch Bureaucracy and Identity Cards

The German method of tracking down Jews was similar across Western Europe, but there were four elements unique to the Netherlands.

Firstly, the Netherlands had a German civilian government rather than a military one, as was the case in Belgium and France. Himmler, Goebbels, Ribbentrop and Hess had people inside the Netherlands and used them to peruse their anti-Semitic aims. This served to accelerate the process of isolation and deportation. There were 5,000 German police in the Netherlands, compared to 3,000 in France.

Secondly, the Dutch bureaucracy and civil service were wedded to principles of administrative and public order above all other considerations. Specifically, comprehensive population registration was a key difference compared to Belgium and France. The registers were used to compile and check lists for arrest and deportation. Their very existence often convinced Jews that there was little point in trying to evade later censuses on the basis that the authorities already had the information. The registers were used as the basis for introducing sophisticated ID cards using watermarked paper and special inks. They contained personal information about the owner, alongside a photo and fingerprint. These were so successful that they were deemed much better than the German equivalent and they became a major headache for the underground.

One leading resistance member, Gerrit-Jan van der Veen, spent two years trying to perfect a way of reproducing the ID card. **Harry was a member of his group**, which produced between 60,000 and 70,000 blank cards before the printers were arrested in June 1944. They obtained genuine blank cards and the stamps to validate them. **This links directly to Harry's work**.

Third was the Dutch police. On their arrival, the Germans restructured them both ideologically and organisationally. A special section were trained to carry out measures against the Jews and in May 1942 a Voluntary Auxiliary Police force of 2,000 was set up made up of Dutch SS and NSB. Deployed in their home towns under the command of local police chiefs, they had a reputation for brutality and illegality and became invaluable to the Germans with their specialist local knowledge. They were almost solely used in the pursuit of Jews and were disbanded two years later.

The Dutch police seemed to accept without opposition German orders to carry out measures against Jews. Some did resist and faced consequences. Some turned a blind eye to forged or invalid documents **(in one instance this saved Fré)**.

By September 1942 it was clear that Jews were not going to report voluntarily for deportation so the police were used to round up those selected. If there was resistance, the Germans used the auxiliaries mentioned above.

In France it was a different story. Owing to the antipathy of the French towards Jews, there was not much resistance initially. However, when French police were ordered to round up a target of 40% of the Jewish population this was regarded as an attack on French sovereignty. The Germans didn't have the resources to collect up the Jews without the help of the French so had to compromise. In July and August

1942, the round-up of Jews provoked negative reactions from French society and there was a steep decline in numbers arrested.

The fourth factor was the Jew-hunters – their role is explained in Chapter 18. *(source: Bob Moore, Chapter 9)*

8. Memorial to Wally Van Hall in Frederiksplein by the Dutch Central bank.

Known as "The Banker of the Resistance", he founded the National Support Fund (NSF) and generated an amount equivalent to €450 million to support Jews in hiding and other resistance activities. In January 1945 he was arrested by the Nazis and executed in Haarlem.

9. The Jewish Council

The Germans blamed the Jews for the February strike, though they had nothing to do with organising it. The Jewish Council was told that, unless it was called off, 300 more Jews would be deported. So the industrial leaders were implored to end it. The strike, far from persuading the Germans to stop persecuting the Jews, gave them another pretext for doing so. And, according to Harry, it gave them the understanding that they should undertake the persecutions and deportations more covertly. How was it that the people who went on strike in early 1941 in support of their Jewish countrymen were able to turn the other cheek during the systematic round-up, deportation and daylight robbery of Jews the following year? What went through their minds?

The Germans had requested the formation of the Jewish Council to help them preserve order in the Jewish Quarter and to assist with the deportations. It was run by Abraham Asscher and David Cohen. Cohen had been president of the Committee for Jewish Refugees, set up in 1933. So Willem probably knew him. My mother can remember her father going to meetings held at the Diamond Exchange.

10. Exemption stamps

The only concession for people who worked for the Jewish Council or Jewish schools, for baptised Jews, for Jews married to non-Jews and having children and for those working for the German war effort was to have a special exemption stamp in their ID cards. These stamps became a matter of life and death for Jews, though in the end even the exemptions proved worthless. For the Germans it was a cat and mouse game. "Their main object was to get rid of the Jews smoothly, and by stages, in order to cause the minimum disruption in Dutch public life. To do that they needed the cooperation of the victims themselves – by granting temporary privileges to a minority, they succeeded in liquidating the rest without too much fuss or bother." (Presser)

When the Jewish Council agreed to apply for exemptions in the spring of 1942, it appointed itself the arbiter of life and death. At the end of July it was asked to create "a very careful and final list" of indispensable Jews. The families of those on the list would also be "exempted from labour service until further notice". The whole issue brought the Jewish Council into disrepute as members sought to save their own.

II. Extracts from Counting My Steps, the autobiography of Jacov Lind (1927–2007)

Jacov's account provides more information about Jaap Granaat and insight into the period when the threat of being rounded up was at its height. Originally from Vienna, Jacov was evacuated to Amsterdam at the age of 11. He evaded Nazi capture by hiding in the attic of Jaap Granaat's house.

At this point the war was going badly for Germany on the Russian front, but against the Jews the Nazis had a good chance of winning. The eight o'clock curfew kept the Jews and the resistance off the streets, while the rest of the population did not seem to care, except for getting food, fuel and cigarettes.

Jacov, then aged 16, needed forged papers, an address to hide, ration cards and contacts with those who could help him. The refugee committee found Jacov a home with Jaap Granaat. Jaap was 35 years old and married to Aleida (previously a stenographer), with a small baby and his mother (Tante Mietje) living in the house. He had been an accountant but his non-Jewish bosses had been forced to discharge him.

It was a clean and comfortable apartment, neither rich nor poor. There were also two German boys aged 10 and 12 staying there, whose upkeep was paid by the Committee. Aleida looked after the baby and the house. Mietje peeled the potatoes.

Jaap went to day classes to learn a new trade. "What can I do with my accountancy in Germany? But as a blacksmith they will need me everywhere, even in Poland."

After six weeks he came home proudly with a seven-armed candelabrum. "To forge a gun or ammunition would have been more worthwhile under the circumstances. But who could tell? Seven candles to light up a fading memory of self-reliance might well be all that could be done. Granaat was an accountant, not a soldier. He was a family man, not a guerrilla. He had responsibilities and wanted to take care of his dependants, 'even in Poland'".

Jacov went to the same school and also learnt metalwork. At the Granaat household he fell in love with Cilly Levitus. She was doing similar work to Fré, helping babies whose parents had been taken to the theatre.

Deportation notices were sent out: letters A–L on Tuesday, K–P on Wednesday, Q–Z on Thursday. Grim rumours spread and no one wanted to go. The Germans had to think of something new. The non-Jews in the old ghetto had to move out and Jews from other places were moved in. The ghetto had to be extended into part of the Afrikaner quarter. The ghetto was not sealed; barbed wire was all that was needed, along with some signs and more policemen to stop and search. The Granaats had to move from 1 Niersstraat – not too difficult as people were leaving all the time. They moved to at 39 Retiefstraat, though without the baby, who was given to farmers to look after until after the war, and also without Tante Mietje, who was taken away by two policemen. She had no exemption stamp and was sent to Westerbork: "There is no safer place than Westerbork, but safer still is to be dead, people said."

The raids increased and hospitals and nursing homes were emptied one after another. The diamond workers received their notices and the textile workers a week later. Even some of the big bosses of the Jewish Council disappeared. The babies in the crèche opposite the theatre were used as ransom – "parents go quietly or we will do something to your new-born!" Then one day in June or July the babies were sent after their parents.

Street by street the old ghetto was cleared out, then it was the turn of the new ghetto. The last big raid took place on 20 June. It started at six in the morning. Many families sat waiting with suitcases neatly packed (30 kilos), houses spic and span and dust sheets over the furniture.

Jaap sold what he could of his furniture in the hope that the Germans wouldn't get it all. By half past five in the afternoon the noise of the lorries was loud. They all went upstairs with their luggage. They sat at the back of the attic waiting and listening. They heard shouting across the street: "All Jews out of their homes!" in Dutch, followed by a loudspeaker in Dutch and German: "Whoever does not come down now, with his luggage, will be put on transport to a special punishment camp. This is your last warning. Bring your keys for your apartments with you and hand them in on demand."

This was repeated three or four times and then men were heard coming upstairs rattling and hammering at doors. They did not see the manhole above the Granaats' second floor.

A few minutes after the last shouting had died away they all went down one by one, except for Jacov. He climbed out onto the roof, lying flat to avoid being spotted by a searching flashlight from across the street. By 10.30 it became normal outside. He crept downstairs into the apartment and found it had been locked and sealed. Now it all belonged to the Reich. He waited until 6am, the end of the curfew, then, breaking a small kitchen window, he left disguised by wearing riding boots, riding trousers, a dark shirt and a jacket with the red and black triangle of the NSB on his lapel.

12. About Westerbork

The camp of Westerbork was situated about 15 km from the village of Westerbork. This camp had been opened by the Dutch authorities in order to receive Jewish refugees from Germany. The first refugees arrived in October 1939. When the Germans invaded Holland there were 750 refugees in the camp.

In July 1942 the German authorities took control of the camp and Westerbork became officially a "transit camp", part of the "Final Solution". The first train left the camp on 16 July with 1,135 of the first selected Jews. By the end of the month, nearly 6,000 Dutch Jews had reached Auschwitz, where the majority were gassed. In November 1942, after new rail lines were constructed, trains arrived directly into the camp. More than 103,000 Jews were transported from Westerbork to Auschwitz or Sobibor. When the Allies liberated Westerbork, 900 prisoners remained in the camp.

The camp of Westerbork was a strange place. There was a school (only for "orphans", i.e. children who arrived without their parents), a hairdresser, an orchestra and a restaurant. If a prisoner had enough money, it was possible to buy goods that were unobtainable elsewhere in Holland at that time. This "comfort" was designed by the SS in order to avoid any problem during the transfers to Auschwitz. A lot of prisoners were therefore hopeful that the condition of life would be the same in the camps of Poland.

The Germans had very little to do with the selections; the Nazi commandant gave the orders and the Jewish "governing" body carried them out, in fear of themselves being deported. Before each Tuesday's transport the camp was in panic, with every prisoner worried they would be selected. The criteria for this kept changing: sometimes pregnant women or the bedridden were exempted and sometimes they were the very ones who had to go. If there happened to be fewer people on the list than needed, "exemptions" became worthless. This is why the Jewish elite tended to provide surplus names to make sure they, their friends and their family were safe.

This demonstrates the risky situation that Lily and her family were in and, later, the perilous and most anxious times faced by the more elite Granaats as one by one their names were inevitably placed on the deportation list.
(source: jewishgen.org/ForgottenCamps)

13. Organisation at Westerbork

Everyone at Westerbork was struck by how well organised it was. Consider the task of removing 100,000 Jews so smoothly and silently from the country to realise the scale of efficiency and organisation.

There was a complex hierarchy under the camp commandant, with many subdivisions, each with leaders and sub-leaders. This a parallel with the Jewish Council in Amsterdam. "Here the awful truth about collaboration – an ever decreasing number of Jews helping to deport an ever decreasing number of their fellows – stood out more starkly, not least because at Westerbork this task was carried out with such exemplary efficiency."

There was Administration, the registering of newcomers (including Jacob Granaat) and the Housing Bureau. Most people were allocated to barracks with triple-decker bunks. Barracks were wooden huts 84 by ten metres wide and six metres high.

There were a few small apartments allotted to highly privileged people and affording the only privacy that was obtainable. **Aunt Carolina and Uncle Simon were allocated one of these, due to their son Hijman Bromet's position as one of the camp leaders – Lily, Tootje and Kitty visited them there.**

In the camp canteen, food not normally available, such as fish, cucumber, pudding mixes and lemonade powder, could be bought. The few able to leave astonished friends with unheard-of luxuries such as bunches of flowers or pot plants.

It was a German Jewish immigrant and eminent academic, Dr Hans Ottenstein, who set up the Antragstelle office in Westerbork, exploring every possible means to apply for exemptions on behalf of Jews doomed to deportation. Ottenstein would ask everyone coming into the camp: "Are you married to a Gentile? Have you any children? Are you a half-Jew, quarter-Jew? A Portuguese Jew? Baptised? Are you of foreign nationality? Can you prove it? An immigration stamp, any special qualifications? Are you on any list that might help you?

Any pretext, however flimsy, could be investigated. The process could go on right up to point of departure and not a few were snatched off the train just before the whistle blew.

(source: Presser, Chapter 7)

Without Hans Ottenstein, I wouldn't have written this story.

14. Eden's address to the House of Commons, 17th December 1942, reported on the BBC:

The British Foreign Secretary, Anthony Eden, has told the House of Commons about mass executions of Jews by Germans in occupied Europe.

Mr Eden also read out a United Nations declaration condemning "this bestial policy". He said news of German atrocities sent in by the Polish Government and widely reported in the press this month would only serve to strengthen allied determination to fight Nazism and punish all those responsible.

Mr Eden described how the German authorities, who have already stripped the Jews of their basic human rights, were now carrying out "Hitler's oft repeated intention to exterminate the Jewish people in Europe".

He described how hundreds of thousands of men, women and children were being transported from all German-occupied territory "in conditions of appalling horror and brutality" to Eastern Europe.

In Poland, Jewish ghettoes were being "systematically emptied" except for the able-bodied who were being sent to labour camps. "None of those taken away are ever heard of again," he said. Those who are sick or injured are left to die of exposure or starvation or killed in mass executions.

The House then heard him read out a declaration made by the governments of Belgium, Czechoslovakia, Greece, Luxembourg, the Netherlands, Norway, Poland, the United States, the UK, the USSR, Yugoslavia and the French National Committee.

It condemned "in the strongest possible terms this bestial policy of cold-blooded extermination" and made a "solemn resolution to ensure that those responsible for these crimes shall not escape retribution". He said the United Nations would try to give asylum to as many refugees as possible but that there were "immense geographical difficulties" as well as security procedures to overcome.

After his announcement, the House rose and held a one-minute silence in sympathy for the victims.

(source: news.bbc.co.uk/onthisday)

15. The Journey

A resourceful medical orderly in Westerbork noticed it was the same train making the journey every week and so he made a little hiding place in which messages could be sent home. He then carefully copied all the messages and smuggled them out of the camp, in order for a record to be kept, before sending them to the correct addresses. Thanks to him, Presser, as part of his research, could read the contents of several letters written in December 1942. These give a clear account of the journey, which lasted three days and two nights. Although the number of testimonies is small, the terrible journey would have been similar for many thousands of others: "All these people who had worked so hard throughout their lives, who had been such solid citizens, were now being carted like cattle into a dark future."

Only a few managed to escape, probably because the Germans let it be known that the truck leader would be held responsible. "The whole thing was sheer farce however, for on arrival in the East, the doors of the trucks were thrown open, and, not stopping to count, the Germans drove them out as fast as they could. To them the Jews were less than cattle, for cattle are worth something and must be counted…"

As an example of how they were treated on the journey, at one stop the father of six-month old twins asked the guard for permission to fill a feeding bottle. The guard said he would do it for him, took the bottle and smashed it against the wall of the truck. There was no water for anyone on that journey.

And the German population? "Hundreds of trains, consisting of thousands of cars, jammed with Jews from Western Europe, being taken to the extermination centres in the east, passed through Germany. These trains would stop at German railway stations for days and sometimes for weeks. Many Jews suffocated in those trains or died of thirst, yet not a single act of assistance is known" (Jacob Lestschinsky).

A letter from a nurse ended, "We're there, just past Auschwitz… In the distance we can see a building all lit up…" Was this the flames from the chimney? We don't know because within two hours she, and all those with her, were no more.

A total of 98 transports left the Netherlands, of which 93 were from Westerbork. Twenty-six transports had no survivors at all. From many others, only a single person survived.

Sixty-seven trains carrying 60,000 people went to Auschwitz; only 500 returned: less than a 1% chance of survival. Nineteen trains went to Sobibor transporting 34,000 people, of whom only 19 survived.
(source: Presser, Chapter 8)

16. Dr Hans Georg Calmeyer

Without Calmeyer none of my family would be here. Calmeyer was a German lawyer who ran a private practice. He had just two employees, one of whom was a Jewish woman. He was not aligned to any political party and when the Nazis rose to power in January 1933 he was forbidden to practice on suspicion of being "politically unreliable". In May 1940 Calmeyer arrived in the Netherlands with the invading forces and he joined the occupation administration.

In the Nazis' view, the Dutch were considered pure Aryans and the need to purify the Netherlands of alien races became a paramount goal. A special office led by Calmeyer was established to examine doubtful cases and decide whether they were to be considered Aryans. In January 1941, Dutch Jews were ordered to register with the authorities; even those who were half or quarter Jewish were included in the list. Unaware of the fate that awaited them, Jews abided by the edict. However, when the deportations began and the significance of being registered as Jews was revealed, these and others applied to Calmeyer's office in order to change their classification.

Calmeyer realised he had the opportunity to help Jews, but knew he would have to act with utmost care not to arouse suspicion within the fiercely anti-Semitic environment in which he worked. He avoided any personal contact with lawyers acting on behalf of Jewish clients, so he would not be suspected of friendliness to Jews.

To shield his department from hostile interference, he chose assistants opposed to the Nazi regime. Calmeyer's bureau was a singular anti-National-Socialist "cell" within the occupation government. Next, he created a passage through which Jews might be assisted in escaping from the German registration trap. According to the German Nuremberg Laws, membership in a Jewish community was considered proof of a person's Jewishness. It was a judicial proposition impervious to proof of the contrary. Only the Führer himself was capable of invalidating a person's Jewish descent.

In March 1941, Calmeyer argued that, within the framework of the racial laws, membership in a religious community could not possibly be regarded as a decisive factor. He also pointed out that, in practice, the application of this ruling was stricter in Holland than in Germany, owing to the absence in the Netherlands of a supreme authority to whom problem cases could be referred. Calmeyer cited several examples of the resulting quandaries, including that of a prominent member of the Dutch National Socialist Party (NSB) who had a Jewish grandfather.

Consequently, Calmeyer proposed that, unlike the situation in Germany, the possibility of counter-proof of Jewish racial descent despite membership in a Jewish community should considered. In approving the proposal, the Nazis failed to realise that they had created a loophole through which numerous Jews would be able to escape the fate that was in store for them.

As soon as this decision became known in Jewish circles, petitions began to arrive at Calmeyer's department requesting that the status of a parent or grandparent be changed from Jewish to half Jewish or even "Aryan".

Another means was to try and prove that the grandparent or parent in question had been an "illegitimate" child of a Jewish mother and an Aryan father and had subsequently been formally adopted by a Jewish husband. Such proof required an official extract from the population register. It is unnecessary to stress that the production of genuine-looking "Calmeyer-certificates" required considerable archival experience and artistic skill.

Ultimately, Calmeyer's decision to support a particular request would depend on whether or not a fairly superficial examination might reveal the spuriousness of the claim, thus endangering all his subsequent approvals. The more fanatical and racist

Nazis called Calmeyer's activities genealogical fraud, and they demanded a case-by-case check of all his approvals.

Particularly problematic was the request on behalf of a group of 4,304 Portuguese Jews. The request was endorsed by several well-known anthropologists, who acted on the assumption that all Portuguese Jews in the Netherlands were descended from Marrano forebears. Calmeyer reacted by saying that "he had only a small vessel, that would surely sink by accommodating such a large number of passengers." Sinking, in this case, would have meant the revision of all requests, including those that had been approved earlier.

The results of Calmeyer's interventions were impressive: out of a total number of 4,767, he recognised 2,026 as half Jewish, 873 as Aryans and rejected 1,868. In analysing these figures, it should also be taken into account that the descendants of those cleared were also exempted from further persecution. In addition, the petitioners themselves were protected against deportation while their applications were being processed, enabling them, if necessary, to go underground. It is known that some petitioners were warned by secretaries at Calmeyer's office as soon as their requests had been turned down, enabling them to disappear from their homes before the German police reached them.

The above figures show that 60 percent of all applications were approved, the majority on the basis of clearly fictitious documentation. Consequently, we can say that at least 3,000 Jewish lives were saved.

So secret and discreet were Calmeyer's machinations that even Lages, the German chief of the Amsterdam police, felt constrained to declare after the war that "to him Calmeyer's activities had always been a book with seven seals."

On 4 March 1992 Yad Vashem recognised Hans Calmeyer as Righteous Among the Nations.

(source: yadvashem.org/yv/en/righteous/stories/calmeyer.asp)

There arose a whole industry of forging and there was a rush to dig out old baptismal and marriage certificates which could mean the difference between life and death. "Old love letters were forged on paper that was fifty to sixty years old and had been rummaged out from some merchant. Ink that looked in every way as though it was many years old was concocted. Ingenuity was boundless, particularly when it came to rubber stamps, for which it was said that all German officials had a weakness; letters from various Consulates bearing foreign postage stamps were collect by resistance workers pretending to be Post Office employees and the postmarks altered" Hertzberg.

False certificates of baptism were available and one could choose between 15 Christian denominations; best of all was the so-called Synodal imprint, which was a pure fiction but, oddly enough, the one that most impressed the Germans. "It is easy to smile at all this today, but less easy to recapture the atmosphere in which these things went on."

(source: Presser, Chapter 5)

17. The Identity of Liesje's Captor

On my trip to Amsterdam with Jamie in April 2015 we asked at NIOD, but there was no information about Seveke and Spillenaar, for example in the telephone directories. However, at the Amsterdam Archives we were directed to a website, "Ontrouw and Zuivering" (Infidelity and Purification), in other words a place where police collaborators were named and shamed. On the "Ontrouw and Zuivering" website we found this entry:

"The Minister of Justice; having consulted the Advisory Committee, referred to in article 5, paragraph 4, the Purification Decree 1945.

"Considering that the persons listed below, also of the opinion the aforementioned committee, have expressed an infidelity, as intended in Article 2, first paragraph, sub-paragraph 1 of the Purification Decree, 1945. In accordance with the opinion of abovementioned commission around 11,500 Dutch officials have been prosecuted under this treatment decision.

"This database contains the names of about 4,500 people, mostly policemen, who been prosecuted under the treatment decision, and reprimanded, suspended or fired.

"Individuals also fell under this legislation were banned from practicing law.

"Information: oorlogshistorie@gmail.com Inspection of files under certain conditions: Central Archive Special Criminal."

Searching this database we found:

SEVEKE	Josephus Franciscus Alphonus Seveke, born 1 December 1917 Amsterdam
SPILLENAAR	Willem Spillenaar, born 4 October 1919 te Duisburg

We think it is likely that the older of the two, Seveke, who was Dutch and seemed to be in charge at the arrest of Nico, was Kitty's contact; and Spillenaar would have been the blond Nazi with his gun trained on Tootje. He was younger and was born in Germany, though he spoke fluent Dutch.

18. The Eighteen Dead by Jan Campert 1941

Translation by Sibylla Chan, included with her permission,

My cell is but two metres long,
a bare two metres wide,
much smaller still the plot of ground
that's not yet recognised,
but there I nameless go to rest
in company of friends,
eighteen we were in number and
not one sees dusk again.

O loveliness of light and land,
of Holland's coast unbound,
when vanquished by our evil foe
I had no peace of mind;
what boots a man, upright and true,
to do in such a plight,
but kiss his child and kiss his wife
and fight the futile fight.

I knew the task that I took on
was fierce and painful work,
but my heart could not let it go,
nor would the spirit shirk.
It knew how foretimes in our land
our freedom was so prized,
before th' invader's cursed hand
had otherwise devised,

But ere he breaks his oaths and brags
the sickening stage did stand
to overrun dear Holland's realm
and rape its hallowed land,
ere Germans gave him their respect
and held him in belief,

he bent our people to his rule
and plundered like a thief.
The rodent catcher of Berlin
now pipes his melody;
as sure as I soon dead shall be,
my love no more to see
and nevermore to break the bread
or sleep with her again –
reject all that he vows or said,
that sly fox of a man.

Whoever reads these words, recall,
my comrades in distress
and their loved ones most of all,
their utter wretchedness,
know this that we too brought to mind
our kin and country dear,
from every night a new day dawns,
and every sky will clear.

Behold the early morning light
upon the pane up high –
please God to lighten my demise,
I failed though I did try,
like any other could have done,
grant me your mercy then,
so let me meet my death a man:
the barrel of a gun.

19. Auschwitz

When the railway was built, Auschwitz was a small town close to the borders of Germany, Austria and the Sudetenland (in what is now the Czech Republic). With 44 train lines coming into Auschwitz, it became an important junction: the crossroads of Europe. There was a camp for migrant workers from all over Europe, who were sent from Auschwitz to the large German estates. With its beautiful brick barracks this was the place that eventually became the Auschwitz concentration camp.

In 1919, Poland became an independent country again and Auschwitz became a Polish town called Oswiecim. The camp was used as a garrison by the Polish Army.

The Auschwitz main camp originally had 20 brick buildings; 14 of them were single-storey buildings and six were two stories high. When this camp was converted into the concentration camp, a second storey was added to the 14 single-storey buildings and eight new two-storey buildings were added, making a total of 28 barracks. Between 13,000 and 16,000 prisoners were crowded into these buildings, where they slept in three-tiered bunks. At one point, in 1942, there were 20,000 prisoners at the Auschwitz main camp.

(source: furtherglory.wordpress.com/oshpitzin-auschwitz)

20. Yad Vashem

YAD VASHEM Martyrs' and Heroes' Remembrance Authority

DAF-ED

A Page of Testimony

P.O.B. 3477 Jerusalem, Israel

THE MARTYRS' AND HEROES' REMEMBRANCE LAW, 5713—1953 determines in Article No. 2 that

The task of YAD VASHEM is to gather into the homeland material regarding all those members of the Jewish people who laid down their lives, who fought and rebelled against the Nazi enemy and his collaborators, and to perpetuate their memory and that of the communities, organizations, and institutions which were destroyed because they were Jewish.

1. Family name *
GRANAAT

2. First Name (maiden name)
WILLEM

3. Date of birth
28 mei 1892

4. Place of birth (town, country)
Amsterdam—Holland

5. Name of father
Hijman Granaat

6. Name of mother
Keetje Tafelkruijer

7. Name of spouse (if a wife, add maiden name)
Lilian May GRANAAT— HOLLINGSWORTH

8. Place of residence before the war
Amsterdam — Holland

9. Places of residence during the war
Amsterdam — 's-Gravenhage— Westerbork.

10. Circumstances of death (place, date, etc.)
Sobibor   20 mei 1943

I, the undersigned Keetje Scheffer — Granaat
residing at (full address) Vlierstraat 24. BADHOEVEDORP. HOLLAND
relationship to deceased dochter (daughter)
hereby declare that this testimony is correct to the best of my knowledge.

Signature   M. Scheffer-Granaat
Place and date Jeruzalem 25 april 1977

...even unto them will I give in mine house and within my walls a place and a name...that shall not be cut off...

234

21. The Digital Monument to the Jewish Community in the Netherlands

The Digital Monument to the Jewish Community in the Netherlands is an Internet monument dedicated to preserving the memory of all the men, women and children who were persecuted as Jews during the Nazi occupation of the Netherlands and did not survive.

Every person in the Monument has a separate page commemorating his or her life. This provides the person's personal details and, where possible, contains a reconstruction of his or her family relationship and the circumstances of each individual life. Addresses are added, enabling visitors to take a virtual walk through streets and towns. The Digital Monument also contains a good deal of other information and there are notes to explain how the site has been set up and how it can be used.

The home page (the image above) is the actual "monument", consisting of a screen with thousands of tiny coloured bars. The bars are grouped together in blocks, with each block representing a family and each little bar within a block representing someone who died in the war.

Tall blue bars represent adult men; tall red bars represent adult women. Half-length green bars represent boys aged six to 21, yellow bars of the same length represent girls aged six to 21. The shortest bars represent children under six: boys are light blue and girls are pink. Surviving family members (about whom the Monument does not feature any other information) appear not on the home page but only on the family pages, as clear bars without any information about gender or age.

The digital nature of the Monument means that there is almost unlimited scope for adding information and photographs. It can therefore grow into a unique presentation of Jewish life in the Netherlands in the 1930s and early 1940s.

Inventories of household effects have been preserved for several thousand families. Over 3,300 of these have been posted to the Monument.

Updated information about the monument
The monument has been updated since writing this book and is now called the Jewish Monument. The updated overview is this.

About the Jewish Monument
The Jewish Monument commemorates the more than 104,000 persons who were persecuted as Jews in the Netherlands and who did not survive the Holocaust.

Within this monument, visitors, editors, family members and historians work together to combine stories and memories. For example, the monument paints a multifaceted picture of the history of the Second World War, the Shoah and the Jewish community in the Netherlands. The Jewish Monument is part of the Jewish Cultural Quarter.

The new website can be found at:

https://www.joodsmonument.nl/en/

https://www.joodsmonument.nl/en/page/571160/about-the-jewish-monument

https://www.joodsmonument.nl/en/page/575912/introduction-video-jewish-monument

List of Sources

Books and Publications

Appleman-Jurman, Alicia, Alicia: My Story. (USA: Bantam Books 1990).

Boeken-Velleman, Leny, Breekbaar, Maar niet gebroken: Het verhaal van een Auschwitz-overlevende. (Laren, (NH): Uitgeverij Verbum 2008).

de Cort, Bart, De Groep Gerretsen: Kroniek van een Verzetsgroep 1940-1945. (Den Haag: Sdu Uitgevers 1998).

Dwork, Deborah, Children with a Star: Jewish Youth in Nazi Europe (Yale University Press 1991).

Frank, Anne, with forward by Storm Jameson, The Diary of Anne Frank (London: Pan Books Ltd 1954).

Hillesum, Etty, Introduced by JG Gaarland, translated by Arnold J. Pomerans, Etty: A Diary 1941-43. (Great Britain: Triad Grafton Books 1985).

Hillesum, Etty, Letters From Westerbork: Before Auschwitz there was Westerbork. (London: Grafton Books, a division of the Collins Publishing Group 1987).

Kulka, Otto Dov, Landscapes of the Metropolis of Death: Reflections on Memory and Imagination. (London: Allen Lane, an imprint of Penguin Books 2013).

Lee, Carol Ann, The Hidden Life of Otto Frank. (London: Penguin Books 2003).

Lind, Jakov, Counting my steps. (London: Jonathan Cape Ltd 1970).

Lindwer, Willy, translated from the Dutch by Alison Meersshaert, The Last Seven Months of Anne Frank: The Stories of Six Women who Knew Anne Frank. (London: Young Picador 2004).

Moore, Bob, Victims & Survivors: The Nazi Persecution of the Jews in The Netherlands 1940-45. (London: Arnold, a member of the Hodder Headline Group 1997).

Presser, Dr Jacob, translated by Arnold Pomerans, Ashes in the Wind: The Destruction of Dutch Jewry. (Great Britain: Souvenir Press Ltd 1968).

Schelvis, Jules, Sobibor: A History of a Nazi Death Camp. (Oxford: Berg 2007).

Schoumans, Jan, The Lost Years (Cambridge: Janus Publishing Co 1994).

Vuijsje, Marja, Ons Kamp: Een Min of Meer Joodse Geschiedenis. (Amsterdam: Atlas 2012).

Waterford, Helen, Commitment to the Dead: One Woman's Journey Toward Understanding. (USA: Renaissance House Publishers 1993).

Other Sources

BBC: news.bbc.co.uk/1/hi/8381413.stm

BBC: news.bbc.co.uk/onthisday/hi/dates/stories/december/17

Boektje, Betje Rachel and Boektje, Sera Sophia, transcript of recorded testimony (The Hague, 1947).

Deathcamps.org/reinhard/dutchclashes.html

Furtherglory.wordpress.com/oshpitzin-auschwitz

Furtherglory.wordpress.com/category/holocaust

Hagalil.com/archiv/2008/10/troebitz.htm

Holocaustresearchproject.org

Jewishgen.org/ForgottenCamps

Jewish Historical Museum, Amsterdam: jck.nl/jewish-historical-museum

The Jewish Monument, Amsterdam: joodsamsterdam.nl

Maps.amsterdam.nl/woii

Maxvandam.info: family trees of Dutch Jewish families

Museum Actueel, Amsterdam: museumactueel.nl

National Library of the Netherlands, The Hague: kb.nl

Nederlands Fotomuseum: nederlandsfotomuseum.nl;

New York Times: nytimes.com/2009/06/03/bamboozling-ourselves

NIOD Netherlands Institute for War, Holocaust and Genocide Studies: niod.nl

Oranjehotel, German Prison in Scheveningen: oranjehotel.org

Plantageamsterdam.nl/en/museums/hollandsche_schouwburg/

Schryver, Samuel, Video Testimony, Florida Holocaust Museum: flholocaustmuseum.org

Stadsarchief Amsterdam (municipal archives): stadsarchief.amsterdam.nl

Streekmuseum Jan Anderson, Vlaardingen: jananderson.nl

Travelpast50.com

US Holocaust Memorial Museum: collections.ushmm.org

Verzets Resistance Museum, Amsterdam: verzetsmuseum.org

The War Graves Foundation: oorlogsgravenstichting.nl

Waterford, Helen, Oral History (US Holocaust Memorial Museum)

Westerbork Museum, Hooghalen: campwesterbork.nl

Wikipedia: en.wikipedia.org/wiki/Dutch_famine_of_1944

Wikipedia.org/wiki/Sobibor_extermination_camp

Yadvashem.org - The World Holocaust Remembrance Center